DISCARDED
P9-ECL-315

ENGLISH RECUSANT LITERATURE
1558–1640

Selected and Edited by
D. M. ROGERS

Volume 127

GREGORY MARTIN

A Discoverie of the
Manifold Corruptions of the
Holy Scriptures
1582

GREGORY MARTIN

A Discoverie of the Manifold Corruptions of the Holy Scriptures

1582

The Scolar Press
1973

ISBN 0 85417 908 9

Published and Printed in Great Britain by
The Scolar Press Limited, 20 Main Street,
Menston, Yorkshire, England

NOTE

Reproduced (original size) from a copy in the library of Ampleforth Abbey, by permission of the Abbot and Community.

References: Allison and Rogers 525; STC 17503.

A DISCOVERIE OF THE MANIFOLD CORRVPTIONS OF THE HOLY SCRIPTVRES BY THE Heretikes of our daies, ſpecially the Engliſh Sectaries, and of their foule dealing herein, by partial & falſe tranſlations to the aduantage of their hereſies, in their Engliſh Bibles vſed and authoriſed ſince the time of Schiſme.

By GREGORY MARTIN one of the readers of Diuinitie in the ENGLISH COLLEGE OF RHEMES.

2 Cor. 2,

Non ſumus ſicut plurimi, adulterantes verbum Dei, ſed ex ſinceritate, ſed ſicut ex Deo, coram Deo, in Chriſto loquimur.

That is,

VVe are not as very many, adulterating the word of God, but of ſinceritie, & as of God, before God, in Chriſt vve ſpeake.

Printed at RHEMES,
By Iohn Fogny.

1582.

THE PREFACE CONTEINING FIVE SVNDRIE ABVSES OR CORRVPTIONS OF HOLY Scriptures, common to al Heretikes, & agreing ſpecially to theſe of our time: vvith many other neceſſarie aduertiſements to the reader.

Heretikes fiue vvaies ſpecially abuſe the Scriptures.

AS it hath been alvvaies the faſhiõ of Heretikes to pretẽd Scriptures, for ſhevv of their cauſe: ſo hath it been alſo their cuſtom and propertie to abuſe the ſaid Scriptures many vvaies, in fauour of their errours.

1 Denying certaine bookes or partes of bookes.

1 One vvay is, to deny vvhole bookes thereof or partes of bookes, vvhen they are euidently againſt them. So did (for example) Ebion al S. Paules epiſtles, Manicheus the Actes of the Apoſtles, Alogiani S. Iohns Goſpel, Marcion many peeces of S. Lukes Goſpel, and ſo did both theſe and other heretikes in other bookes, denying and allovving vvhat they liſt, as is euident by S. Ireneus, S. Epiphanius, S. Auguſtine, and al antiquitie.

2 Doubting of their authoritie, and calling them into queſtiõ

2 An other vvay is, to call into queſtion at the leaſt and make ſome doubt of the authoritie of certaine bookes of holy Scriptures, thereby to diminiſh their credite. ſo did Manicheus affirme of

the vvhole nevv Teſtament,that it vvas not vvritten by the Apoſtles:& peculiarly of S. Matthevves Goſpel,that it wasſome other mās vnder his name: and therfore not of ſuch credite,but that it might in ſome part be refuſed.ſo did Marciō & the Ariās deny the epiſtle to the Hebrues to be S Paules, Epiphan. li. 2.hær.69 Euſeb.li 4. hiſt.c.27.:& Alogiani the Apocalypſe to be S.Iohns the Euāgeliſt. Epiph.& Auguſt.in hær.Alogianorum.

3 Voluntarie expoſitions according to euery ones fanſie or hereſie.

3 An other way is, to expound the Scriptures after their ovvne priuate conceite and phantaſie, not according to the approued ſenſe of the holy auncient fathers and Catholike Church. ſo did Theodorus Mopſueſtites(Act. Synod.5.)affirme of al the bookes of the Prophets,and of the Pſalmes, that they ſpake not euidently of Chriſt, but that the auncient fathers did voluntarily dravv thoſe ſayings vnto Chriſt vvhich vvere ſpoken of other matters ſo did al heretikes, that vvould ſeeme to groūd their hereſies vpon Scriptures, & to auouch them by Scriptures expounded according to their ovvne ſenſe and imagination.

4 Changing ſome vvordes or ſentēces of the very original text. Tertul.cont. Marcio. li.1. in princ. Tertull. li.5.

4 An other vvay is, to alter the very original text of the holy Scripture,by adding,taking away or changing it here and there for their purpoſe.ſo did the Arians in ſundrie places, and the Neſtoriās in the firſt epiſtle of S. Iohn, and eſpecially Marcion,vvho was therfore called; *Mus Ponticus*, the mouſe of Pontus, becauſe he had gnavven (as it vvere) certaine places vvith his corruptions, whereof ſome are ſaid to remaine in the Greeke text vntil this day.

5 Falſe and heretical tranſlation.

5 An other way is,to make falſe tranſlations of the Scriptures for the maintenance of errour and hereſie.ſo did the Arians (as S.Hierom noteth in 26.Eſa.) read and tranſlate Prouerb 8.*Dominus creauit me in initio viarum ſuarum.*that is, *The Lord created*

ted me in the beginning of his vvaies, so to make Christ the vvisedom of God, a mere creature. S. Augustin also li. 5. cont. Iulian. c. 2. noteth it as the interpretation of some Pelagian Gen 3. *Fecerunt sibi vestimenta,* for, *perizómata* or *campestria.* that is, *They made them selues garments.* whereas the vvord of the Scripture is, breeches or aprons proper & peculiar to couer the secrete partes. Againe, the self same Heretikes did reade falsely Ro. 5. *Regnauit mors ab Adam vsque ad Moysen etiā in eos qui peccauerūt in similitudinē præuaricationis Adæ,* that is, *Death reigned from Adam to Moyses euen on them that sinned after the similitude of the preuarication of Adam,* to maintaine their heresie against original sinne, that none vvere infected therewith, or subiect to death & damnatiō, but by sinning actually as Adam did. Thus did the old Heretikes.

ἐκτήσατο, possedit.

קָנָנִי

περιζώματα

חגרת

Aug. ep. 89. & de pecc. mer. c. 11.

ἐπὶ τοὺς μὴ ἁμαρτήσαντας.

6 What these of our daies? is it credible that being so vvel vvarned by the condemnation and detestation of them, they also vvould be as mad and as impious as those? Heretikes (gentle Reader) be alvvaies like Heretikes, and hovvsoeuer they differ in opinions or names, yet in this point they agree, to abuse the Scriptures for their purpose by al meanes possibly. I vvil but touche foure points of the fiue before mentioned, because my purpose is to stay vpon the last only, and to discipher their corrupt translations. But if I vvould stand vpon the other also, vvere it not easy to shevv the maner of their proceding against the Scriptures to haue been thus: to deny some vvhole bookes and parts of bookes, to call other some into question, to expound the rest at their pleasure, to picke quarels to the very original and Canonical text, to fester and infect the vvhole body of the Bible vvith cankred translations?

That the Protestants and Caluinistes vse the foresaid fiue meanes of defacing the Scriptures.

7 Did not Luther deny S. Iames epistle and so contemne it that he called it an epistle of strawv, & not vvorthie of an Apostolical spirit? must I proue this to M. Vvhitakers, vvho vvould neuer haue *denied it so vehemently in the superlatiue degree for shame, if he had not thought it more shame to graunt it? I neede not goe far for the matter: Aske M. Fulke, and he vvil flatly confesse it vvas so. Aske Caluin *in arg. ep. Iacobi.* aske Flaccus Illyricus, *in argum. ep. Iacobi.* and you shal perceiue it is very true. I vvil not send you to the Catholike Germans and others, both of his ovvne time and after, that vvrote against him in the question of iustification: among vvhom not one omitteth this, being a thing so famous and infamous to the confusion of that Arch-heretike.

Cont. rat. Edm. Camp. pag. 11.

Retent. pag. 32. dist. of the Rocke p. 307. Luther. in nouo Test. Germa. in Præf. Iacob.

8 To let this passe · Tobie, Ecclesiasticus, & the Machabees are they not most certainely reiected? and yet they vvere allovved and receiued for Canonical, by the same authoritie that S. Iames epistle vvas. This epistle the Caluinists are content to admit, because * so it pleased Caluin: those bookes they reiect, because so also it pleased him. And vvhy did it so please Caluin? vnder pretence forsooth that they vvere once doubted of, and not taken for Canonical. but is that the true cause in deede? Hovv do they then * receiue S. Iames epistle as Canonical, hauing been before doubted of also, yea (as * they say) reiected?

Côc. Carth. 3 can. 47.

Argum. in ep. Iac.

Vvhitak. p. 10.

ibid.

9 Marke gentle Reader for thy soules sake, and thou shalt finde, that heresie and only heresie is the cause of their denying these bookes: so far, that against the orders and Hierarchies and particular patronages of Angels, one of them vvriteth thus in the name of the rest, *Vve passe not for that Raphael of Tobie, neither do vve acknovvledge those seuen Angels vvhich he speaketh of. al this is far from Canonical Scrip-*tures

ibid. p. 17. M. Whitak. by these vvordes cōdemneth

tures, that the same Raphael recordeth, and sauoureth I vvot not vvhat superstition. Against free vvil thus: *I litle care for the place of Ecclesiasticus, neither vvil I beleeue free vvil, though he affirme an hundred times, That before men is life and death.* And against praier for the dead, and intercession of Saincts, thus: *As for the booke of the Machabees, I do care lesse for it then for the other. Iudas dreame cōcerning Onias I let passe as a dreame.* This is their reuerence of the Scriptures vvhich haue vniuersally been reuerenced for Canonical in the Church of God aboue 1100 yeres, *Conc. Carth. 3.* and particularly of many fathers long before, *August. de doct. Christ. lib. 2 ca. 8.*

their ovvne Seruice booke, which appointeth these bookes of Tobie & Ecclesiasticus, to be readde for holy Scripture, as the other. Do they readde in their Churches Apocryphal and superstitious bookes for holy Scripture? or is he a Puritane, that thus disgraceth their order of daily Seruice?

10 As for partes of bookes do they not reiect certaine peeces of Daniel and of Hester, because they are not in the Hebrue, vvhich reason S. Augustine reiecteth: or because they vvere once doubted of by certaine of the fathers? by vvhich reason some part of S. Marke and S. Lukes Gospel might novv also be called in controuersie, specially if it be true vvhich M. Vvhitakers by a figuratiue speache more then insinuateth, *That he can not see by vvhat right that vvhich once vvas not in credite, should by time vvinne authoritie.* Forgetting him self by & by, and in the very next lines admitting S. Iames epistle (though before doubted of) for Canonical Scriptures. vnles they receiue it but of their courtesie, and so may refuse it vvhen it shal please them, vvhich must needes be gathered of his vvordes, as also many other notorious absurdities, contradictions, and dumme blāckes. Vvhich only to note, were to confute M. whitakers by him self, being the Ansvverer for both Vniuersities.

pag 10.

M. Vvhitak. booke.

11 For the second point, vvhich is not the grosse denial of bookes, but yet calling of them in question, mouing scruples about them, & diminishing their authoritie and credite, I vvil goe no further

 then

In the argument Bib. an. 1579.

then to S. Paules epistle to the Hebrues, vvhich I vvil not aske vvhy they doubt of, or rather thinke it not to be S. Paules, for they vvil tel me, because it vvas once in doubt (not considering that it vvas in like maner doubted vvhether it vvere Canonical, & yet they vvil not novv deny but it is Canonical) but I must aske them and request them to make a reasonable ansvver, vvhy in their English Bible of the yere 1579 and 1580 they presume to leaue out S. Paules name out of the very title of the said epistle, vvhich name is * in the Greeke, and in Bezas Latin translation, both vvhich they professe to folovv. See the title of the new Test an. 1580. Doth not the title tel them that it is S. Paules? vvhy seeke they further: or vvhy do they change the title, striking out S. Paules name, if they meant to deale simply and sincerely? and vvhat an heretical peeuishnes is this, because Beza telleth them of one obscure Greeke copie that hath not Paules name, and onely one: that they vvil rather folovv it, then al other copies both Greeke and Latin? I report me to al indifferent men of common sense, vvhether they do it not to diminish the credite of the epistle.

* ἡ πρὸς ἑβραίους ἐπιστολὴ Παύλου

12 I knovv very vvel that the authoritie of Canonical Scripture standeth not vpon the certaintie of the author, but yet to be Paules or not Paules, Apostolical or not Apostolical, maketh great difference of credite and estimation. For, vvhat made S. Iames epistle doubted of sometime, or the secōd of S. Peter, and the rest, but that they vvere not thought to be the epistles of those Apostles? This Luther savv very vvel, vvhen he denied S. Iames epistle to be Iames the Apostles vvriting. If titles of bookes be of no importāce, then leaue out Matthevv, Marke, Luke, and Iohn, leaue out Paul in his other epistles also, and you shal much pleasure the

the Manichees and other old Heretikes: and if the titles make no difference, vrge no more the title of the Apocalypſe, *S. Iohn the Diuines*, as though it vvere not S. Iohns the Euangeliſtes, and you ſhal much diſpleaſure ſome Heretikes novv a daies. breefely, moſt certaine it is, and they knovv it beſt by their ovvne vſual doings, that it is a principal vvay to the diſcredite of any booke, to deny it to be that authors, vnder vvhoſe name it hath been receiued.

13 But I come to the third point of volũtarie expoſitions of the Scripture, that is vvhen euery man expoũdeth according to his errour & Hereſie. This needeth no proofe, for vve ſee it vvith our eies. Looke vpon the Caluiniſts and Puritanes at home, the Lutherans, Zuinglians, and Caluiniſts abrode: read their bookes vvritten vehemently, one ſect againſt an other: are not their expoſitions of one and the ſame Scripture as diuerſe and contrarie, as their opinions differ one from an other? Let the example at home be, their controuerſie about the diſtinction of Eccleſiaſtical degrees, Arch-biſhop, Biſhop, and miniſter: the example abrode, their diuers imaginations & phantaſies vpon theſe moſt ſacred vvordes, *Hoc eſt corpus meum.*

14 And if you vvil yet haue a further demonſtration, this one may ſuffice for al. They reiect Councels, and Fathers, and the Catholike Churches interpretation, vnles it be agreable to Gods vvord, and vvhether it be agreable or no, that Luther ſhal iudge for the Lutherans, Caluin for the Caluiniſts, Cartvvright for the Puritanes, and an other for the Brethren of loue: breefely *them ſelues vvil be iudges both of Councels and Fathers vvhether they expound the Scriptures vvel or no, & euery youth among them vpon confidence of his ſpirit and knovvledge vvil ſaucily controule not onely one but

* Vvhitak. pa 17. & 120.

but al the fathers cõsenting together, if it be against that vvhich they imagine to be the truth.

15 Vvherevpon it riseth that one of them defen-
Ib. pag. 101. deth this as very vvel said of Luther, *That he esteemed not the vvorth of a rush a thousand Augustines, Cyprians, Churches, against him self.* And an other very finely and figuratiuely, (as he thought) against the holy
Præf. ad 6 theses Oxon pag. 25. Doctor and Martyr S. Cyprian affirming *that the Church of Rome can not erre in faith*, saith thus: *Pardon me Cyprian, I vvould gladly beleeue thee, but that beleeuing thee, I should not beleeue the Gospel.* This is that
Li. Confess. 1. ca. 14. li. 7. c. 20. vvhich S. Augustine saith of the like men, *dulcissimè vanos esse, non peritos sed perituros, nec tam disertos in errore, quā desertos a veritate.* And I thinke verily that not only vve, but the vviser men among them selues smile at such eloquence, or pitie it, saying
Cicero de Senect. this or the like most truely, *Prodierunt oratores noui, stulti adolescentuli.*

16 The 4 point is, of picking quarels to the very original text: for alter & change it I hope they shal not be able in this vvatchful vvorld of most vigilant Catholikes. But vvhat they vvould doe, if
Beza the mouse of Geneua, gnavveth the text of Scripture. al Bibles vvere only in their handes and at their commaundement, ghesse by this: that Beza against the euidence of al copies both Greeke and Latin, (In his Annot. vpon the new Test. set forth in the yere 1556.) thinketh πρῶτος is more then should be in the text Mat. 10: & τὸ ἐκχυνόμενον Luc. 22. and προσκυνεῖν αὐτοῖς Act. 7: the first, against Peters supremacie: the second, against the real presence of Christs bloud in the B. Sacrament: the third, against the making of vvhatsoeuer images, vvhether they be adored or no. Thus you see hovv the mouse of Geneua (as I told you before of Marcion the mouse of Pontus) knibbleth and gnavveth about it, though he can not bite it of altogether.

17 He doth the like in sundrie places vvhich you may see in his Annotations Act. 7. v.16. Vvhere he is saucie against al copies Greeke and Latin to pronounce corruption, corruption, auouching and endeuouring to proue that it must be so, and that vvith these vvordes, *To vvhat purpose should the holy Ghost, or Luke, adde this?* Act.8.v.26. But because those places concerne no cōtrouersie, I say no more but that he biteth at the text, and vvould change it according to his imagination, if he might: vvhich is to proud an enterprise for Beza, and smal reuerence of the holy scriptures, so to call the very text into controuersie, that vvhatsoeuer pleaseth not him, crept out of the margent into the text, vvhich is his common and almost his only coniecture.

18 He biteth sore at the vvord ἀνατολὴ Luc.1.v. 78. and vvil not trāslate that, but the Hebrue word of the old Testament. but at ὠδῖνας (Act. 2. v. 24.) much more, & at ἑβδομήκοντα πέντε (Act. 7. v. 14.) excedingly: but yet after he hath said al that he could against it, he concludeth, that *he durst not, and that he had a conscience, vpon coniecture to change any thing.* And therfore al this is gnavving only. but in the 3 of Luke he maketh no conscience at al, to leaue out these wordes vers. 36, *Qui fuit Cainan*, not only in his owne translation, but in the vulgar Latin vvhich is ioyned therewith, saying in his Annot. *Non dubitauimus expungere*, that is, *Vve doubted not to put it out*: & vvhy? *by the authoritie of Moyses Gen.* 11. Vvhereby he signifieth, that it is not in the Hebrue Gen.11. vvhere this posteritie of Sem is reckened: and so to mainteine the Hebrue veritie (as they call it) in the old Testament he careth not vvhat become of the Greeke in the nevv Testament: vvhich yet at other times, against the vulgar Latin text,

צֶמַח

No. Test. an. 1556.

τοῦ καϊνάν.

Beza reconcileth the Greeke text of the nevv Testament vvith the Hebrue text of the old, by putting out of the Greeke text so much as pleaseth him.

text, they call the Greeke veritie , and the pure fountaine , and that text vvhereby al tranſlations muſt be tried.

19 But if he haue no other vvay to reconcile both Teſtaments, but by ſtriking out in the Greeke of the new , al that agreeth not vvith the Hebrue of the old Teſtament, then let him alter and chāge ſo many wordes of our Sauiour him ſelf, of the Euangeliſtes, and of the Apoſtles, as are cited out of the old Teſtament , and are not in Hebrue. Vvhich places they know are very many, & when neede is, they ſhal be gathered to their handes. Let him ſtrike out (Mat. 13. v. 14. 15. & Act. 28. v 26. 27)
Eſa. 6, 9. 10. the vvordes of our Sauiour and S. Paul , cited out of Eſay, becauſe they are far otherwiſe in the He-
Gal. 3, 13. brue. Strike out of the epiſtle to the Galatiās theſe
πᾶς κρεμάμενος ἐπὶ ξύλου. vvordes, *vpon a tree* : becauſe in the Hebrue it is only thus *Curſed is he that is hanged.* Deut. 21 in fine. Yea ſtrike out of Dauids Pſalmes that which con-
כָּאֲרִי cerneth our redemption vpon the Croſſe much neerer, *They haue pearced my handes & my feete*, Pſ. 21. becauſe in the Hebrue there is no ſuch thing. Let
ἔλαβες them cōtroule the Apoſtle, *Eph.* 4, for ſaying, *dedit*
לָקַחְתָּ *he gaue giftes* : becauſe it is both in the Hebrue and Greeke, (Pſal. 67) *Accepiſti, thou tookeſt giftes.* and (Hebr. 10) for, *corpus aptaſti*, let them put, *aures per-*
אָזְנַיִם *foraſti*, becauſe it is ſo in the Hebrue Pſal. 40. To be
כָּרִיתָ ſhort , if al muſt be reformed according to the Hebrue , vvhy doth he not in S. Steuens ſermon cut
לִּי of the number of fiue ſoules from ſeuentie fiue, becauſe it is not in the Hebrue?

20 Muſt ſuch difficulties and diuerſities be reſolued by chopping and changing , hacking and hewing the ſacred text of holy Scripture ? See into vvhat perplexities wilful hereſie and arrogācie hath driuen them . To diſcredite the vulgar Latin tranſlation of the Bible, and the fathers expoſitiós accor-

according to the ſame (for that is the original cauſe of this) and beſides, that they may haue alwaies this euaſion, *It is not ſo in the Hebrue, it is othervviſe in the Greeke*, and ſo ſeeme ioly fellowes and great clerkes vnto the ignorant people, what doe they? they admit only the Hebrue in the old Teſt. and the Greeke in the nevv, to be the true and authentical text of the Scripture Vvhervpō this folovveth, that they reiect, and muſt needes reiect the Greeke of the old Teſt. (called the Septuaginta) as falſe, becauſe it differeth frō the Hebrue. Vvhich being reiected therevpon it folovveth againe, that whereſoeuer thoſe places ſo diſagreing from the Hebrue are cited by Chriſt or the Euangeliſtes & Apoſtles, there alſo they muſt be reiected, becauſe they diſagree from the Hebrue. and ſo yet againe it folovveth, that the Greeke text of the nevv Teſtament is not true, becauſe it is not according to the Hebrue veritie: and conſequently the wordes of our Sauiour, and vvritings of his Apoſtles muſt be reformed (to ſay the leſt) becauſe they ſpeake according to the Septuaginta, and not according to the Hebrue.

Their perplexitie in defending both the hebrue text of the old Teſtament, and Greeke text of the new.

21 Al which muſt needes folow, if this be a good conſequēce, *I finde it not in Moyſes, nor in the Hebrue, therfore I ſtrooke it out*, as Beza doth and ſaith concerning the foreſaid vvordes, *Qui fuit Cainan*. This conſequence therfore let vs ſee hovv they vvil iuſtifie: and vvithal let them tel vs, vvhether they vvil diſcredite the nevv Teſtament, becauſe of the Septuaginta, or credite the Septuaginta, becauſe of the nevv Teſtamēt, or hovv they cā credite one, & diſcredite the other, vvhere both agree & conſent together: or, vvhether they vvil diſcredite both, for credite of the Hebrue: or rather, whether there be not ſome other way to reconcile both Hebrue and Greeke, better then Bezas impudent preſumption

ption. Vvhich if they vvil not mainteine, let them flatly confeſſe that he did vvickedly, and not (as they doe) defend euery vvord and deede of their Maiſters, be it neuer ſo heinous, or ſalue it at the leaſt.

Hovv the fathers reconcile the ſaid Hebrue and Greeke.

22 Alas hovv far are theſe men from the modeſtie of the auncient fathers, and from the humble ſpirit of obedient Catholikes, vvho ſeeke al other meanes to reſolue difficulties, rather then to doe violence to the ſacred Scripture, and vvhen they finde no vvay, they leaue it to God. S. Auguſtine concerning the difference of the Hebrue and the Greeke, ſaith often to this effect, that it pleaſed the holy Ghoſt to vtter by the one, that vvhich he vvould not vtter by the other. And S. Ambroſe thus, *Vve haue found many things not idly added of the 70 Greeke interpreters.* S. Hierom, though an earneſt patrone of the Hebrue (not vvithout cauſe, being at that time perhaps the Hebrue veritie in deede) yet giueth many reaſons for the differences of the Septuaginta, and concerning the foreſaid places of S. Luke, he doth giue a reaſon thereof, both for the 70, and for the Euangeliſt that folovved them, neither doubting of the truth thereof, nor controuling them *by the authoritie of Moyſes* (as Beza ſpeaketh) that is, by the Hebrue. Others ſay concerning Cainan, that Moyſes might leaue him out in the Genealogie of Sem, by the inſtinct of the ſame Spirit, that S. Matthevv left out three kings in the genealogie of our Sauiour. Vvhere if a man vvould controule the Euangeliſt by the Hebrue of the old Teſtament that is read in the bookes of the kings, he ſhould be as vviſe and as honeſt a man as Beza. Laſtly, Venerable Bede thinketh it ſufficient in this very difficultie of Cainan, to maruel at it reuerently, rather then to ſearche it dangerouſly. And thus far of picking

Li.18. de Ciuit. c. 43. 2 Lib. de Doct. Chr. c. 15.

Hexam. li. 3. cap. 6.

In Procem. li. Paralip.

Cōment. in 28. Eſa. and in quæſtion. Hebrai.

Mat. c. 1.

Præf. in Act. Apoſt.

quarels

quarels to the original text, and their good vvil to alter and change it as they list, if they might be suffered.

23 Vvhich also may be proued by al their false translations (being the principal point I meane to speake of) most euidently. For as novv they translate falsely to their purpose, because they can not alter the text: so vvould they, if it vvere possible, haue the text agreable to their translation. For example, he that translateth, *ordinances*, vvhen it is in the original Greeke text, *iustifications*, and, *traditions*, he vvould rather that it vvere, *ordinances*, also in the Greeke: but because he cannot bring that about, he doth at the least vvhat he can, to make the ignorant beleeue it is so, by so translating it.

The 5. abuse of Scriptures, *Corrupt translation*. vvhich is the argumét and purpose of this booke.

24 And this of al other is the most fine and subtil treacherie against the Scriptures, to deceiue the ignorant readers vvithal, (vvhich S. Paul calleth *the secrete things of dishonestie, and adulterating of the vvord of God*, as it vvere mingling vvater vvith vvine like false vinteners) vvhen they giue them for Gods vvord, & vnder the name of Gods word, their ovvne vvordes, and not Gods, forged and framed, altered and changed, according to differences of times, and varietie of nevv opinions, and diuersitie of humors and spirits, diuersely and differently, one Heretike not-only correcting his fellovv euery day, but one egrely refuting and refelling an other. *Bucer, and the Osiandrians and c Sacramentaries against Luther for false translations: Luther against Munster, Beza against Castaleo, Castaleo against Beza, Caluin against Seruetus, Illyricus both against Caluin and Beza: The Puritanes cõtroule the grosser Caluinistes of our Countrie, yea the later translations of the self same Heretikes controule the former excedingly, not only of ouersights, but of vvilful falsifications, as it is noto-

2 Cor. 4

The Heretikes dissension about their translations.

* Dial. cont. Melanćth. Lind. dubit. pag. 84, 56. 98.

c See Zuingl. resp. 1. and Confess. Tigurinorum.

ibid.pag. 83. 97.

notorious in the * later editions of Luther and Beza, and in our Englifh Bibles fet forth in diuers yeres, from Tindal their firft tranflatour vntil this day: yea (vvhich is more) the Englifh trãflatours of Bezas nevv Teftament, controule him and his tranflation vvhich they proteft to folovv, * being afraid fometime and afhamed to expreffe in Englifh his falfe tranflations in the Latin.

The nevv Teft. of the yere 1580.

* Luc. 3, 36. Act. 1, 14. & 2, 23. Act. 3, 21.

25 But in this Catalogue of diffentious falfifiers and difagreing tranflatours, I vvil not greatly rippe vp old faultes neither abrode, nor at home. I leaue Luthers falfe tranflations into the German tongue, to the credite of Staphylus, *Apolog. part. 2.* and Emferus, *præf. Annot. in no. Teft. Luth.* and other German vvriters of his ovvne time, that favv them and readde them, and reckened the nũber of them in the nevv Teftamẽt only, about * 1400 heretical corruptions: I leaue Caluins and Bezas frenche corruptions, to fo many vvorthie men as * haue noted them in their frẽche bookes againft the faid heretikes: Tindals and his companions corruptiõs in their firft Englifh bible, to our learned coũtriemen of that age, & namely to the right Reuerend Father and Confeffor Bifhop Tonftal, vvho in a fermon openly protefted that he had found in the nevv Teftament only, no leffe then two thoufand. If vve knovv it not, or vvil not beleeue it, * ftrangers in their Latin vvritings teftifie it to the vvorld.

The Germã, Frenche, and Englifh corruptions of the nevv Teftament.

* See Lind. Dubit. p. 84 85, &c.

* Vigor and the reft.

* Lind. Dub. pag. 98.

26 But I omit thefe as vnknovven to our countrie, or to this age, and vvil deale principally vvith the Englifh tranflations of our time, vvhich are in euery mans handes vvithin our countrie the corruptions vvhereof, as they are partly touched here and there in the Annotations vpon the late nevv Englifh Teftament Catholikely tranflated & printed at Rhemes, fo by occafion thereof, I vvil by Gods

The authors intẽt in this booke.

Gods help,to the better comoditie of the reader, and euidence of the thing, lay them closer together,and more largely display them,not counting the number,because it vvere hard, but esteeming the vveight & importance of so many as I thought good to note, specially in the nevv Testament. Vvhere I haue to aduertise the Reader of certaine special things, vvhich he must obserue.

Certaine aduertisemēts to the Reader.

27 First, that in this booke he may not looke for the proofe or explication & deciding of controuersies, Vvhich is done in the Annotations vpon the new Testament,but only the refuting or controuling of their false translations concerning the said controuersies, vvhich is the peculiar argumēt of this treatise.

28 Secondly, that vve refute sometime one of their translations, sometime an other, and euery one as their falshod giueth occasion. Neither is it a good defense for the falshod of one, that it is truely translated in an other: the reader being deceiued by any one; because commonly he readeth but one. Yea one of them is a cōdemnation of the other.

29 Thirdly,that we speake indifferently against Protestants, Caluinistes, Bezites, and Puritans, vvithout any curious distinction of them, being al among them selues brethren and pewfellowes, and sometime the one sort of them, sometime the other more or lesse corrupting the holy Scriptures.

30 Fourthly,that we giue but a tast of their corruptions,not seing so far, nor marking al so narrowly and skilfully, as them selues knovv their ovvne subtelties and meanings, vvho vvil smile at the places vvhich we haue not espied.

31 Fifthly, that the very vse and affectation of certaine termes,and auoiding other some, though

it be no demonſtration againſt them, but that they may ſeeme to defend it for true tráſlation, yet was it neceſſarie to be noted, becauſe it is & hath been alvvaies a token of heretical meaning.

32 Sixtly, that in explicating theſe things, vve haue endeuoured to auoid (as much as vvas poſſible) the tedious ſnes of Greeke & Hebrue vvordes, vvhich are only for the learned in theſe tongues, and vvhich made ſome litle doubt vvhether this matter (vvhich of neceſſitie muſt be examined by them) vvere to be vvritten in Engliſh or no. but being perſuaded by thoſe (vvho them ſelues haue no ſkill in the ſaid tõgues) that euery reader might reape commoditie thereby, to the vnderſtanding & deteſting of ſuch falſe and Heretical tranſlations, it vvas thought good to make it vulgar and common to al our deere countrie men, as the nevv Teſtament it ſelf is cõmon, vvhereof this Diſcouerie is as it vvere an handmaid, attending therevpon for the larger explication and proofe of corruptions there breefely touched, and for ſupplie of other ſome not there mentioned.

33 Seuenthly, that al the Engliſh corruptions here noted and refuted, are either in al or ſome of their Engliſh bibles printed in theſe yeres, 1562. 1577. 1579. And if the corruption be in one Bible, not in an other, commonly the ſaid Bible or bibles are noted in the margent: if not, yet ſure it is that it is in one of them, and ſo the reader ſhal finde it, if he finde it not alvvaies in his ovvne Bible. And in this caſe the reader muſt be very vviſe and circũſpect, that he thinke not by and by vve charge them falſly, becauſe they can ſhevv him ſome later edition that hath it not ſo as vve ſay. for it is their common and knovven faſhion, not onely in their tranſlations of the Bible, but in their other bookes and vvritinges, to alter and change, adde and put

out,

out, in their later editiõs, according as either them selues are ashamed of the former, or their scholers that print them againe, dissent and disagree from their Maisters. So hath Luthers, Caluins, and Bezas vvritinges and translations been changed both by them selues and their scholers in many places, so that Catholike men when they cõfute that which they finde euident faultes in this or that edition, feare nothing more then that the reader hath some other edition, where they are corrected for very shame, and so may conceiue that there is no such thing, but that they are accused vvrongfully. for example. Call to minde the late pretended conference in the tower, where that matter vvas denied and faced out for Luthers credite, by some one booke or edition of his, vvhich them selues, and al the vvorld knoweth was most truely laid to his charge.

Touching S. Iames epistle.

34 Eightly, in citing Beza, I meane alvvaies (vnles I note othervvise) his Latin translation of the nevv Testament vvith his annotations adioyned therevnto, printed in the yere 1556.

35 Lastly and principally is to be noted that we wil not charge them vvith falsifying that vvhich in deede is the true and authentical Scripture, I meane the vulgar Latin Bible, vvhich so many yeres hath been of so great authoritie in the Church of God, and with al the auncient fathers of the Latin Church, as is declared in the preface of the Nevv Testament: though it is much to be noted, that as Luther, only in fauour of his heresies did vvilfully forsake it, so the rest folowed and do folovv him at this day, for no other cause in the vvorld but that it is against them. & therfore they inueigh against it, and against the holy Councel of Trent for confirming the authoritie thereof, both in their special treatises thereof, and in al their

Vve charge them not with forsaking the old approued Latin text, though it be an il signe, & to their euident confusion.

Kemnitius. Caluin.

vvritinges, vvhere they can take any occaſion.

36 And concerning their vvilful and heretical auoiding thereof in their nevv tranſlations, vvhat greater argumēt can there be then this, that Luther, vvho before alvvaies had readde vvith the Cath. Church and vvith al antiquitie, theſe vvordes of S. Paul, *Haue not vve povver to leade about* A WOMAN A SISTER, *as alſo the reſt of the Apoſtles?* and in S. Peter, theſe vvordes, *Labour that* BY GOOD WORKES *you may make ſure your vocation and election:* ſodenly, after he had cōtrarie to his profeſſion taken *a vvife* (as he called her) and preached that al other votaries might do the ſame, and that faith only iuſtified, *good vvorkes* vvere not neceſſarie to ſaluation: ſodenly (I ſay) after he fell to theſe heresies, he began to reade and tranſlate the former Scriptures accordingly, thus: *Haue not vve povver to leade about a* SISTER A WIFE, *as the reſt of the Apoſtles?* and, *Labour that you may make ſure your vocation and election:* leauing out the other vvordes, *by good vvorkes*. And ſo doe both the Caluiniſts abrode, and our Engliſh Proteſtants at home reade and tranſlate at this day, becauſe they hold the ſelf ſame hereſies.

1 Cor. 9. *Mulierem ſororem.* 2 Pet. 1.

37 So doe they in infinite places alter the old text, vvhich pleaſed them vvell before they vvere Heretikes, and they doe it vvith braſen faces, and plaine proteſtation, hauing no ſhame nor remorſe at al, in fleeing from that vvhich all antiquitie vvith one conſent allovved and embraced vntil their vnhappie daies. Vvhich though it be an euident cōdemnation of their nouelties in the ſight of any reaſonable man that hath any grace, yet as I began to admoniſh thee (gentle Reader) vve vvil not charge them for altering the auncient approued Latin tranſlation, becauſe they pretend to folovv the Hebrue and Greeke, and our purpoſe is not here,

here, to proue that they should not folovv the Hebrue and Greeke that now is, before the auncient approued Latin text, which is done breifely already in the preface to the nevv Testament.

38 Neither vvil vve burden them, for not folovving the vulgar Latin text, vvhen the same agreeth with most auncient Greeke copies: vvhich notvvithstāding is great partialitie in them, & must needes be of an heretical vvilful humor, that amōg the Greeke copies them selues, they reiect that vvhich most agreeth vvith the vulgar Latin text, in places of controuersies: Yet vvil vve not I say, neither in this case, lay falshod and corruption to their charge, because they pretend to translate the common Greeke text of the nevv Testament, that is, one certaine copie. but here at the least let them shevv their fidelitie, & that they be true and exacte translatours. for here onely shal they be examined and called to account.

Vve charge them not vvith forsaking the Greeke copies that agree vvith the auncièt approued Latin text, though this be a signe of their incredible partialitie.

39 And if they folovv sincerely their Greeke and Hebrue text, vvhich they professe to folovv, and which they esteeme the only authentical text, so far vve accuse them not of heretical corruption. but if it shal be euidētly proued, that they shrinke from the same also, and translate an other thing, and that vvilfully, and of ful intention to countenance their false religion and wicked opinions, making the Scriptures to speake as they list: then vve trust, the indifferēt reader for his ovvne soules sake, vvil easily see and conclude, that they haue no feare of God, no reuerence of the Scriptures, no conscience to deceiue their readers: He vvil perceiue that the Scriptures make against them, vvhich they so peruert and corrupt for their purpose: that neither the Hebrue nor Greeke text is for them, vvhich they dare not translate truely and sincerely: that their cause is naught, which needeth such foul

Vve charge them for forsaking & false translating their ovvne Hebrue and Greeke texts.

 shiftes

ſhiftes: that they muſt needes knovv al this, and therfore doe vvilfully againſt their conſcience, & conſequently are obſtinate Heretikes.

40 And the more to vnderſtand their miſerie & vvretchednes, before vve enter to examine their trãſlations, marke & gather of al that vvhich I haue ſaid in this preface, their manifold ſlightes & iumpes, from one ſhift to an other, & hovv Catholike writers haue purſued and chaſed them, & folovved them, and driuen them euen to this extreme refuge and ſeely couert of falſe tranſlation, vvhere alſo they muſt of neceſſitie yeld, or deuiſe ſome nevv euaſion, which vve can not yet imagin.

The diuers ſhiftes and ſlighces that the Proteſtants are driuen vnto by the Catholikes, as it vvere the iumpes and turnings of an hare before the houndes.

41 Firſt we are vvont to make this offer (as we thinke) moſt reaſonable and indifferent: that foraſmuch as the Scriptures are diuerſely expounded of vs and of them, they neither be tied to our interpretation, nor vve to theirs, but to put it to the arbitrement and iudgement of the auncient fathers, of general Councels, of vniuerſal cuſtom of times and places in the Catholike Church. No, ſay they, vve wil be our ovvne iudges and interpreters, or folow Luther, if we be Lutherans: Caluin, if we be Caluiniſtes: and ſo forth.

42 This being of it ſelf a ſhameles ſhift, vnles it be better coloured, the next is to ſay, that the Scriptures are eaſie and plaine & ſufficient of them ſelues to determine euery matter, and therfore they wil be tried by the Scriptures only. we are cõtent, becauſe they wil needes haue it ſo, and vve alleage vnto them the bookes of Tobie, Eccleſiaſticus, Machabees. No, ſay they: we admit none of theſe for Scripture. Vvhy ſo? are they not approued Canonical by the ſame authoritie of the Church, of auncient Councels and fathers, that the other bookes are? No matter, ſay they, Luther admitteth them not, Caluin doth not allovv them.

40 Vvel

43 Vvel, let vs goe forvvard in their ovvne daunce. You allow at the least the Ievves Canonical bookes of the old Testament, that is, al that are extant in the Hebrue Bible: and al of the new Testament vvithout exception. Yea, that we doe. In these bookes then, wil you be tried by the vulgar auncient Latin Bible, only vsed in al the vvest Church aboue a thousand yeres? No. Vvil you be tried by the Greeke Bible of the Septuaginta interpreters, so renovvmed and authorised, in our Sauiours ovvne speaches, in the Euangelistes and Apostles writings, in the whole Greeke Church euermore? No How then wil you be tried? They ansvver, Only by the Hebrue Bible that now is, and as novv it is pointed with vovvels. Vvil you see? and do you thinke that only, the true authentical Hebrue which the holy Ghost did first put into the pennes of those sacred writers? Vve do thinke it (say they) and esteeme it the only authentical and true Scripture of the old Testament.

44 Vve aske them againe, what say you then to that place of the psalme, where in the Hebrue it is thus, *As a lion my handes and my feete*: for that which in truth should be thus, *They digged* or *pearced my handes and my feete*: being an euident prophecie of Christs nailing to the Crosse. There in deede (say they) we folow not the Hebrue, but the Greeke text. Sometime then you folow the Greeke and not the Hebrue only. And what if the same Greeke text make for the Catholikes, as in these places for example, *I haue inclined my hart to keepe thy iustifications for revvard*: and, *Redeeme thy sinnes vvith almes*: might we not obtaine here the like fauour at your hands for the Greeke text, specially when the Hebrue doth not disagree? No, say they, nor in no other place vvhere the Greeke is neuer so plaine, if the Hebrue word at the least may be any other-

כָּאֲרִי

 wise

wise interpreted, and drawen to an other signification.

45 Vve replie againe and say vnto them, vvhy, Is not the credite of those Septuaginta interpreters, vvho them selues vvere Ievves, and best learned in their owne tongue, and (as S. Augustine often, and other auncient fathers say) vvere inspired vvith the holy Ghost, in translating the Hebrue bible into Greeke: Is not their credite (I say) in determining and defining the signification of the Hebrue vvord, far greater then yours? No. Is not the authoritie of al the auncient fathers both Greeke and Latin, that folovved them, equiualent in this case to your iudgement? No, say they, but because vve finde some ambiguitie in the Hebrue, we wil take the aduantage, and we wil determine and limite it to our purpose.

46 Againe vve condescend to their vvilfulnes, and say: vvhat if the Hebrue be not ambiguous, but so plaine & certaine to signifie one thing, that it can not be plainer? As, *Thou shalt not leaue my soule in Hel*, vvhich proueth for vs, that Christ in soule descended into Hel. Is not the one Hebrue vvord as proper for soule, as *anima* in Latin, the other as proper and vsual for Hel, as *Infernus* in Latin? Here then at the least vvil you yeld? No, say they, not here neither. for Beza telleth vs that the Hebrue vvord, vvhich commonly and vsually signifieth, *soule*, yet for a purpose, if a man vvil straine it, may signifie, not only *body*, but also, *carcas* and so he translateth it. But Beza (say vve) being admonished by his frendes, corrected it in his later edition. Yea, say they, he was content to change his translation, but not his opinion concerning the Hebrue word, as him self protesteth.

Psal. 15. נַפְשִׁי בִּשְׁאוֹל

47 Vvel then, doth it like you to reade thus according to Bezas translation, *Thou shalt not leaue my*

carcas

carcas in the graue? No, we are content to alter the word carcas (which is not a seemely word for our Sauiours body) and yet we are loth to say soule, but if we might, we vvould say rather, *life, person*, as appeareth in the margent of our Bibles. but as for the Hebrue word that signifieth Hel, though the Greeke and Latin Bible through out, the Greeke and Latin fathers in al their writinges, as occasion serueth, do so reade it and vnderstand it, yet wil we neuer so translate it: but for *Hel*, we vvil say *graue*, in al such places of Scripture as might inferre *Limbus patrum*, if we should translate, *Hel*. These are their shiftes, and turninges, and windinges, in the old Testament.

48 In the new Testament, we aske them, wil you be tried by the auncient Latin translation, which is the text of the fathers and the whole Church? No, but we appeale to the Greeke. Vvhat Greeke, say we, for there be sundrie copies, and the best of them (as Beza confesseth) agree with the said auncient Latin. for example in S. Peters wordes, *Labour that by good vvorkes you may make* 2 Pet. ca. 1.
sure your vocation and election. doth this Greeke copie please you? No, say they: we appeale to that Greeke copie, which hath not those wordes, *by good workes*, for otherwise we should graunt the merite and efficacie of good workes tovvard saluation: and generally to tel you at once, by what Greeke we wil be tried, we like best the vulgar Greeke text of the new Testament, which is most common and in euery mans handes.

49 Vvel, say we, if you wil needes haue it so, take your pleasure in choosing your text. and if you wil stand to it, graunt vs that Peter was cheese among the Apostles, because your ovvne Greeke text saith, *The first, Peter.* No, saith Beza: we vvil Mat. 10.
graunt you no such thing, for these wordes were

added

added to the Greeke text by one that fauoured Peters primacie. Is it so? then you wil not stand to this Greeke text neither. Not in this place, saith Beza.

50 Let vs see an other place. You must graunt vs (say we) by this Greeke text, that Christs very bloud which was shed for vs, is really in the chalice, because S. Luke saith so in the Greeke text. No, saith Beza, those Greeke wordes came out of the margent into the text, & therfore I trāslate not according to them, but according to that which I thinke the truer Greeke text, although I finde it in no copies in the world, and this his doing* is mainteined & iustified by our English Protestants in their writinges of late.

* See chap. 1. nu. 37. chap. 17. nu. 11.

51 Vvel yet, say we, there are places in the same Greeke text, as plaine for vs as these novv cited, where you can not say, it came out of the margent, or, it was added falsely to the text. As, *Stand and hold fast the traditions &c.* by this text we require that you graunt vs traditions deliuered by word of mouth, as wel as the vvritten word, that is, the Scriptures. No, say they, we knovv the Greeke word signifieth tradition as plaine as possibly, but here and in the like places, we rather translate it, *ordinances*, *instructions*, and what els soeuer. Nay Sirs, say vve, you can not so ansvver the matter, for in other places, you translate it duely and truely, *tradition*: and vvhy more in one place then in an other? They are ashamed to tel vvhy, but they must tel, and shame both them selues and the Diuel, if euer they thinke it good to ansvver this treatise, as also why they chinged *congregation*, which vvas alvvaies in their first translation, into *Church*, in their later translations, & did not change likevvise *ordinances* into *traditions*, *Elders* into *Priests*.

2 Thess. 2.

52 The

52 The cause is, that the name of Church was at the first odious vnto them, because of the Catholike Church which stoode against them: but afterward this name grevve into more fauour vvith them, because of their English Church, so at length called and termed. but their hatred of Priests and traditions continueth still, as it first began, and therfore their translation also remaineth as before, suppressing the names both of the one and of the other. But of al these their dealings they shal be told in their seueral chapters and places.

53 To conclude as I began, concerning their shiftes, and iumpes, and vvindinges, and turninges euery way, from one thing to an other, til they are driuen to the extreme refuge of palpable corruptions and false translations: consider vvith me in this one case only of traditions, as may be likevvise considered in al other controuersies, that the auncient fathers, councels, antiquitie, vniuersalitie, & custom of the vvhole Church allovv traditions: the canonical Scriptures haue them, the latin text hath them, the Greeke text hath them: only their translations haue them not. Likevvise in the old Testament, the approued latin text hath such and such speaches that make for vs, the renovvmed Greeke text hath it, the Hebrue text hath it: only their translations haue it not.

These are the translations vvhich vve cal heretical and vvilful, and vvhich shal be examined & discussed in this booke.

THE ARGVMENTS OF EVERY CHAPTER, VVITH THE PAGE VVHERE euery Chapter beginneth.

A DISCOVERIE OF THE MANIFOLD CORRVPTIONS OF THE HOLY SCRIPTVRES, by the Heretikes of our daies, specially the English Sectaries, & of their foule dealing herein, by partial and false translations to the aduantage of their heresies, in their English Bibles vsed and authorised since the time of Schisme.

CHAP. I.

That the Protestants translate the holy Scriptures falsely of purpose, in fauour of their heresies.

THOVGH this shal euidently appeare through out this vvhole booke in euery place that shal be obiected vnto them: yet because it is an obseruation of greatest importance in this case, and vvhich stingeth them sore, & toucheth their credite exceedingly, in so much that one of them setting a good face vpon the matter, * saith confi- dently

* Confutation of Io. Hovvlet fol. 35. pag. 2.

dently, that al the Papists in the vvorld are not able to shevv one place of Scripture mistrāslated wilfully and of purpose: therfore I vvil giue the reader, certaine breife obseruations and euident markes to knovv vvilful corruptions, as it vvere an abridgement and summe of this treatise.

Euidēt markes or signes to knovv vvilful corruptions in translating.

2 The first marke and most general is: If they translate els vvhere not amisse, and in places of controuersie betvvene them and vs, most falsely: it is an euident argument that they doe it not of negligence, or ignorance, but of partialitie to the matter in cōtrouersie. This is to be seen through the vvhole Bible, vvhere the faultes of their translations are altogether, or specially, in those Scriptures that concerne the causes in question betvvene vs. For other smal faultes, or rather ouersightes, vve vvil no further note vnto them, then to the end, that they may the more easily pardon vs the like, if they finde them.

3 If, as in their opinions & heresies, they forsake the auncient fathers: so also in their translations, they goe from that text & auncient reading of holy Scriptures, vvhich al the fathers vsed and expounded: is it not plaine that their translation folovveth the veine and humor of their heresie? And againe if they that so abhorre from the auncient

auncient expoſitions of the fathers, yet if it ſeeme to ſerue for them, ſticke not to make the expoſition of any one Doctor, the very text of holy Scripture: vvhat is this but heretical wilfulnes? See this 1. chap. nu. 43. ch. 10. nu. 1. 2. cha. 18. numb. 10. 11. and chap. 19. nu. 1.

4 Againe, if they that profeſſe to tranſlate the Hebrue and Greeke, and that becauſe it maketh more for them (as they ſay) and therfore in al cõferences and diſputatiōs appeale vnto it as to the foũtaine & touchſtone, if they (I ſay) in tranſlating places of controuerſie, flee from the Hebrue and the Greeke, it is a moſt certaine argumẽt of vvilful corruption. This is done mañy vvaies, and is to be obſerued alſo through out the vvhole Bible, and in al this booke.

5 If the Greeke be, *Idololatria*, and *idololátra*: and they tranſlate not, *Idolatrie*, and, *idolater*: but, *vvorſhipping of images*, & *vvorſhipper of images*, and that ſo abſurdly, that they make the Apoſtle ſay, *Couetouſnes is vvorſhipping of images*: this none vvould doe but fooles or mad men, vnles it vvere of purpoſe againſt ſacred images. See chap. 3. numb 1. 2.

εἰδωλολατρεία. εἰδωλολάτρης. Eph. 5. Col. 3 Bib. an. 1577.

6 If the Apoſtle ſay, A pagan *idolater*, and a Chriſtian *idolater*, by one and the ſame Greeke vvord, in one and the ſame meaning: and they tranſlate, A pagan *idolater*, & a Chr

1 Cor. 5. εἰδωλολάτρης. Bib. an. 1562

a Chriſtian *vvorſhipper of images*, by tvvo diſtinct vvordes and diuerſe meanings: it muſt needes be done vvilfully to the foreſaid purpoſe. See chap.3.nu.8.9.

παράδοσις 7 If they trāſlate one & the ſame Greeke vvord, *Tradition*, vvhenſoeuer the Scripture ſpeaketh of euil traditions: and neuer tranſlate it ſo, vvhenſoeuer it ſpeaketh of good and Apoſtolical traditions: their intention is euident againſt the authoritie of Traditions. See chap.2.numb.1.2.3.

τί δογματίζεσθε. 8 Yea if they tranſlate, *Tradition*, takē in il part, vvhere it is not in the Greeke: & trāſlate it not ſo, where it is in the Greeke, takē

Col.2.v.20. in good part: it is more euidence of the foreſaid wicked intention. See chap. 2. nu. 5.6.

9 If they make this a good rule, to tranſlate according to the vſual ſignification, and not the original deriuation of wordes,

* Pag. 209. as Beza and * M. Vvhitakers doe: and if they tranſlate contrarie to this rule, vvhat is it but vvilful corruption? So they doe in tranſlating, *idolum*, an image, *Presbyter*, an elder: and the like. See chap. 4. & chap.6. nu.6.7.8. &c. nu.13.&c.

10 If *Presbyter*, by Eccleſiaſtical vſe, be appropriated to ſignifie a Prieſt, no leſſe then, *Epiſcopus*, to ſignifie a Biſhop, or *Diaconus*, a Deacon: and if they tranſlate theſe tvvo later

later accordingly, and the first neuer in al the nevv Testament: vvhat can it be but vvilful corruption in fauour of this heresie, * That there are no Priests of the nevv Testament? See chap. 6. numb. 12.

Vvhitak. p. 199.

11 If for Gods *altar*, they translate, *Temple*: & for Bels idololatrical *table*, they translate, *altar*: iudge vvhether it be not of purpose against our altars, and in fauour of their communion table. See chap. 17. numb. 15. 16.

12 If at the beginning of their heresie, vvhen sacred images vvere broken in peeces, altars digged dovvne, the Catholike Churches authoritie defaced, the king made supreme head, then their translation vvas made accordingly, and if aftervvard vvhen these errours vvere vvel established in the realme, and had taken roote in the peoples hartes, al vvas altered and changed in their later translations, and novv they could not finde that in the Greeke, vvhich vvas in the former translation: vvhat vvas it at the first but vvilful corruption to serue the time that then vvas? See chap. 3. 5. chap. 17. nu. 15. chap. 15. nu. 22.

Bib. in king Edvv. time, printed againe 1562.

13 If at the first reuolt, vvhen none were noted for Heretikes and Schismatikes, but them selues, they did not once put the names of Schisme or Heresie in the Bible, but

in steede thereof, *diuision*, and, *secte*, in so
Bib. 1562. much that for an Heretike, they said, *an*
Tit. 3. *author of Sectes*, vvhat may vve iudge of it
but as of vvilful corruption? See chap. 4, numb. 3.

14 If they trāslate so absurdly at the first, that them selues are driuen to change it for shame: it must needes be at the first vvilful corruption. for example, vvhen it vvas in the first, *Temple*, and in the later, *Altar*: in the first alvvaies, *Congregation*, in the later alvvaies, *Church*: in the first, *To the king as cheefe head*, in the later, *To the king as hauing preeminence*. So did Beza first translate, *carcas*, and afterward, *soule*. Which alteration in al these places is so great, that it could not be negligence at the first or ignorance, but a plaine heretical intention. See chap. 17. numb. 15. chap. 5. nu. 4. 5. chap. 15. numb. 22. chap. 7. nu. 2.

15 If they vvil not stand to al their translations, but flee to that namely vvhich novv is readde in their churches: & if that vvhich is novv read in their churches, differ in the pointes aforesaid, from that that vvas readde in their churches in king Edvvards time: & if from both these, they flee to the Geneua Bible, and from that againe, to the other aforesaid: vvhat shal vve iudge of the one or the other, but that al is voluntarie and as

they

they liſt? See chap. 3. numb. 10. 11. 12. cha. 10. numb. 12.

16 If they gladly vſe theſe wordes in il part, vvhere they are not in the original text, *Proceßion, ſhrines, deuotions, excommunicate, images:* and auoid theſe vvordes, vvhich are in the original, *Hymnes, grace, myſterie, Sacrament, Church, altar, Prieſts, Catholike, traditions, iuſtifications:* is it not plaine that they doe it of purpoſe to diſgrace, or ſuppreſſe the ſaid things and ſpeaches vſed in the Catholike Church? See chap. 21. numb. 5. & ſeq. chap. 12. numb. 3.

17 If in a caſe that maketh for them, they ſtraine the very original ſignification of the vvord, and in a caſe that maketh againſt them, they neglect it altogether: vvhat is this but vvilful and of purpoſe? See chap. 7. nu. 36.

18 If in vvordes of ambiguous and diuers ſignification, they vvil haue it ſignifie here or there, as it pleaſeth them: and that ſo vehemently, that here it muſt needes ſo ſignifie, and there it muſt not: and both this, and that, to one end and in fauour of one and the ſame opinion: vvhat is this but vvilful tranſlation? So doth Beza vrge γυναῖκα to ſignifie, *vvife*, and not to ſignifie, *vvife*, both againſt virginitie and chaſtitie of Prieſts: and the Engliſh Bible tranſlateth accordingly. See chap. 15. nu. 11. 12.

Beza in 1. Cor. 7. v. 1. & 9. v. 5.

Bib. an. 157[illegible]

19 If the Puritanes and grosser Caluinistes disagree about the translations, one part preferring the Geneua English Bible, the other the Bible read in their Church: and if the Lutherans condemne the Zuinglians & Caluinistes translations, and contrariwise: and if al Sectaries reproue eche an others translation: Vvhat doth it argue, but that the translations differ according to their diuers opinions? See their bookes vvritten one against an other.

Luc. 3. v. 36. Act. 1. v. 14. c. 2. v. 23. c. 3. v. 21. c. 26. v. 20. 2 Thes. 2. v. 15. & c. 3. v. 6.

20 If the English Geneua Bibles thẽ selues dare not folovv their Maister Beza, vvhom they professe to translate, because in their opinion he goeth vvide, and that in places of controuersie: hovv vvilful vvas he in so translating? See chap. 12. numb. 6. 8. cha. 13. numb. 1.

21 If for the most part they reprehend the old vulgar translation, and appeale to the Greeke: and yet in places of controuersie sometime for their more aduantage (as they thinke) they leaue the Greeke, and folovv our Latin translation: vvhat is it els, but voluntarie and partial translation? See chap. 2. nu. 8. chap. 6. nu. 10. 21. chap. 7. nu. 39. chap. 10. nu. 6.

Beza Luc. 1. Ro. 2. Apoc. 19, 8.

22 If othervvise they auoid this vvord, *iustificationes*, altogether, & yet trãslate it When they can not choose, but vvith a cõmẽtarie that

*that it signifieth good vvorkes that are te-stimonies of a liuely faith: doth not this heretical commentarie shevv their heretical meaning, vvhen they auoid the vvord altogether? See chap. 8. nu. 1. 2. 3. Beza in c.19. Apoc. v. 8.

23 Vvhen by adding to the text at their pleasure, they make the Apostle say, that by Adams offence, *sinne came* on al men, but that by Christs iustice, *the benefite* only *abounded tovvard* al men, not that iustice *came* on al, vvhereas the Apostle maketh the case alike, vvithout any such diuers additions, to vvit, * that vve are truely made iust by Christ, as by Adam vve are made sinners: is not this most vvilful corruption for their heresie of imputatiue and phantastical iustice. See chap. 11. nu. 1 Ro. 5. v. 18. No. Test. an. 1580. Bib. 1579. Ro. 5. v. 19.

24 But if in this case of iustification, vvhen the question is vvhether only faith iustifie, & vve say no, hauing the expresse vvordes of S. Iames: they say, yea, hauing no expresse scripture for it: if in this case they vvil adde, *only*, to the very text: is it not most horrible and diuelish corruption? So did Luther, * vvhom our English Protestants honour as their father, and in this heresie of *only faith*, are his ovvne children. See chap. 12. Ia. 2. v. 24. Ro. 3. v. 28. Luth. tom. 2. fol. 405. edit. Witteb. an. 1551. Whitak. pag. 198.

25 If these that account them selues the great Grecians & Hebricians of the vvorld, vvil so translate for the aduantage of their cause, as though they had no skil in the Their ignorance of the Greeke and Hebrue tongue, or their

ſalſe & wilful tranſlation thereof againſt their knowledge.

vvorld, and as though they knevv neither the ſignification of vvordes, nor proprietie of phraſes in the ſaid languages: is it not to be eſteemed ſhamleſſe corruption?

Brétius. Melancth. See Linda. Dubi. Dial. 1. c. 12
Pſal. 51.
σοὶ μόνῳ
לְבַדְּךָ

26 I vvil not ſpeake of the German Heretikes, vvho to mainteine this hereſie, that al our vvorkes, be they neuer ſo good, are ſinne, tranſlated, for *Tibi ſoli peccaui, to the only haue I ſinned*, thus, *Tibi ſolùm peccaui.* that is, *I haue nothing els but ſinned: vvhatſoeuer I doe, I ſinne:* vvhereas neither the Greeke nor the Hebrue vvil poſſibly admit that ſenſe. Let theſe paſſe as Lutherans, yet vvilful corrupters, ⋆ and acknovvledged of our Engliſh Proteſtants for their good brethren. But if Beza trãſlate, ἔτι ὄντων ἡμῶν ἀσθενῶν, *vvhen vve vvere yet of no ſtrength*, as the Geneua Engliſh Bible alſo doth interprete it, vvhereas euery yong Grecian knovveth that ἀσθενὴς is vveake, feeble, infirme, and not altogether without ſtrength: is not this of purpoſe to take avvay mans free vvil altogether? See chap. 10. nu. 13.

Whitak. pag. 198.
Ro. 5, v. 6.

1 Cor. 15.
ἡ σὺν ἐμοί.

27 If Caluin tranſlate, *Non ego, ſed gratia Dei quæ mibi aderat*: may not meane Grecians controule him, that he alſo tranſlateth falſely againſt free vvil, becauſe the prepoſition σὺν doth require ſome other participle to be vnderſtood, that ſhould ſignifie a cooperation vvith free vvil to vvit, συγκοπιάσασα, *vvhich laboured vvith me?* See chap. 10. nu. 2.

If,

28 If, vvhen the Hebrue beareth indifferẽt-
ly, to ſay, Sinne *lieth* at the doore: and, vnto
thee the deſire *thereof* ſhal be ſubiect, & thou Gen. 4. v. 7.
ſhalt rule *ouer it*: the Geneua Engliſh Bi- an. 1579.
ble tranſlate the firſt vvithout ſcruple, &
the later not, becauſe of the Hebrue grammar: is not this alſo moſt vvilful againſt
free vvil? See chap. 10. nu. 9.

29 If Caluin affirme that ἀπὸ εὐλαβείας cannot Calu. in 5.
ſignifie, *propter reuerentiam*, becauſe ἀπὸ is not Hebr.
ſo vſed, and Beza auoucheth the ſame more
earneſtly, and the Engliſh Bible tranſlateth Bib. an. 1579
accordingly, vvhich may be confuted by
infinite examples in the Scripture it ſelf, and
is confuted by Illyricus the Lutheran: is it
not a ſigne either of paſſing ignorance, or
of moſt wilful corruption, to mainteine the
blaſphemie that herevpon they conclude?
See chap. 7. nu. 42. 43,

30 If Beza in the ſelf ſame place contend,
that εὐλάβεια doth not ſignifie reuerence or
pietie, but ſuch a feare as hath horrour and
aſtoniſhmẽt of minde: & in an other place
ſaith of this ſelf ſame vvord, cleane contrarie: vvhat is it but of purpoſe to vphold
the ſaid blaſphemie? See cha. 7. nu. 39. 40.

31 If he tranſlate for, Gods *foreknovvledge*,
Gods *prouidence*, for *ſoule*, *carcas*, for *hel*, *graue*: πρόγνωσις
to vvhat end is this but for certaine here- Act. 2. v. 23.
tical concluſions? And if vpon admonitiõ ψυχὴ. ᾅδου.
ibid. v. 27.

he

Annota. in no. Teſt. poſt.edit. he alter his tranſlation for ſhame, and yet *proteſteth that he vnderſtandeth it as he did before, did he not tranſlate before vvilfully according to his obſtinate opinion? See chap. 7.

Annot. in Act. 2. v. 24. שְׁאוֹל 32 If to this purpoſe he auouch that, *Sheol*, ſignifieth nothing els in Hebrue but a graue, vvhereas al Hebricians knovv that it is the moſt proper and vſual vvord in the קֶבֶר Scripture for Hel, as the other vvord *Keber*, is for a graue: vvho vvould thinke he vvould ſo endanger his eſtimation in the Hebrue tongue, but that an heretical purpoſe againſt Chriſts deſcending into hel, blinded him? See chap. 7.

33 And if al the Engliſh Bibles trãſlate accordingly, to vvit, for Hel, *graue*, vvhereſoeuer the Scripture may meane any lower place that is not the Hel of the damned: and vvhere it muſt needes ſignifie that Hel, there they neuer auoid ſo to tranſlate it: is it not an euident argument that they know very vvel the proper ſignification, but of purpoſe they wil neuer vſe it to their diſaduantage in the queſtions of *Limbus*, Purgatorie, Chriſts deſcending into Hel? cha. 7.

34 If further yet in this kinde of contro-Annot. in Act. 2. v. 24. uerſie, Beza vvould be bold to affirme (for ſo he ſaith) if the Grammarians would giue חֶבֶל him leaue, that *Chebel* vvith fiue points ſignifieth

nifieth, *funem,* no lesse then *Chebel* vvith sixe points: is he not vvonderfully set to mainteine his opiniõ, that wil change the nature of vvordes, if he might, for his purpose? חֶבֶל That is, he vvould trãslate, *Solutis funibus mortis,* not, *Solutis doloribus inferni.*

35 If passiues must be turned into actiues, and actiues into passiues, participles disagree in case from their substantiues, or rather be plucked and separated from their true substantiues, solœcismes imagined, vvhere the construction is most agreable, errours diuised to creepe out of the margẽt, and such like: vvho vvould so presume in the text of holy Scripture, to haue al Grammar, and vvordes, and phrases, and constructions at his commaundement, but Beza & his like, for the aduantage of their cause? See chap. 5. nu. 6. and the numbers next folovving in this chapter.

36 For example S. Peter saith, *Heauen must receiue Christ.* He translateth, *Christ must be conteined in heauen,* vvhich Caluin him self misliketh, the Geneua English Bible is afraid to folovv, Illyricus the Lutheran reprehendeth: and yet M. Vvhitakers taketh the aduantage of this trãslation, to proue that Christs natural body is so conteined in heauen, that it can not be vpon the altar. For he knevv that this vvas his maisters purpose and intent in so translating. This it is, vvhen the blinde folovv the blinde, yea rather vvhen

Act. 3, 21. δέξασθαι.

Pag. 43.

vvhen they see and vvil be blinde: for certaine it is (& I appeale to their greatest Græciãs) that howsoeuer it be taken for good in their diuinitie, it wil be esteemed most false in their Greeke scholes both of Oxford and Cãbridge: & howsoeuer they may presume to translate the holy Scriptures after this sort, surely no man, no not them selues, would so translate Demosthenes, for sauing their credite and estimation in the Greeke tongue. See chap. 17. nu. 7. 8. 9.

37 But there is yet vvorse stuffe behind: to vvit, the famous place Luc. 22. vvhere Beza translateth thus, *Hoc poculum nouum testamentũ per meũ sanguinẽ*, qui *pro vobis funditur*: whereas in the Greeke, in al copies vvithout exception, he confesseth that in true Grammatical construction it must needes be said, *quod pro vobis funditur*, and therfore he saith it is either a plaine *solœcophanes*, (and according to that presumption he boldly translateth) or a corruption crept out of the margent into the text. And as for the vvord *solœcophanes*, vve vnderstand him that he meaneth a plaine solœcisme and fault in grammar, & so doth

Pag. 34. 35. M. Vvhitakers: but M. Fulke saith that he

Against D. Sand. Rocke pag. 308. meaneth no such thing, but that it is an elegancie and figuratiue speache, vsed of most eloquent authors: and it is a vvorld to see, and a Græcian must needes smile at his deuises,

uiſes, ſtriuing to make S. Lukes ſpeache here as he cōſtrueth the vvordes, an elegancie in the Greeke tōgue. He ſendeth vs firſt to Budees cōmentaries, where there are examples of *ſolœcophanes*: and in deede Budee taketh the vvord for that vvhich may ſeeme a ſolœciſme, and yet is an elegancie, and al his examples are of moſt fine and figuratiue phraſes, but alas hovv vnlike to that in S. Luke. and here M. Fulke vvas very fouly deceiued, thinking that Beza and Budee tooke the vvord in one ſenſe: and ſo taking his marke amiſſe, as it vvere a counter for gold, vvhere he found *ſolœcophanes* in Budee, there he thought al vvas like to S. Lukes ſentence, and that vvhich Beza meant to be a plaine ſolœciſme, he maketh it like to Budees elegancies. Much like to thoſe good ſearchers in Oxford (as it is ſaid) maiſters of art, vvho hauing to ſeeke for Papiſtical bookes in a lavvyers ſtudie, and ſeing there bookes vvith redde letters, cried out, Maſſe bookes, Maſſe bookes: vvhereas it vvas the Code or ſome other booke of the Ciuil or Canon Lavv.

See Com. Bud. *Figurata cōſtructio*, or, σχῆμα Ἀττικόν.

38 This was lacke of iudgemēt in M. Fulke at the leaſt, and no great ſigne of ſkill in Greeke phraſes, and he muſt no more call D. Sanders vnlearned for not vnderſtāding Bezas meaning, but him ſelf, vvho in deede vnder-

vnderstood him not. For, if Beza meant that it vvas an elegancie vsed of the finest authors, and such as Budee doth exemplifie of, vvhy doth he say, *that he seeth not vvhy Luke should vse solœcophanes*, but thinketh rather, *it is a corruptiō crept into the margent?* Tel vs, M. Fulke vve beseche you, vvhether is the better and honester defense, to say, that it is an elegācie & fine phrase in S. Luke, or to say, it is a fault in the text, it came out of the margent, the Gospel is here corrupted. Thinke you Beza such a foole, that he vvould rather stand vpon this later, if he might haue vsed the former, and had so meant by *solœcophanes?* yea vvhat needed any defense at al, if it had been an vsual & knovvē elegancie, as you vvould proue it?

39 For you say further, that τὸ is takē for ὃ, & ἐστὶ is vnderstood, & that this is a cōmon thing in the best Greeke authors. but you must adde, that the said relatiue must alwaies be referred to the antecedent of the same case, as this speache τὸ ποτήριον τὸ ἐκχυνόμενον may be resolued thus, τὸ ποτήριον ὃ ἐκχυνόμενόν ἐστι, or rather ὃ ἐκχύνεται. but that ἐν τῷ αἵματί μου, τὸ ἐκχυνόμενον, may be resolued, ὃ ἐκχυνόμενόν ἐστι, you shal neuer be able to bring one example, & you vvilfully abuse vvhatsoeuer knowledge you haue of the Greeke tōgue, to deceiue the ignorant, or els you haue no

skil

ſkill at al, that ſpeake ſo barbarouſly and ruſtically of Greeke elegancies. for if you haue ſkil, you knovv in your conſcience, that ἐν τῷ ἐμῷ αἵματι τὸ ὑπὲρ ὑμῶν ἐκχυνόμενον, is as great a ſolœciſme in Greeke, & no more elegancie, then to ſay in Latin, *In meo ſanguine fuſus pro vobis*, vvhich in the ſchole deſerueth vvhipping. And yet you aſke very vehemently (concerning theſe vvordes, *Hic calix nouum Teſtamentum in meo ſanguine qui pro vobis fundetur:*) what meane Grammarian vvould referre, *qui*, to *calix*, and not to *ſanguis*? I anſvver, that a mere latiniſt, for ignorance of the Greeke tongue, vvould referre it rather as you ſay: but he that knovveth the Greeke, as you ſeeme to doe, though he be a very yong Grammarian, vvil eaſily ſee it can not ſo be referred: as in the like Act. 14. *Sacerdos quoque Iouis qui erat ante ciuitatem eorum.* Here, *qui*, is ambiguous, but in the Greeke vve ſee that, *qui*, muſt be referred to, *Iouis*, and can not be referred to, *Sacerdos*.

ὁ ἱερεὺς τοῦ Διὸς τοῦ ὄντος.

40 And this is one commoditie among others, that vve reape of the Greeke text, to reſolue the ambiguitie that is ſometime in the Latin: vvhereas you neither admit the one nor the other, but as you liſt, neither doth the Greeke ſatisfie you, be it neuer ſo plaine and infallible, but you vvil deuiſe that it is corrupted, that there is a ſolœciſme,

that the same solœcisme is an elegancie, and therevpō you translate your ovvne deuise, and not the vvord of God. vvhich vvhence can it procede, but of most vvilful corruption? See chap. 17. nu. 10. 11. 12.

41 If in ambiguous Hebrue vvordes of doubtful signification, vvhere the Greeke giueth one certaine sense, you refuse the Greeke, & take your aduantage of the other sense: vvhat is this but vvilful partialitie? so you doe in, *Redime eleemosynis peccata tua. Dan.* 4. & *Inclinaui cor meū ad faciendas iustificationes tuas propter retributionē.* and, *Nimis honorati sunt amici tui Deus &c.* and yet at an other time you folovv the determination of the Greeke for an other aduantage: as Psal. 98. Adore his footestoole, *because he is holy.* Whereas in the Hebrue it may be as in our Latin, *because it is holy.* See cha. 13. nu. 18. chap. 9. nu. 23. 24. chap. 18. nu. 1. 2. So you flee from the Hebrue to the Greeke, and from this to that againe, from both to the vulgar Latin, as is shevved in other places: and as S. Augustine saith to Faustus the Manichee, You are the rule of truth: vvhatsoeuer is for you, is true: vvhatsoeuer is against you, is not true.

Ps. 118 Octon. Nun.

Ps. 138.

קָדוֹשׁ הוּא

Li. 11. cont. Faust. c. 2.

42 Vvhat shal I speake of the Hebrue particle *vau?* vvhich (Gen. 14. v. 18) must in no case be translated, *because*, lest it should proue that Melchisedec offered sacrifice of bread

וְהוּא כֹּהֵן

and

and vvine, as al the fathers expound it: but (Luc. 1. v. 42) vvhere they tranſlate the equiualent Greeke particle καὶ, there Beza proueth the ſaid particle to ſignifie, *becauſe*, & tranſlateth accordingly, & the Engliſh Bezites likevviſe. I vvil not vrge them vvhy, vve like the ſenſe vvel, and Theophylacte ſo expoundeth it. but if the Greeke copulatiue may be ſo tranſlated, vvhy not the Hebrue copulatiue much more, vvhich often in the Scripture is vſed in that ſenſe? See chap. 17. nu. 13. 14.

Quia benedictus, for, & benedictus fructus ventris tui.

43 But I vvould aſke rather, vvhy κεχαριτωμένη may not in any caſe be tranſlated, *ful of grace*: vvhereas ἡλκωμένος is tranſlated, *ful of ſores*. both vvordes being of like forme and force. See chap. 18. nu. 4. 5.

Luc. 1. v. 28.
Luc. 16. v. 20

44 Againe, vvhy ſay they (Hebr. 13) *Let your conuerſation be vvithout couetouſnes*, and ſay not, *Let mariage be honorable in al, and the bed vndefiled.* both being expreſſed a like by the Apoſtle, and by vvay of exhortation, as the reſt that goeth before and folovveth? See chap. 15. nu. 15.

ἀφιλάργυρος ὁ τρόπος.
τίμιος ὁ γάμος.

45 Are vve to ſuſpicious thinke you? hovv can *feare*, be tráſlated, that vvhich he feared: ⋆ *repentance*, them that repent or amend their life: *tradition*, the doctrine deliuered: *temples*, ſhrines: *idols*, deuotions: *euery humane creature*, al ordinances of man: *foreknovvledge*, proui-

Hebr. 5. v. 7.
⋆ Beza. Act. 26. v. 20.
2 Theſ. 2 & 3.

dence: *soul*, carcas: *hel*, graue: *altar*, temple: *table*, altar: and such like?

46 Vvhat caused these strange speaches in
Psal. 86,13. Bib. 1579. their English Bibles, *Thou shalt not leaue my soul in the graue. Thou hast deliuered my soule from the lowest graue. A couetous mā is a worshipper of images. By laying on of the hands of the Eldership. Haile freely beloued.* SINNE *lieth at the doore, and thou shalt rule ouer* HIM. *Breake of thy sinnes vvith righteousnes.* for, *Redeeme vvith almes. Ielousie is cruel as the graue.* for, *as hel.* Cant. Cant. 8. Bib. an. 1579. *The greifes of the graue caught me.* Psal. 116. And, *God vvil redeeme*
Psal. 48. *my soule from the povver of the graue. O graue I vvil be thy destruction. Os.* 13. and such like? vvhat made Caluin so translate into Latin, that if you turne it into English, the sense is, that
Tit. 3. God povvred vvater vpon vs aboundantly, meaning the holy Ghost: vvhat els but because he vvould take avvay the necessitie of material vvater in Baptisme, as in his commentarie and Bezas, it is euident?

47 I had meant to haue but breifely skimmed ouer these things, but multitude of matter maketh me to long, as it chaunceth to a man that vvadeth through myrie and foule places, and yet the greatest demonstration that they are vvilful corrupters, is behind, vvhich only I vvil adde, and for the rest, referre the reader to the vvhole booke.

48 Doubt you vvhether they translate of purpose and partialitie, in fauour of their opinions? you shal heare them selues say so

and proteſt it. If I dealt vvith Lutherans, this one teſtimonie of Luther vvere ſuffi-cient, vvho being aſked vvhy he added, *only*, into the text Ro. 3: anſvvered that he did it to explicate the Apoſtles ſenſe more plainely. that is, to make the Apoſtle ſay more plainely, that faith only iuſtified. and his diſciple Illyricus diſputeth the matter, that the Apoſtle ſaying, *by faith vvithout vvorkes*, ſaith in deede, *only faith*. but becauſe I deale rather vvith our Engliſh Caluiniſtes, and Beza is their cheefe trāſlatour, & a captaine amōg them, whom they profeſſe to folovv in the title of the new Teſt. an. 1580, and by the very name of their Geneua Bibles, let vs ſee vvhat he ſaith.

Tom. 2. fol. 405. edit. Vvitteb. an. 1551.

The expreſſe teſtimonies of Beza (vvhom the Engliſh Heretical tranſlatiōs folow herein) that he doth wilfully and of purpoſe trāſlate againſt ſuch & ſuch Catholike aſſertions.

49 Firſt concerning, μετανοεῖτε, vvhich the vulgar Latin and Eraſmus tranſlate, *Agite pœnitentiam, Repent*, or, *Doe penance. This interpretation* (ſaith he) *I refuſe for many cauſes, but for this eſpecially, that many ignorāt perſons haue taken hereby an occaſion of the falſe opinions of* SATISFACTION, *vvherevvith the Church is troubled at this day.* Loe, of purpoſe againſt ſatisfaction he vvil not tranſlate the Greeke vvord, as it ought to be, and as it is proued to ſignifie, both in this booke, and in the Annotations vpon the nevv Teſtament. A litle after ſpeaking of the ſame vvord, he ſaith, *vvhy I haue changed the name, pœnitentia, I haue told a litle before*, * proteſting that he vvil neuer vſe thoſe

Mat. 3. v. 8.

Loco ſupra citato.

vvordes, but *resipiscere*, and *resipiscentia*, that is, amendment of life: because of their heresie, that repentance is nothing els but a mere amendment of former life, without recompense or satisfaction or penance for the sinnes before committed. See chap. 13.

δικαιώματα. 50 Againe concerning the vvord, *Iustifications*, vvhich in the Scripture very often signifie the commaundements, he saith thus. Luc. 1. v. 6. *The Greeke interpreters of the Bible* (meaning the Septuaginta) *applied this vvord to signifie the vvhole Lavv of God, and therfore commonly it is vvont to be translated vvord for vvord, Iustificationes: vvhich interpretation therfore only I reiected, that I might take avvay this occasion also of cauilling against iustification by faith.* and so for, *iustificationes*, he putteth *constituta*, Tullies word forsooth, as he saith. Can you haue a more plaine testimonie of his heretical purpose?

51 Againe, vvhen he had reiected this translation (Act. 2. v. 27) *Non derelinques animam meam in inferno, Thou shalt not leaue my soule in Hel:* because (as he saith) herevpon grevve the errours of Christs descending into Hel, of Limbus, and of Purgatorie: at length he concludeth thus, *Vvhereas the doubtful interpretation of one or tvvo vvordes hath brought forth so many monsters, I chose rather * simply, for soule, to say, carcas, for hel, graue: then to foster these foule errors.*

* Loe hovv simply: *Anima*, carcas. *Infernus*, graue.

ὃν δεῖ οὐρανὸν δέξασθαι. Act. 3. v. 21. 52 Againe, vvhen he had translated for, *Vvhom heauen must receiue*, thus, *vvho must be conteined in heauen*: he saith, *vvhereas vve haue vsed the passiue*

kind

kinde of speache, rather then the actiue (vvhich is in the Greeke:) *vve did it to auoid al ambiguitie. for it is very expedient, that there should be in the Church of God, this perspicuous testimonie, against them, that for ascending by faith into heauen, so to be ioyned to our head, obstinatly mainteine that Christ must be called againe out of heauen vnto vs.* Meaning his presence in the B. Sacrament, & inueighing no lesse against the Lutherans then the Catholikes, as the *Lutherās do here against him for this vvilful interpretatiō, & that by Caluins ovvne iudgement, vvho thinketh it a forced translation. Flac. Illyr.

53 But Beza goeth forvvard stil in this kinde. Ro. 5. v. 18. whereas Erasmus had put *propagatum est*, indifferently, both of Adams sinne vvhich made vs truely sinners, and of Christs iustice, vvhich maketh vs truely iust: he reiecting it, among other causes vvhy it displeased him, saith: *That old errour of the Sophists* (meaning Catholikes) *vvhich for imputatiue iustice put an inherent qualitie in the place, is so great, and so execrable to al good men, that I thinke nothing is so much to be auoided as it.*

54 These fevv examples proue vnto vs that the Scriptures translated verbatim, exactly, & according to the proper vse and signification of the vvordes, do by the Heretikes confession make for the Catholikes, and therfore Beza saith he altereth the vvordes into other: & (I thinke) it may suf-

fice any indifferent reader to iudge of his purpose and meaning in other places of his translation, and consequently of theirs that either allovv him, or folovv him, vvhich are our English Caluinists, and Bezites. Many other vvaies there are to make most certaine proofe of their wilfulnes, as vvhen * the trãslation is framed according to their false and heretical commentarie: and, When they vvil auouch their translations out of profane vvriters, Homer, Plutarch, Plinie, Tullie, Virgil, and Terence, and reiect the Ecclesiastical vse of vvordes in the Scriptures and fathers: vvhich Beza doth for the most part alvvaies. but it vvere infinite to note al the markes, and by these, the vvise reader may conceiue the rest.

Calu. Heb. 5, 7. & Tit. 3, 6. Beza 2 Thess. 2, 15. & 3, 6.

55 But vvould you thinke that these men could notvvithstanding speake very grauely and honestly against voluntarie and vvilful translations of Scripture, that so notoriously offend therein them selues? Harken vvhat Beza saith against Castaleo and the like: *The matter* (saith he) *is novv come to this point, that the trãslatours of Scripture out of the Greeke into Latin, or into any other tongue, thinke that they may lavvfully doe any thing in translating Vvhom if a man reprehend, he shal be ansvvered by and by, that they doe the office of a translatour, not that translateth vvord for vvord, but that expresseth the sense. So it commeth to passe, that, vvhiles euery man vvil rather freely folovv* his

Annot. act. 10. v. 46.

his ovvne iudgement, then be a religious interpreter of the Holy Ghoſt, he doth rather peruert many things then tranſlate them. Is not this vvel ſaid, if he had done accordingly? but doing the cleane contrarie, as hath been proued, he is a diſſembling hypocrite in ſo ſaying, & a vvilful Heretike in ſo doing, and condemned by his ovvne iudgement.

56 But after this general vewe of their wilful purpoſe and heretical intention, let vs examine their falſe tranſlations more particularly, and argue the caſe vvith them more at large, & preſſe them to anſvver, vvhether in their cōſcience it be ſo or no, as hitherto is ſaid: and that by ſeueral chapters of ſuch CONTROVERSIES as their corruptions concerne: and firſt of al (vvithout further curioſitie vvhence to begin, in caſes ſo indifferent) of TRADITIONS.

CHAP. II.

Heretical tranſlation of holy Scripture againſt Apoſtolical TRADITIONS.

THIS is a matter of ſuch importance, that if they ſhould graunt any traditions of the Apoſtles, and not pretend the vvritten vvord only: they knovv that by [c] ſuch traditions mentioned in al antiquitie, their religion 1

[c] See the annotations of the nevv Teſtament. 2 Theſſ. 2, 15.

ligion vvere vvholy defaced and ouerthro-vven. for remedie vvhereof, and for the defacing of al such traditions, they bend their translations against them in this wonderful maner. Vvheresoeuer the Holy Scripture speaketh against certaine traditions of the Ievves, partly friuolous, partly repugnant to the Lavv of God, there al the English
παραδόσεις. translations folovv the Greeke exactly, neuer omitting this vvord, *tradition.* Contrarievvise vvheresoeuer the holy Scripture speaketh in the commendation of Traditions, to vvit, such traditions as the Apostles deliuered to the Churche, there al their said trāslations agree, not to folovv the Greeke, vvhich is still the self same vvord, but for, *traditions*, they translate, *ordinances*, or *instructions.* Vvhy so and to vvhat purpose? vve appeale to the vvorme of their conscience, vvhich continually accuseth them of an heretical meaning, vvhether, by vrging the vvord, *traditions*, vvheresoeuer they are discommended, and by suppressing the vvord, vvheresoeuer they are commended, their purpose and intent be not, to signifie to the Reader, that al traditions are naught, & none good, al reprouable, none allovvable.

2 For example. Mat. 15. Thus they translate,
παράδοσιν. *Vvhy do thy disciples transgresse the* TRADITION *of the Elders?* And againe, *Vvhy do you also transgresse the*

the commaundement of God by your TRADITION? And againe, *Thus haue you made the commaundement of God of no effect by your* TRADITION: here (I vvarant you) al the belles ſound tradition, and the vvord is neuer omitted, and it is very vvel and honeſtly tranſlated, for ſo the Greeke vvord doth proprely ſignifie. But novv on the other ſide, concerning good traditions, let vs ſee their dealing. The Apoſtle by the ſelf ſame vvord both in Greeke and Latin, ſaith thus: *Therfore, brethren, ſtand & hold faſt the* TRADITIONS *vvhich you haue learned either by vvord, or by our epiſtle.* And againe, *Vvithdravv your ſelues from euery brother walking inordinatly, & not according to the* TRADITION *vvhich they haue receiued of vs.* And againe (according to the Greeke vvhich they profeſſe to follovv:) *I praiſe you brethren, that in al things you are mindeful of me, and as I haue deliuered vnto you, you keepe my* TRADITIONS.

2 Theſ. 2. v. 15 παραδό-
σεις, traditiones.

2 Theſſ. 3, 6.

1 Cor. 11, 2.
καθὼς παρ-
έδωκα,
τὰς παρα-
δόσεις κα-
τέχετε.

3 Here vve ſee plaine mention of S. Paules traditions, and cõſequently of Apoſtolical traditions, yea and traditions by vvord of mouth, deliuered to the ſaid Churches vvithout vvriting or Scripture. In al vvhich places looke, gentle reader, & ſeeke al their Engliſh tranſlations, & thou ſhalt * not once finde the vvord, *tradition*, but in ſteede thereof, *ordinances, inſtructions, preachings, inſtitutions*, and any vvord els rather then, *tradition.* in ſo much that Beza their maiſter tranſ-

* Yet M. Fulke ſaith, it is found there. pag. 153 againſt D. Sand. Rocke. If he giue not vs an inſtance, let him giue him ſelf the lie.

2 Theſſ. 2 & 3.

παραδό-σεις. trãſlateth it *traditam doctrinã, the doctrine deliuered,* putting the ſingular number for the plural, & adding, *doctrine,* of his ovvne. ſo framing the text of holy Scripture according to his falſe cõmẽtarie, or rather putting his cõmẽtarie in the text, & making it the text of Scripture. Vvho would thinke their malice and partialitie againſt traditions vvere ſo great, that they ſhould al agree vvith one conſent ſo duely and exactly in theſe and theſe places to cõceale the word, vvhich in other places do ſo gladly vſe it, the Greeke vvord being al one in al the ſaid places?

4 Yea they doe els vvhere ſo gladly vſe this vvord, tradition, vvhen it may tend to the diſcredite thereof: that they put the ſaid vvord in al their Engliſh Bibles, vvith the like ful conſent as before, vvhen it is not in the Greeke at al. As vvhen they tranſ-

Col. 2. 20. τί δογματίζεσθε. late thus, *If ye be dead vvith Christ from the rudiments of the vvorld: vvhy as though liuing in the vvorld,* ARE YE LEDDE VVITH TRADITIONS? & as an other* Engliſh tranſlation of theirs readeth more heretically, *Vvhy are ye burdened vvith traditions?* Tel vs ſincerely you that profeſſe to haue ſkill in the Greeke, & to tranſlate according to the Greeke: tell vs vve beſeche you, vvhether this Greeke vvord δόγμα do ſignifie tradition, and δογματίζεσθαι, to be ledde or burdened vvith traditions.

* of the yere 1579.

You

You can not be ignorant that it doth not ſo ſignifie, but as a litle before in the ſame chapter, & in other places, your ſelues tranſlate *δόγματα, ordinances, decrees:* ſo τί δογματίζεσθε, muſt be (as in the vulgar Latin it is) *Quid decernitis?* Vvhy do you *ordaine* or *decree*, or, vvhy are you ledde vvith *decrees?*

Col. 2, 14. Epheſ. 2, 15. δόγμασιν. ἐν δόγμασιν.

5 Iuſtifie your tranſlation if you can, either out of Scriptures, fathers, or Lexicon. and make vs a good reaſon vvhy you put the vvord, *traditions*, here, vvhere it is not in the Greeke: and vvould not put it in the places before, vvhere you knovv it is moſt euidently in the Greeke. Yea you muſt tel vs, vvhy you tranſlate for tradition, *ordinance*, and contrarie for ordinance, *tradition*: ſo turning catte in panne (as they ſay) at your pleaſure, and wreſting both the one and the other to one end, that you may make the very name of traditions odious among the people, be they neuer ſo authentical, euen from the Apoſtles: vvhich your conſcience knovveth, and you ſhal anſvver for it at the dreadful day.

παράδοσις they tranſlate, *ordinance*: and δόγμα, *tradition*: cleane contrarie.

6 Somevvhat more excuſable it is, but yet proceding of the ſame heretical humor, and on your part (that ſhould exactly folovv the Greeke) falſely tranſlated, vvhen you tranſlate in S. Peters Epiſtle thus: *You vvere not redeemed vvith corruptible things from your vaine* 1 Pet. 1, 18.

conuer-

conuersation receiued by the tradition of the fathers. Vvhere the Greeke is thus rather to be translated, *from your vaine conuersation deliuered by the fathers.* but your fingers itched to foist in the vvord, *tradition,* and for, *deliuered,* to say, *receiued,* because it is the phrase of the Catholike church, that it hath *receiued* many things *by tradition,* vvhich you vvould here controule by likenes of vvordes in this false translation.

ἐκ τῆς ματαίας ὑμῶν ἀναστροφῆς πατροπαραδότου.

7 But concerning the vvord *tradition,* you vvil say perhaps the sense thereof is included in the Greeke vvord, *deliuered.* Vve graunt. but vvould you be content, if vve should alvvaies expresly adde, *tradition,* vvhere it is so included? then should vve say 1 Cor. 11, 2. *I praise you that as I haue deliuered you* (by tradition,) *you keepe my precepts* or *traditions.* And againe v. 23. *For I receiued of our Lord, vvhich also I deliuered vnto you* (by tradition) &c. And Luc. 1. v. 2. *As they* (by tradition) *deliuered vnto vs, vvhich from the beginning savv &c.* and such like, by your example, vve should translate in this sort. but vve vse not this licentious maner in trãslating holy Scriptures, neither is it a translators part, but an interpreters, and his that maketh a commentarie: neither doth a good cause neede other translation then the expresse text of the Scripture giueth.

Tradidi παρέδωκα

8 And

8 And if you vvil yet ſay, that our vulgar Latin tranſlation hath here the vvord, *tradition*: vve graunt it hath ſo, and therfore vve alſo tranſlate accordingly. but you profeſſe to tranſlate the Greeke, and not the vulgar Latin, vvhich you in England condemne as Papiſtical, and* ſay it is the vvorſt of al, though *Beza your maiſter pronoũce it to be the very beſt: and vvil you notvvithſtanding folovv the ſaid vulgar Latin rather then the Greeke, to make traditions odious? Yea ſuch is your partialitie one vvay, and inconſtancie an other vvay, that for your heretical purpoſe you are content to folovv the old Latin tranſlation, though it differ from the Greeke, & againe an other time you vvil not folovv it, though it be al one vvith the Greeke moſt exactly. as in the place before alleaged, vvhere the vulgar Latin trãſlation hath nothing of traditions, but, *Quid decernitis*, as it is in the Greeke: you tranſlate, *Vvhy are ye burdened vvith traditions?*

Diſcouer. of the Rocke. pag. 147.

Prefat. in no. Teſt. 1556.

Col. 2, 20.

9 So that a blinde man may ſee, you frame your tranſlations to bolſter your errours & hereſies, without al reſpect of folovving ſincerely either the Greeke or the Latin. But for the Latin no maruel, the Greeke at the leaſt vvhy doe you not folovv? Is it the Greeke that induceth you to ſay ordinãces for traditions, traditions for decrees, ordinances

παραδόσεις.

δόγματα.

δικαιώματα. πρεσβύτερος. ᾅδης. εἴδωλον.

nances for iustifications, Elder for Priest, graue for hel, image for idol? tel vs before God and in your conscience vvhether it be, because you wil exactly folow the Greeke: nay tel vs truely, and shame the Diuel, vvhether the Greeke wordes do not sound and signifie most properly that, vvhich you of purpose vvil not translate, for disaduantaging your heresies? And first let vs see concerning the question of Images.

CHAP. III.

Heretical translation against sacred IMAGES.

1 I BESECHE you vvhat is the next and readiest and most proper English of *Idolum, idololatra, idololatria?* is it not *Idol, idolater, idolatrie?* are not these plaine English vvordes, and vvel knovven in our language? Vvhy sought you further for other termes and vvordes, if you had meant faithfully? Vvhat needed that circumstance of three vvordes for one, *vvorshipper of images*, and, *vvorshipping of images?* vvhether (I pray you) is the more natural & conuenient speache, either in our English tõgue, or for the truth of the thing, to say as the holy Scripture doth, *Couetousnes is idolatrie,* and

εἴδωλον. εἰδωλολάτρης. εἰδωλολατρεία.

Bib. 1577. Eph. 5. Col. 3.

and consequently, *The couetous man is an idolater:* or as you translate, *Couetousnes is vvorshipping of images*, and, *The couetous man is a vvorshipper of images?*

2 Vve say commonly in English, Such a riche man maketh his money his God: and the Apostle saith in like maner of some, *Vvhose belly is their God. Phil. 3.* & generally euery creature is our idol, vvhen vve esteeme it so excedingly that vve make it our God. but vvho euer heard in English, that our money, or bellie, vvere our images, and that by esteeming of them to much, vve become vvorshippers of images? Among your selues are there not some euen of your Superintendents, of vvhom the Apostle speaketh, that make an idol of their money and belly, by couetousnes & belly cheere? Yet can vve not call you therfore in any true sense, *vvorshippers of images*, neither would you abide it. You see then that there is a great difference betvvixt idol and image, idolatrie and vvorshipping of images: and euen so great difference is there betvvixt S. Paules vvordes and your translation.

The absurditie of this translation, *A couetous man is a Worshipper of images.*

3 Vvil you see more yet to this purpose? In the English Bible printed the yere 1562 you reade thus: *Hovv agreeth the Temple of God vvith images?* Can vve be ignorant of Satans cogitations herein, that it vvas translated

2 Cor. 6.

of purpose to delude the simple people and to make them beleeue that the Apostle speaketh against sacred images in the churches, vvhich were then in plucking dovvne in England, vvhen this your translation vvas first published in print? Vvhereas in very truth you know, that the Apostle here partly interpreteth him self to speake of men, as of Gods temples wherein he dvvelleth, partly alludeth to Salomons Temple, vvhich did very vvell agree vvith images (for it had the Cherubins, vvhich vvere the representations of Angels, and the figures of oxen to beare vp the lauatorie) but vvith idols it could not agree: and therfore the Apostles vvordes are these, *Hovv agreeth the Temple of God vvith idols?*

Salomons Temple did vvel agree vvith images, but not vvith idols.

μετ' τῶν εἰδώλων.

4 Vvhen Moyses by Gods appointement erected a brasen serpent, and commaunded the people that vvere stung vvith serpents, to behold it, & thereby they vvere healed: this vvas an image only, and as an image vvas it erected and kept and vsed by Gods commaundement. but vvhen it grevve to be an idol (saith S. Augustine) that is, vvhen the people began to adore it as God, then king Ezechias brake it in peeces to the great cōmendation of his pietie and godly zeale. So vvhen the children of Israel in the absence of Moyses made a calfe, and said, These

The brasen serpent, first an image, & lavvful: aftervvard an idol, and vnlavvful.

Num. 21.

Li. 10 de Ciuit. c. 8.

4 Reg. 18.

Exod. 32.

These are thy Gods ô Israel that brought thee out of Ægypt, vvas it but an image vvhich they made? vvas that so heinous a matter that God vvould so haue punished them as he did? No they made it an idol also, saying, *These are thy gods ô Israel.* And therfore the Apostle saith to the Corinthians, *Be not idolaters, as some of them.* Vvhich also you translate most falsely, *Be not worshippers of images, as some of them.*

The molten calfe, an idol.

1 Cor. 10. εἰδωλολάτραι.

5 Vve see then that the Ievves had images vvithout sinne, but not idols. Againe for hauing idols they vvere accounted like vnto the Gentiles, as the Psalme saith, *They learned their workes, and serued their grauen idols.* but they vvere not accounted like vnto the Gentiles for hauing images, vvhich they had in Salomons Temple, and in the brasen serpent. S. Hierom vvriteth of the Ammonites and Moabites (vvho vvere Gentiles and Idolaters) that comming into the temple of Hierusalem, and seeing the Angelical images of the Cherubins couering the Propitiatorie, they said, Loe, euen as the Gentiles, so Iuda also hath idols of their religiō. These men did put no difference betvvene their ovvne idols, and the Ievves lavvful images. and are not you ashamed to be like to these? They accused Salomons Temple of Idols, because they savv there lavvful images: you accuse the Churches of God of

Psal. 105.

In c. 25. Ezech.

The Protestants are like to the Ammonites & Moabites.

idolatrie, because you see there the sacred images of Christ and his Saincts.

6 But tel vs yet I pray you, doe the holy Scriptures of either Testament speake of al maner of images, or rather of the idols of the Gentiles? your cõscience knoweth that they speake directly against the idols & the idolatrie that vvas among the Pagans and Infidels: frõ vvhich as the Ievves in the old Testamẽt, so the first Christians in the nevv Testament vvere to be prohibited. but vvil you haue a demonstration that your owne conscience condemneth you herein, & that you apply al translation to your heresie? Vvhat caused you being othervvise in al places so ready to translate, images: yet Esa. 31 and Zachar. 13 to translate, *idols*, in al your Bibles vvith ful cõsent? Vvhy in these places specially and so aduisedly? No doubt because God saith there, speaking of this time of the nevv Testament: *In that day euery man shal cast out his idols of siluer and idols of gold.* And, *I vvil destroy the names of the idols out of the earth, so that they shal no more be had in remembrance.* In vvhich places if you had trãslated, *images*, you had made the prophecie false, because images haue not been destroied out of the vvorld, but are, and haue been in Christian countries vvith honour & reuerence, euen since Christes time. Mary in the idols of the

The holy Scripture speaketh against the idols of the Gẽtiles, not against al maner of images.

Gen

Gentiles vve ſee it verified, vvhich are deſtroied in al the world ſo far as Gentilitie is conuerted to Chriſt.

7 And vvhat vvere the Pagans idols or their idolatrie? S. Paul telleth vs, ſaying: Ro. 1. *They changed the glorie of the incorruptible God into the ſimilitude of the image of a corruptible man, and of birdes and beaſtes and creeping things: and they ſerued (or vvorſhipped) the creature more then the creator.* Doth he charge them for making the image of man or beaſt? Your ſelues haue hangings and clothes ful of ſuch paintings and embroderings of imagirie. Wherevvith then are they charged? vvith giuing the glorie of God to ſuch creatures, vvhich vvas to make them idols, and them ſelues idolaters.

Vvhat vvere the *idols* of the Pagans.

8 The caſe being thus, vvhy do you make 1 Cor. 5.
it tvvo diſtinct things in S. Paul, calling the Bib. 1562.
Pagans, idolaters: and the Chriſtians doing the ſame, vvorſhippers of images: and that in one ſentence, vvhereas the Apoſtle vſeth but one and the ſelf ſame Greeke vvord in ſpeaking both of Pagans and Chriſtians? It is a maruelous and vvilful corruption, and vvel to be marked, and therfore I vvil put dovvne the vvhole ſentence, as it is in your Engliſh tranſlatiõ. *I vvrote to you that you ſhould not companie vvith fornicators: and I meant not at al of the fornicators of this vvorld, either of the couetous, or extortioners, either* [c] *the idolaters &c. but that ye companie not together, if any that is called a brother, be a fornicator*

[c] εἰδωλολάτραις.

c εἰδωλολά-τρης.

nicator, or couetous, or c A VVORSHIPPER OF IMAGES, *or an extortioner.* In the first, speaking of Pagans, your translatour nameth *idolater* according to the text, but in the later part speaking of Christians, you translate the very self same Greeke vvord, *vvorshipper of images.* Vvhy so? forsooth to make the reader thinke that S. Paul speaketh here, not only of Pagan idolaters, but also of Catholike Christians that reuerently kneele in praier before the Crosse, the holy Roode, the images of our Sauiour Christ and his Saincts: as though the Apostle had commaunded such to be auoided.

9 Vvhere if you haue yet the face to deny this your malitious and heretical intent, tell vs, vvhy al these other vvordes are translated and repeated alike in both places, *couetous, fornicators, extortioners,* both Pagans and Christians: and only this vvord (idolaters) not so, but Pagans, idolaters: & Christians, vvorshippers of images. At the least you can not deny but it vvas of purpose done, to make both seeme al one, yea and to signifie that the Christians doing the foresaid reuerence before sacred images (which you call vvorshipping of images) are more to be auoided then the Pagan idolaters. Vvhereas the Apostle speaking of Pagans and Christians that committed one and the self

ſelf ſame heinous ſinne vvhatſoeuer, commaundeth the Chriſtian in that caſe to be auoided for his amendement, leauing the Pagan to him ſelf & to God, as hauing not to doe to iudge of him.

10 But to this the anſvver belike vvil be made, as one of them hath already anſvvered in the like caſe, that in the Engliſh Bible appointed to be read in their churches it is othervviſe, and euen as vve vvould haue it corrected: and therfore (ſaith he) *it had been good before vve entred into ſuch heinous accuſations, to haue examined our groundes that they had been true.* As though vve accuſe them not truely of falſe tranſlation, vnles it be falſe in that one Bible vvhich for the preſent is read in their churches: or as though it pertained not to thē hovv their other Engliſh Bibles be trāſlated: or as though the people read not al indifferently vvithout prohibition, and may be abuſed by euery one of thēm: or as though the Bible vvhich novv is read (as vve thinke) in their churches, haue not the like abſurd tranſlations, yea more abſurd, euen in this matter of images, as is before declared: or as though vve muſt firſt learne what Engliſh tranſlation is read in their church (vvhich vvere hard to knovv, it changeth ſo oft) before vve may be bold to accuſe them of falſe tranſlation: or

W. Fulke, a Confut. of Iohn Hovvlet fo. 35.

Bib. 1577. Col. 3. v. 5.

or as though it vvere not the ſame Bible that Was for many yeres read in their churches, & is yet in euery mans handes, vvhich hath this abſurd tranſlation vvhereof vve haue laſt ſpoken.

Bib. 1562. 11 Surely the Bible that vve moſt accuſe not only in this point, but for ſundrie other moſt groſſe faultes and heretical tranſlations, ſpoken of in other places, is that Bible vvhich vvas authoriſed by Cramner their Archbiſhop of Canterburie, and read al king Edvvards time in their churches, & (as it ſeemeth by the late printing thereof againe an. 1562) a great part of this Queenes reigne. And certaine it is, that it vvas ſo long read in al their churches vvith this venemous & corrupt tranſlation of images alvvaies in ſteede of idols, that it made the deceiued people of their ſecte, to deſpiſe, contemne, and abandon the very ſigne and image of their ſaluatiō, the croſſe of Chriſt, the holy roode or crucifixe repreſenting the maner of his bitter paſſion and death, the ſacred images of the bleſſed Virgin Marie the mother of God, & of S. Iohn Euangeliſt, repreſenting their ſtanding by the

Io. 19. v. 26. Croſſe at the very time of his Paſſion. in ſo much that novv by experience vve ſee the foule inconuenience thereof, to vvit, that al other images and pictures of infamous harlots

harlots and Heretikes, of Heathen tyrants and persecutors, are lavvful in England at this day, and their houses, parlours and chambers are garnished vvith them: onely sacred images, and representations of the holy mysterie of our redemption, are esteemed idolatrous, and haue been openly defaced in most spiteful maner and burned, to the great dishonour of our Sauiour Christ and his Saincts.

12 And as concerning the bible that at this day is read in their churches, if it be that of the yere 1577, it is vvorse sometime in this matter of images, then the other. for vvhere the other readeth, *Couetousnes, vvhich is vvorshipping of idols*: there this later (vvhereunto they appeale) readeth thus, *Couetousnes, vvhich is vvorshipping of images.* and Eph. 5. it readeth as absurdly as the other, *A couetous man, vvhich is a vvorshipper of images.* Loe this is the English bible vvhich they referre vs vnto, as better translated, and as correcting the fault of the former. But because it is euident by these places, that this also is partly vvorse, and partly as il as the other, therfore this great cõfuter of M. Iohn Houlet fleeth once more, to the Geneua English Bible, saying, *Thus vve reade*, and, *so vve translate*: to wit, *A couetous person, vvhich is an idolater.* Vvhere shal vve haue these good fellovves, and

Col. 3. v. 5.

W. Fulke Confut. fol. 35.

Fol. 36. Bib. 1579.

hovv

hovv shal vve be sure that they vvill stand to any of their translations? from the first readde in their churches, they flee to that that is now readde, & frō this againe, to the later Geneua English Bibles, neither readde in their churches (as vve suppose) nor of greatest authoritie among them: and vve doubt not but they vvil as fast flee from this, to the former againe, vvhen this shal be proued in some places more false & absurd then the other.

13 But vvhat matter is it hovv they reade in their churches, or hovv they correct their former trāslations by the later: vvhen the old corruption remaineth stil, being set of purpose in the toppe of euery doore vvithin their churches, in these vvordes:

1 Io. 5. *Babes keepe your selues from images?* Vvhy remaineth that vvritten so often and so conspicuously in the vvalles of their churches, vvhich in their Bibles they correct as a fault? their later bibles say, *keepe your selues from idols*: their church vvalles say, *keepe your selues from images.* S. Iohn speaking to the lately conuerted Gentiles, biddeth them beware of the idols from vvhence they vvere conuerted: they speaking to the old instructed Christians, bid them bevvare of the sacred image of Christ our Sauiour, of the holy Crucifixe, of the crosse, of euery such repre-

repreſentation and monument of Chriſts paſſion, and our redemption. And therfore in the very ſame place vvhere theſe holy monuments vvere vvont to ſtand in Catholike times, to vvit, in the roode loft and partition of the Church and chauncel: there now ſtand theſe vvordes as confronting and cōdemning the foreſaid holy monumēts, *Babes keepe your ſelues frō images.* Vvhich vvordes vvhoſoeuer eſteemeth as the wordes of Scripture, and the vvordes of S. Iohn, ſpoken againſt Chriſtes image, is made a very babe in deede, and ſottiſhly abuſed by their ſcribled doores, and falſe tranſlations, to count that idolatrie, vvhich is in deede to no other purpoſe then to the great honour of him vvhoſe image and picture it is.

14 But the gay confuter vvith vvhom I began, ſaith for further anſvver: *Admit that in ſome of our tranſlations it be, Children keepe your ſelues from images* (for ſo he vvould haue ſaid if it vvere truely printed) *Vvhat great crime of corruption is here committed?* And vvhen it is ſaid againe, this is the crime and fault thereof, that they meane by ſo tranſlating to make the ſimple beleeue that idols and images are al one, vvhich is abſurd: he replieth that it is no more abſurditie, *then in ſteede of a Greeke vvord, to vſe a Latin* of the ſame ſignification. W. Fulke. Fo. 35.

And

And vpon this position he graunteth that according to the propertie of the Greeke vvord a man may say, *God made man according to his idol*, and that generally, *idolum* may as truely be translated an image, as *Tyrannus* a king (vvhich is very true, both being absurd) & here he citeth many authors and dictionaries idly, to prooue that *idolum* may signifie the same that *Image*.

Gen. 1. κατὰ τὴν εἰκόνα

εἴδωλον εἰκὼν

15 But I beseeche you Sir, if the dictionaries tel you that εἴδωλον may by the original propertie of the vvord signifie an image, (vvhich no man denieth) do they tel you also that you may commonly and ordinarily translate it so, as the common vsual signification thereof? or do they tel you that image and idol are so al one, that vvheresoeuer you finde this vvord image, you may truely call it, idol? for these are the points that you should defend in your ansvver. for an example, do they teach you to translate in these places thus, *God hath predestinated vs to be made conformable to the idol of his sonne.* And againe, *As we haue borne the idol of the earthly* (Adam:) *so let vs beare the idol of the heauenly* (CHRIST). And againe, *Vve are transformed into the same idol, euen as of our Lordes spirit.* And againe, *The Lavv hauing a shadovv of the good things to come, not the very idol of the things.* And againe, Christ *vvho is the idol of the inuisible God?* Is this (I pray you) a true translation? *yea*, say you, *according to the propertie of* the

Rom. 8. *imagini.* 1 Cor. 15. *imaginem* 2 Cor. 3. Hebr. 10. Col. 1. 2 Cor. 4.

the vvord: but because the name of idols, in the English tonge, for the great dishonour done to God in vvorship-ping of images, is become odious, no Christian man vvould say so.

16 First note hovv folishly and vnaduisedly he speaketh here, because he vvould confound images and idols, & make them falsely to signifie one thing: vvhen he saith, the name of *idol*, is become odious in the English tongue because of vvorshipping of *Images*, He should haue said, The dishonour done to God in vvorshipping Idols, made the name of Idols odious. As in his ovvne exāple of *Tyrant*, and king: he meant to tel vs that *Tyrant* sometime vvas an vsual name for euery king, and because certaine such Tyrants abused their povver, therfore the name of Tyrant became odious. for he vvil not say (I trovv) that for the fault of kings, the name of Tyrant became odious. Likevvise the Romanes tooke avvay the name of Manlius for the crime of one Mālius, not for the crime of Iohn at Nokes, or of any other name. The name of Iudas is so odious that men novv commonly are not so called. Vvhy so? because he that betraied Christ, vvas called Iudas: not because he vvas also Iscariote. The very name of Ministers is odious and contemptible. vvhy? because Ministers are so levvd, vvicked, & vnlearned, not because some Priests be naught

naught. Euen so the name of idol grevve to be odious, because of the idols of the Gentiles, not because of holy images. For if the reuerence done by Christians to holy images vvere euill, as it is not, it should in this case haue made the name of images odious: & not the name of Idols. But God be thanked, the name of Images is no odious name among Catholike Christians, but onely among heretikes & Imagebreakers, such as the second general Councel of Nice hath condemned therfore vvith the sentence of *Anáthema*. No more then the Crosse is odious, vvhich to al good Christians is honorable, because our Sauiour Christ died on a Crosse.

17 But to omit this mans extraordinarie and vnaduised speaches vvhich be to many and to tedious (as when he saith in the same sentence, *Hovvsoeuer the name idol is grovven odious in the English tongue*, as though it vvere not also odious in the Latin & Greeke tonges, but that in Latin and Greeke a man might say according to his fond opinion, *Fecit bonem ad idolum suum*, and so in the other places vvhere is *imago*) to omit these rashe assertions I say, and to returne to his other vvordes vvhere he saith, that though the original propertie of the vvordes hath that signification, yet *no Christian man vvould say that* God

God made man according to his idol, no more then a good ſubiect vvould call his lavvful Prince a tyrant. doth he not here tell vs that, vvhich vve vvould haue, to vvit, that vve may not ſpeake or trāſlate according to the original propertie of the vvord, but according to the cōmon vſual and accuſtomed ſignification thereof? As vve may not tranſlate, *Phalaris tyrannus, Phalaris the king*, as ſometime *tyrannus* did ſignifie, and in auncient authors doth ſignifie: but, *Phalaris the tyrant*, as novv this vvord *tyrannus* is commonly taken & vnderſtood. Euen ſo vve may not novv tranſlate, *My children keepe your ſelues from images*, as the vvord may and doth ſometime ſignifie according to the original propertie thereof, but vve muſt trāſlate, *keepe your ſelues from idols*, according to the common vſe and ſignification of the vvord in vulgar ſpeache, and in the holy Scriptures. Vvhere the Greeke vvord is ſo notoriouſly & vſually peculiar to idols, and not vnto images: that the holy fathers of the ſecond Nicene Councel (vvhich knevv right vvel the ſignification of the Greeke vvord, them ſelues being Græcians) do pronounce *Anáthema* to al ſuch as interpret thoſe places of the holy Scripture that concerne idols, of images or againſt ſacred images, as novv theſe Caluiniſts do, not onely in their Commentaries vpon

ab idolis ἀπὸ τῶν εἰδώλων 1 Io. 5.

vpon the holy Scriptures, but euen in their translations of the text.

18 This then being so, that vvordes must be translated as their common vse and signification requireth, if you aske your old question, vvhat great crime of corruption is committed in translating, *keepe your selues from images*, the Greeke being εἰδώλων? you haue ansvvered your self, that in so translating, idol & image are made to signifie one thing, vvhich may not be done, no more then Tyrant and king can be made to signifie al one. And hovv can you say then, that *this is no more absurditie, then in steede of a Greeke vvord, to vse a latin of the same signification.* Are you not here contrarie to your self? Are idol and image, tyrant and king, of one significatiō? said you not that in the English tonge, idol is grovven to an other signification, then image, as tyrant is grovven to an other signification then king? Your false translatiōs therfore that in so many places make idols and images al one, not onely forcing the word in the holy Scriptures, but disgracing the sentence thereby (as Ephes. 5. & Col. 3) are they not in your owne iudgement very corrupt: & as your ovvne consciences must confesse, of a malitious intent corrupted, to disgrace thereby the Churches holy images by pretense of the holy Scriptures that speak

Loco citato fo. 35.

Eph. 5. A couetous mā is a vvorship-per of images. and *Col.* 3. Couetousnes is worshipping of images.

ſpeake onely of the Pagans idols.

19 But of the vſual, and original ſignification of vvordes (vvhereof you take occaſion of manifold corruptions) vve vvil ſpeake more anon, if firſt vve touche ſome other your falſifications againſt holy images: as, vvhere you affectate to thruſt the vvord image into the text, vvhen there is no ſuch thing in the Hebrue or Greeke, as in that notorious example 2. Par. 36. (Bib. 1562.) *Carued images that vvere laid to his charge.* τῇ βαάλ. ſubaud. στήλη Num. c.22. Againe, Ro. 11. *To the image of Baal.* and Act. 19. *The image that came dovvne from Iupiter.* τὸ διοπετὲς Vvhere you are not content to vnderſtand image rather then idol, but alſo to thruſt it into the text, being not in the Greeke, as you knovv very vvel.

20 Of this kinde of falſification is that vvhich is crept as a leproſie through out al your bibles, tranſlating, *Sculptile* and *conflatile*, *grauen image*, *molten image*, namely in the firſt commaundement, vvhere you knovv in the Greeke it is idol, & in the Hebrue, ſuch a vvord as ſignifieth onely a grauen thing, not including this vvord image: and you know that God commaunded to make the images of Cherubins, and of oxen in the Temple, and of the braſen ſerpẽt in the deſert, and therfore your vviſedomes might haue cõſidered, that he forbadde not al gra-

εἴδωλον פֶּסֶל

The meaning of the 1. Commaũdement concerning false gods and grauen idols

uen images, but such as the Gentiles made and vvorshipped as goddes: and therfore *Non facies tibi sculptile*, concurreth vvith those vvordes that goe before, *Thou shalt haue none other gods but me*. For so to haue an image as to make it a god, is to make it more then an image: and therfore, vvhen it is an Idol, as vvere the Idols of the Gentiles, then it is forbid by this commaundement. Other-vvise, vvhen the Crosse stood many yeres vpon the Table in the Queenes Chappel, vvas it against this cõmaundement? or vvas it idolatrie in the Quenes Maiestie & her Counsellers, that appointed it there, being the supreme head of your churche? Or do the Lutherans your puefellowes, at this day commit idolatrie against this commaundement, that haue in their churches the crucifixe, and the holy Images of the mother of God, and of S. Iohn the Euangelist? Or if the vvhole storie of the Gospel cõcerning our sauiour Christ, vvere dravven in pictures and Images in your churches, as it is in many of ours, vvere it (trovv you) against this commaundement? fye for shame, that you should thus vvith intolerable impudencie and deceite abuse and bevvitch the ignorãt people, against your ovvne knowledge and conscience. For, vvot you not, that God many times expresly forbade the

The Crosse in the Q. Chappel.

Images in the Lutheran Churches.

Ievves

Ievves both mariages and other conuersation vvith the Gentiles, lest they might fall to vvorship their idols, as Salomon did,& as the Psalme reporteth of them? This then is the meaning of the commaundement, neither to make the idols of the Gentiles, nor any other like vnto them, and to that end, as did Ieroboam in Dan and Bethel.

3 Reg. 11.
Ps. 105.v.35.

21 This being a thing so plaine as nothing more in all the holy Scriptures, yet your itching humour of deceite and falsehod, for the most part doth translate still, *images, images,* vvhen the Latin and Greeke and Hebrue haue diuers other vvordes, and very seldom that vvhich ansvvereth to image. for when it is image in the Latin, or Greeke or Hebrue textes, your translation is not reprehended: for vve also translate sometimes, images, vvhen the text of the holy scripture requireth it. and we are not ignorant that there vvere images, vvhich the Pagans adored for their gods:& vve knovv that some idols are images, but not al images, idols. but vvhen the holy Scriptures call them by so many names, rather then images, because they vvere not onely images, but made idols: vvhy do your translations, like cuckoes birdes, sound continually, images, images, more then idols, or other vvordes equiualent to idols, vvhich

Hebr.
Teraphim.
Matsebah.
Temunah.
Maschith.
Pesel.
Tselamim.
Tabnith.
Hamanim.
Sæmel.
Massecah.
Nesachim.
Gillulim.
Miphletseth

Gr.
εἴδωλα
ἀγάλματα
χειροποίητα
γλυπτὰ
μορφὴ
εἰκὼν
στῆλαι
στύλοι
χωνευτὰ

Al *image* and *images*, in their translations.

are there meant?

22 Tvvo places onely vve vvill at this time aske you the reason of: first vvhy you
Matsebah. translate the Hebrue and Greeke that ans-
στήλη vvereth to *statua, image*, so often as you do? Vvhereas this vvord in the said tonges, is taken also in the better part, as vvhen Ia-
Gen.28.v.22 cob set vp a stone and erected it for a* title, povvring oile vpon it: and the prophet
Esa.19.v.19. saith, *our Lordes altar shal be in Aegypt, and his* title beside it.* So that the vvord doth signifie generally a signe erected of good or euil, and therfore might very well (if it pleased you) haue some other English then, *image*. Vnles you will say that Iacob also set vp an image: &, Our Lordes image shal be in Ægypt: which you will not say, though you might vvith more reason then in other places.

Of the yere 1579. 23 Secondly vve demaund, vvhy your very last English Bible hath (Esa. 30, 22:)
Pésilim. For tvvo Hebrue vvordes, vvhich are in
Massechoth. Latin *Sculptilia* and *conflatilia*, tvvise, *images,*
εἴδωλα. *images*: neither vvord being Hebrue for an image: no more then if a man vvould aske, vvhat is Latin for an image, & you vvould tell him *sculptile*. Vvherevpon he seeing a faire painted image in a table, might happily say, *Ecce egregium sculptile.* Vvhich euery boy in the Grammar schoole vvould laugh at. Vvhich therfore vve tel you, because vve

perceiue

perceiue your tranſlations endeuour and as it vvere affectat, to make *Sculptile* and *image* al one. Vvhich is moſt euidently falſe and to your great confuſiõ appeareth *Abac. 2. v. 13.* Vvhere for theſe vvordes, *Quid prodeſt ſculptile, quia ſculpſit illud fictor ſuus conflatile & imaginẽ falſam?* Vvhich is according to the Hebrue and Greeke: your later Engliſh trãſlation hath, *Vvhat profiteth the image? for the maker thereof hath made it an image, and a teacher of lies.*

פסלכי
פסלו
γλυπτὸν, ὅτι ἔγλυψαν αὐτὸ χώνευμα.
Of the yere 1579.

24 I vvould euery common Reader vvere able to diſcerne your falſhod in this place. Firſt, you make *ſculpere ſculptile,* no more then, *to make an image*: Vvhich being abſurd you knovv (becauſe the painter or embroderer making an image, can not be ſaid *ſculpere ſculptile*) might teach you that the Hebrue hath in it no ſignificatiõ of image, no more then *ſculpere* can ſignifie, to make an image: and therfore the Greeke and the Latin preciſely (for the moſt part) expreſſe neither more nor leſſe, then a thing grauẽ: but yet meane alvvaies by theſe vvordes, *a grauen idol,* to vvhich ſignification they are appropriated by vſe of holy Scripture, as *ſimulacrum, idolum, conflatile,* and ſometime *imago.* In vvhich ſenſe of ſignifying Idols, if you alſo did repeate *images* ſo often, although the tranſlation vvere not preciſe, yet it vvere in ſome part tolerable, becauſe the ſenſe vvere ſo: but vvhen you do it to bring al holy images

Sculptile. γλυπτὸν

 into

into contempt, euen the image of our Sauiour Christ crucified, you may iustly be controuled for false and heretical translators.

Abac. 1. 25 As in this very place (vvhich is an other falshod like to the other) *conflatile* you translate *image*, as you did *sculptile*, and so here againe in Abacucke (as before in Esay is noted) for tvvo distinct vvordes, eche signifying an other diuers thing from image, you translate, *images*, *images*. Thirdly, for *imaginem falsam*, *a false image*, you translate an other thing, vvithout any necessarie pretense either of Hebrue or Greeke, auoiding here the name of image, because this place telleth you that the holy Scripture speaketh against false images, or as the Greeke hath, φαντασίαν ψευδῆ *false phantasies*, or as you translate the Hebrue, such images as teach lies, representing false Gods vvhich are not, as the Apostle saith, 1 Cor. 8. Act. 19. *Idolum nihil est*, And, *Non sunt Dij qui manibus fiunt*. Vvhich distinction of false and true images you vvil not haue, because you condemne al images, euen holy and sacred also, and therfore you make the holy Scriptures to speake herein according to your ovvne fansie.

26 Vvherein you procede so far, that vvhen Daniel said to the king, Dan. 14. v. 4. *I vvorship not idols made vvith handes* (εἴδωλα χειροποίητα) you make

make him ſay thus, *I vvorſhip not things that be* Bib. 1562.
made vvith handes. leauing out the vvord idols 1577.
altogether as though he had ſaid, nothing made vvith hand vvere to be adored, not the Arke, the propitiatorie, no nor the holy Croſſe it ſelf that our Sauiour ſhed his bloud vpon. As before you added to the text, ſo here you diminiſh & take from it at your pleaſure.

27 But concerning the vvord image, vvhich you make to be the Engliſh of al the Latin, Hebrue, and Greeke vvordes, be they neuer ſo many and ſo diſtinct, I beſeeche you vvhat reaſon had you to tranſlate γλυπτὰ *images*, Sap. 15 v. 13: doth the Greeke vvord ſo ſignifie? doth not the ſentence folovving tel you that it ſhould haue been tranſlated, *grauen idols?* for thus it ſaith, *They iudged al the idols of the nations to be Gods.* loe your images, or rather loe the true names of the Pagans goddes, vvhich it pleaſeth you to call, *images, images.*

28 But (to conclude this point) you might, and it vvould haue vvel becommed you, in tranſlating or expounding the foreſaid vvordes, to haue folovved S. Hierom Comment.
the great famous tranſlator and interpreter in Abac. 2.
of the holy Scriptures: vvho telleth you tvvo ſenſes of the foreſaid vvordes: the one literal, of the idols of the Gentiles: the

other mystical, of Heresies and errours. *Sculptile*, saith he, *& conflatile: I take to be peruerse opinions, vvhich are adored of the authors that made them. See Arius, that graued to him self this idol, that Christ vvas onely a creature, & adored that vvhich he had grauen. behold Eunomius, hovv he molted and cast a false image, and bovved to that vvhich he had molten.* Suppose he had exemplified of the tvvo condemned heretikes Iouinian and Vigilātius also: had he not touched your idols, that is, the old condemned heresies vvhich you at this day adore?

29 These onely (I mean heresies & heretikes) are the idols and idolaters (by the auncient Doctors iudgement) vvhich haue been among Christians, since the idolatrie
Zach. 13. of the Gentiles ceased according to the prophets. Therfore S. Hierom saith againe,
Loco citato. *If thou see a man that vvill not yeld to the truth, but vvhen the falshod of his opinions is once shevved, perseuereth still in that he began: thou maist aptly say, Sperat*
Osee 11. *in figmento suo, and he maketh dumme or deafe idols.* And againe, *Al Heretikes haue their gods: & vvhatsoeuer they haue forged, they adore the same as sculptile and conflatile*: that is, *as a grauen and molten idol.* And
Osee 12. againe, *He saith vvel, I haue found vnto my self an idol*: For, *al the forgeries of heretikes are as the idols of the Gentils: neither do they much differ in impietie,*
In 5. Amos. *though in name they seeme to differ.* And againe, *Vvhatsoeuer according to the letter is spoken against the idolatrie of the Ievves, do thou referre al this vnto them vvhich vnder the name of Christ vvorship idols, and forging to them selues peruerse opinions, carie the tabernacle of their*

king

king the Deuil, and the image of their idols. For they vvorſhip not an idol, but for varietie of their doctrine they adore diuerſe Gods. And he put in very vvell, vvhich you made to your ſelues: for they receiued them not of God, but forged them of their ovvne minde. And of the idol of Samaria he ſaith, we alvvaies vnderſtand Samaria (& the idol of Samaria) in the perſon of Heretikes, the ſame Prophet ſaying, VVO BE TO THEM THAT DESPISE SION, AND TRVST IN THE MOVNT OF SAMARIA. *For Heretikes deſpiſe the Church of God, and truſt in the falſhod of their opinions, erecting them ſelues againſt the knovvledge of God: and ſaying, vvhen they haue diuided the people* (by ſchiſme,) *vve haue no part in Dauid, nor inheritance in the ſonne of Iſay.*

In 8. Amos.

c. 6.

30 Thus the Reader may ſee that the holy Scriptures vvhich the Aduerſaries falſely tranſlate againſt the holy images of our Sauiour Chriſt and his ſainctes, to make vs idolaters, do in deede concerne their idols, and condemne them as idolaters, vvhich forge nevv opinions to them ſelues, ſuch as the auncient fathers knevv not, and adore them and their ovvne ſenſe and interpretation of Scriptures, ſo far & ſo vehemently, that they preferre it before the approued iudgement of all the generall councels and holy Doctors, and for maintenance of the ſame, corrupt the holy Scriptures at their pleaſure, and make them ſpeake according

to

to there fansies, as we haue partly shevved, and novv are to declare further.

CHAP. IIII.

The ECCLESIASTICAL *vse of vvordes turned into their* ORIGINAL *and* PROFANE *signification.*

1 WE spake a litle before of the double signification of wordes, the one according to the original propertie, the other according to the vsual taking thereof in all vulgar speache and vvriting. These vvordes (as by the vvay vve shevved before vpon occasion of the Aduersaries graunt) are to be translated in their vulgar and vsual signification, not as they signifie by their original propertie. As for example: *Maior* in the original signification is, *greater*. But vvhen vve say, The *Maior* of London, novv it is taken and soundeth in euery mans eare for such an Officer: and no man vvill say, The *Greater* of London, according to the original propertie of it. likevvise *Episcopus* a Greeke vvord, in the original sense is euery ouerseer, as Tullie vseth it and other profane vvriters: but among Christians in Ecclesiastical speache it is a Bishop. and no man vvil say, My Lord *ouerseer* of London, for my

Chap. 3. nu. 17. 18. See also M. Vvhitaker pag. 209. & the 6 chap. of this booke (nu. 6. 7. 8. & nu. 13. &c.) much more of this matter.

my L. *Bishop*. Likevvise vve say, Seuen *Deacons*, S. Steuen a *Deacon*. no man vvill say, Seuen *Ministers*, S. Steuen a *Minister*. although that be the original signification of the vvord Deacon. but by Ecclesiastical vse & appropriation being taken for a certaine degree of the Clergie, so it soundeth in euery mans eare, and so it must be translated. As vve say, Nero made many *Martyrs*: not, Nero made many *vvitnesses*: and yet Martyr by the first originall propertie of the vvord is nothing els but a vvitnes. Vve say *Baptisme* is a Sacrament: not, *Vvashing* is a Sacrament. Yet Baptisme and vvashing by the first originall propertie of the vvord is all one.

2 Novv then to come to our purpose, such are the absurde translations of the English Bibles, and altogether like vnto these. Namely, vvhen they translate congregation for Church, Elder for Priest, image for idol, dissension for schisme, General for Catholike, secrete for Sacrament, ouer-seer for Bishop, [c] messenger for Angel, embassadour for Apostle, minister for Deacon, and such like: to vvhat other end be these deceitfull translations but to conceale & obscure the name of the Church and dignities thereof mentioned in the holy Scriptures: to dissemble the vvord schisme (as they do also He-

c See chap. 15. nu. 18. & 3. 4. & chap. 21. nu

Gal.5.Tit.3. 1 Cor. 11. * Heresie and Heretike) for feare of disgra-
Bib. 1562. cing their schismes and Heresies, to say of Matrimonie, neither Sacrament vvhich is the Latin, nor mysterie which is the Greeke, but to goe as far as they can possibly from the common vsual and Ecclesiastical
Eph.5, v. 32. vvordes, saying, *This is a great secrete*: in fauour of their heresie, that Matrimonie is no Sacrament.

1 Cor.1.v.10 3 S. Paul saith as plaine as he can speake, *I beseeche you brethren, that you all say one thing, and that there be no schismes among you.* They translate for schismes, dissentions: vvhich may be in profane and vvorldly things, as vvell as in matters of religion. but schismes are those that diuide the vnitie of the Church, vvher-of they knovv them selues guilty. S. Paul
Tit. 3 saith as plainely as is possible, *A man that is an*
αἱρετικὸν *Heretike auoid after the first and second admonition.*
ἄνθρωπον they translated in their Bible of the yere
αἱρέσεις. 1562, *A man that is an authour of Sectes.* and vvhere
Gal 5. the Greeke is, *Heresie*, reckened among damnable sinnes, they say, *Sectes*: fauouring that name for their owne sakes, and dissembling it, as though the holy Scriptures spake not against Heresie or Heretikes, Schisme or Schismatikes.

4 As also they suppresse the very name Catholike, vvhen it is expresly in the Greeke, for malice tovvard Catholikes and Catho

Catholike religion, becauſe they knovv, them ſelues neuer ſhal be called or knowē by that name. And therfore theire tvvo Engliſh Bibles accuſtomed to be reade in theire church (therfore by like moſt authenticall) leaue it cleane out in the title of al thoſe Epiſtles, which haue been knovven by the name of *Catholicæ Epiſtolæ* euer ſince the Apoſtles time: and their later Engliſh Bible (dealing ſomevvhat more honeſtly) hath turned the word *Catholike* into *General*: ſaying, *The General Epiſtle of Iames, of Peter, &c.* As if a man ſhould ſay in his Creede, *I beleeue the general Church*, becauſe he vvould not ſay, *the Catholike Church*: as the Lutheran Catechiſmes ſay for that purpoſe, *I beleeue the Chriſtian Church.* So that by this rule, vvhen S. Auguſtine telleth that the maner vvas in cities vvhere there vvas libertie of religion, to aſke, *Qua itur ad Catholicam?* Vve muſt tranſlate it, *Vvhich is the vvay to the General?* And vvhen S. Hierom ſaith, If vve agree in faith vvith the B. of Rome, *ergo Catholici ſumus*: vve muſt trāſlate it, *Then vve are Generals.* Is not this good ſtuff? Are they not aſhamed thus to inuert and peruert al vvordes againſt common ſenſe and vſe and reaſon? Catholike and General or Vniuerſal (vve knovv) is by the original propertie of the vvord al one: but according to the vſe of both, as it is ridiculous to ſay, A Catholike Councel, for a general

An. 1562. 1577.

Euſeb. li. 2. Ec. hiſt. c. 22 in fine. 1579.

Lind. in Dubitantio.

Councel: so is it ridiculous and impious to say, General for Catholike, in derogation thereof, and for to hide it vnder a bushel.

5 Is it because they vvould folovv the
Catholica. Greeke, that they turne καθολικὴ, general? euen as iust, as vvhen they turne εἴδωλον image, παράδοσιν instruction, δικαίωμα ordinance, σχίσμα dissension, αἵρεσιν sect, μυστήριον secrete, and such like, vvhere they goe as far from the Greeke as they can, & vvill be glad to pretend for ansvver of their vvord, *secte*, that they folovv our Latin translation. Alas poore shift for them that othervvise pretend nothing but the Greeke, to be tried by that Latin vvhich them selues cōdemne. But vve honour the said text, and translate it *sectes* also, as vve there finde it, and as vve do in other places folovv the Latin text, and take not our aduantage of the Greeke text, because vve knovv the Latin translation is good also and sincere, and approued in the Church by long antiquitie, and it is in sense al one to vs vvith the Greeke: but not so to them, vvho in these daies of controuersie about the Greeke and Latin text, by not folovving the Greeke, vvhich they professe sincerely to follovv, bevvray them selues that they do it for a malitious purpose.

CHAP.

CHAP. V.

Heretical tranſlation againſt the CHVRCH.

AS they ſuppreſſe the name, 1
Catholike, euen ſo did they
in their firſt Engliſh bible
the name of *Church* it ſelf:
becauſe at their firſt reuolt &
apoſtaſie from that that vvas vniuerſally
knovven to be the onely true Catholike
Church: it vvas a great obiection againſt
their ſchiſmatical procedings, and it ſtucke
much in the peoples conſciences, that they
forſooke the Church, and that the Church
cōdemned them. Vvherevpon very vvilely
they ſuppreſſed the name Church in their
Engliſh tranſlation, ſo, that in al that Bible Bib. 1562.
ſo lōg read in their cōgregatiōs, we can not
once finde the name thereof. Iudge by theſe
places vvhich ſeeme of moſt importance
for the dignitie preeminence & authoritie
of the *Church*.

2 Our Sauiour ſaith, *Vpon this Rocke I vvil build* Mat. 16.
my Church, and the gates of Hel ſhal not preuaile againſt
it. They make him to ſay, *Vpon this rocke* Mat. 18.
I wil build my cōgregation. Againe, *If he heare not them,*
tel the Church: and if he heare not the Church, let him be
to thee as an Heathen and as a publicane. they ſay, *Con-*
gregation. Againe, vvho vvould thinke they
vvould haue altered the vvord Church in
the

Eph. 5. the epistle to the Ephesians? their English translation for many yeres redde thus, *Ye husbands loue your vviues, as Christ loued the congregation, and clensed it to make it vnto him self a glorious cōgregation vvithout spot or vvrinkle.* And, *This is a great secrete, but I speake of Christ and of the congregation.*

1 Tim. 3. And to Timothee, *The house of God, vvhich is the congregation of the liuing God, the pillar and ground of truth.* Here is no vvord of Church, vvhich in Latin and Greeke is, *Ecclesiæ Dei viui, columna & firmamentum veritatis.* Likevvise to the Ephesians againe,

Eph. 1. *He hath made him head of the congregation, vvhich is his body.* And to the Hebrues they

Heb. 12. v. 23 are al bold to translate: *The congregation of the first-borne,* vvhere the Apostle nameth heauenly Hierusalem, the citie of the liuing God, &c.

3 So that by this translation, there is no more Church militant and triumphant, but congregation, and he is not head of the Church, but of the congregation: and this congregation at the time of the making of this trāslation, vvas in a fevv nevv brethren of England, for vvhose sake the name Church vvas left out of the English Bible, to commend the name of congregation aboue the name of churche. vvhereas S. Au-

In ps. 81. in initio. gustine telleth them, that the Ievves Syna-

συναγωγή. gogue, vvas a congregation: the Church, a

ἐκκλησία. conuocation: and that a congregation, is of beasts also: a conuocation, of reasonable crea-

creatures onely: and that the Ievves congregation is sometime called the *church*, but the Apostles neuer called the Church, *Congregation*. do you see then vvhat a goodly change they haue made, for Church, to say cõgregation: so making them selues a very Synagogue, & that by the propertie of the Greeke vvord, vvhich yet (as S. Augustine telleth them most truely) signifieth rather a conuocation?

4 If they appeale here to their later translations, vve must obtaine of them to condemne the former, and to confesse this vvas a grosse fault committed therein. and that the Catholike Church of our contrie did not il to forbid and burne suche bookes vvhich vvere so translated by Tyndal and the like, as being not in deede Gods booke, vvord, or Scripture, but the Diuels vvord. Yea they must confesse, that the leauing out of this vvord Church altogether, vvas of an heretical spirit against the Catholike Romane Church, because then they had no Caluinistical church in any like forme of religion and gouernement to theirs novv. Neither vvil it serue them to say after their maner, And if a man should translate *Ecclesiam, congregation: this is no more absurditie, then in steede of a Greeke vvord, to vse a Latin of the same signification.* This (vve trovv) vvil not suffise

Confut. of M. Houlet fo. 35.

E them

them in the iudgement of the simplest indifferent Reader.

5 But, my Maisters, if you vvould confesse the former faults and corruptions neuer so plainely, is that ynough to iustifie your corrupt dealing in the holy Scriptures? Is it not an horrible fault so vvilfully to falsifie and corrupt the vvord of God vvritten by the inspiration of the holy Ghost? May you abuse the people for certaine yeres vvith false translations, and aftervvard say, Lo vve haue amended it in our later translations? Then might the Heretike Beza be excused for translating in steede of Christs *soul in hel*, his *carcas in the graue*. and because some freende told him of that corruption, and he corrected it in the later editions, he should neuerthelesse in your iudgemēt, be counted a right honest man. No (be ye sure) the discrete Reader can not be so abused, but he vvil easily see, that there is a great difference in mending some ouersightes vvhich may escape the best men: & in your grosse false translations, vvho at the first falsifie of a prepensed malice, and aftervvards alter it for very shame. Hovvbeit, to say the truth, in the cheefest and principal place that concerneth the Churches perpetuitie and stabilitie, you haue not yet altered the former translation, but it remaineth as before, and

See his nevv Test. in Latin of the yere 1556, printed by Robert Steuen in fol. Act. 2. v. 27.

is

is at this day readde in your churches thus, *Vpon this rocke I vvil build my congregation.* Can it be vvithout some heretical subteltie, that in this place specially and (I thinke) only you change not the vvord congregation into Church? Giue vs a reason & discharge your credite.

Mat. 16. v. 18. Bib. 1577.

6 Vvhat shal I say of Beza, vvhom the English bibles also folovv, translating actiuely that Greeke vvord, (vvhich in common vse, & by S. Chrysostoms and the Greeke Doctors exposition is a plaine passiue:) to signifie, as in his Annotations is cleere, that Christ may be vvithout his Church, that is, a head vvithout a body. The vvordes be these in the heretical translation, *He gaue him to be the head ouer al thinges to the Church, vvhich* (Church) *is his body, the fulnes of him that filleth all in all.* S. Chrysostom, saith Beza, (he might haue said al the Greeke & Latin auncient fathers) taketh it passiuely, in this sense, that Christ *is filled* al in al, because all faithful men as members, and the vvhole Church as the body, concurre to the fulnes and accomplishmēt of Christ the head. *But this* (saith he) *seemeth vnto me a forced interpretation.* Vvhy so beza?

Eph. 1. v. 22. 23

τοῦ πληρουμένου.

7 Marke his Doctors vvhom he opposeth to the fathers both Greeke and Latin. Becaufe Xenophon (saith he) in such a

place, and Plato in such a place, vse the said Greeke word actiuely. I omit this miserable match, & vnvvorthie names of Xenophon & Plato in trial of S. Paules wordes, against al the glorious Doctors: this is his common custom. I aske him rather of these his owne doctors, hovv they vse the Greeke vvord in other places of their vvorkes? hovv vse they it most cõmonly? yea how do al other Greeke vvriters either profane or sacred vse it? Vvhat say the Greeke readers of al vniuersities? Surely not only they, but their scholers for the most part, can not be ignorant, that the vse of this vvord and the like, is passiue, though sometime it may also signifie actiuely: but that is so rare in comparison of the other, that no man lightly vvil vse it, and I am vvel assured it vvould be counted a fault and some lacke of skill, if one novv in his vvritinges that vvould expresse this in Greeke, *God filleth al thinges vvith his blessing*, should say, πληρõυlαι πάνlα: and *The vvine filleth the cuppe*, ὁ οἶνος πληρõυlαι το πολήελον. Aske them that haue skill, and controule me. Contrarievvise, if one vvould say passiuely, *Al thinges are filled vvith Gods blessing*, *The cuppe is filled vvith vvine*, *Such a prophecie is fulfilled*, Vvhat meane Græcian vvould not say, as S. Chrysostom here expoũdeth this vvord, πληρõυlαι, vsing it passiuely?

πληροῦμαι

8 Yet (saith Beza) this is a forced inter-

pretation, because Xenophon forsooth & Plato (once perhaps in al their vvhole vvorkes) vse it othervvise. O heretical blindnes or rather stubburnenes, that calleth that forced, vvhich is most common and vsual: and seeth not that his ovvne translatiō is forced, because it is against the common vse of the vvord. but no maruel. For he that in other places thinketh it no forced interpretation, to translate δέξασθαι, *to be conteined*, Vvhich neither Xenophon, nor Plato, nor any Greeke author vvill allovv him to doe, and ψυχὴν, *carcas*, and πρόγνωσιν, *prouidence*, and μετάνοιαν, *them that amend their liues*, may much more in this place dissemble his forced interpretation of πεπληρουμένου. But vvhy he should call S. Chrysostoms interpretation forced, vvhich is the common & vsual interpretation, that hath no more reason, then if a very theefe should say to an honest man, Thou art a theefe, and not I.

Recipere.

Animam.
Præscientiā.
Pœnitentiā.

9 Is it forced Beza, that Christ *is filled al in al* by the Church? doth not S. Paul in the very next vvordes before, call the Church the fulnes of Christ, saying, *Vvhich is the fulnes of him that is filled al in al?* If the Church be the fulnes of him, then is he filled or hath his fulnes of the Church, so that he is not a maimed head vvithout a body. This would S. Paul say, if you vvould giue him leaue, and this he doth say, vvhether you vvill or

Eph. 1.

 no.

no. But vvhat is the cause that they vvil not suffer the Apostle to say so? because (saith Beza) *Christ needeth no such complement.* And if he neede it not, then may he be vvithout a Church, and consequently it is no absurditie, if the Church hath been for many yeres not only inuisible, but also not at all. Vvould a man easily at the first imagine or conceiue that there vvere such secrete poison in their translation?

10 Againe, it commeth from the same
Bib. 1579. puddle of Geneua, that in their bibles so called, the English Bezites translate against the vnitie of the Catholike Church. For vvhereas them selues are ful of sectes and dissensions, and the true Church is knovven by vnitie, and hath this marke giuen her
Cant. 6. v. 8. by Christ him self, in vvhose person Salo-
μία mon speaking saith, *Vna est columba mea*, that
אחת is, *One is my doue*, or, *My doue is one.* therfore in steede hereof, the foresaid bible saith, *My doue is alone*: Neither Hebrue nor Greeke vvord hauing that signification, but being as proper to signifie one, as *Vnus* in latin.

11 But vve beseeche euery indifferent Reader, euen for his soules health to consider that one point specially before mentioned of their abandoning the name of Church for so many yeres out of their English Bibles: thereby to defeate the stron-

gest

gest argument that might and may possibly be brought against them and all other Heretikes : to vvit , the authoritie of the Church vvhich is so many vvaies and so greatly recommended vnto all Christians in holy Scriptures. consider (I pray you) vvhat a malitious intētion they had herein. First , that the name Church should neuer sound in the common peoples eares out of the Scriptures : secondly , that as in other things , so in this also it might seeme to the ignorant a good argument against the authoritie of the Church, to say, *Vve finde not this vvord (Church) in al the holy Scriptures*. For as in other articles they say so, because they finde not the expresse word in the holy scripture, so did they vvell prouide , that the vvord (Church) in the holy Scriptures should not stay or hinder their schismaticall and hereticall procedings , as long as that vvas the onely English translation , that vvas read and liked among the people: that is, so long till they had by preaching taken avvay the Catholike Churches credite and authoritie altogether , among the ignorant by opposing the Scriptures therevnto, vvhich them selues had thus falsely translated.

CHAP. VI.

Heretical translation against PRIEST *and* PRIESTHOD.

1 BVT because it may be, they vvill stand here vpon their later translations, vvhich haue the name Church, (because by that time they savv the absurditie of changing the name, & now their number vvas increased, & thẽ selues began to chalẽge to be the true Church, though not the Catholike: and for former times vvhen they vvere not, they deuised an inuisible Church) If then they vvill stand vpon their later trãslations, and refuse to iustifie the former: let vs demaund of them concerning al their English translations, vvhy and to vvhat end they suppresse the name *Priest*, translating it *Elder*, in al places vvhere the holy Scripture vvould signifie by *Presbyter* and *Presbyterium*, the Priests and Priesthod of the nevv Testament?

2 Vnderstand gentle Reader, their vvylie pollicie therein is this. To take avvay the holy sacrifice of the Masse, they take avvay both altar and Priest, because they knovv right vvell that these three (Priest, sacrifice, and altar) are dependents and consequents one of an other, so that they can not be separated. If there be an external sacrifice, there

there muſt be an external Prieſthod to offer it, an altar to offer the ſame vpon. ſo had the Gentiles their ſacrifices, Prieſts, and altars: ſo had the Ievves: ſo Chriſt him ſelf being a Prieſt according to the order of Melchiſedec, had a ſacrifice, his body: and an altar, his Croſſe: vpon the vvhich he offered it. And becauſe he inſtituted this ſacrifice to continue in his Church for euer in commemoration and repreſentation of his death, therfore did he vvithal ordaine his Apoſtles Prieſts at his laſt ſupper, there & then inſtituted the holy order of Prieſthod and Prieſts (ſaying, *hoc facite, Doe this*:) Luc. c. 22. v. 19.
to offer the ſelf ſame ſacrifice in a myſtical
and vnblouddy maner, vntil the vvorldes end.

3 To defeate al this and to take avvay all external Prieſthod and ſacrifice, they by corrupt tranſlation of the holy Scriptures, make them cleane dumme as though they had not a word of any ſuch Prieſts or Prieſthod as vve ſpeake of. Their Bibles (vve graunt) haue the name of Prieſts very often, but that is vvhen mention is made either of the Prieſts of the Ievves, or of the Prieſts of the Gentiles (ſpecially vvhen they are reprehended and blamed in the holy Scriptures) and in ſuch places our Aduerſaries haue the name Prieſts in there tranſlations

to make the very name of Priest odious amonge the common ignorant people. Againe they haue also the name Priests, vvhen they are taken for all maner of men, vvomen, or children, that offer internal and spiritual sacrifices, vvhereby our Aduersaries vvould falsely signifie that there are no other Priests, as one of them of late freshly auoucheth, directly against S. Augustine, vvho in one breife sentence distinguisheth Priests proprely so called in the Church, and Priests as it is a common name to al Christians. Lib. 20 de Ciuit. Dei cap. 10. This name then of Priest & Priesthod proprely so called (as S. Augustine saith, which is an order distinct from the laitie & vulgar people, ordained to offer Christ in an vnbloudy maner in sacrifice to his heauenly father for vs, to preach and minister the Sacraments, & to be the Pastors of the people) they vvholy suppresse in their translations, and in al places vvhere the holy Scripture calleth them, *Presbyteros*, there they neuer translate *Priests*, but *Elders*. and that they do obserue so duely and so vvarily and vvith so full and generall consent in al their English Bibles as the Puritans do plainely cōfesse, & M. vvhitgift denieth it not, that a man vvould vvonder to see hovv carefull they are, that the people may not once heare the

Vvhitakers. p. 199.

See the puritans replie. pag. 159. and vvhitgifts defence against the Puritans pag. 722.

the name of any such Priest in all the holy Scriptures.

4 As for example in theire translations. vvhen there fel a questiō about circūcision, *They determined that Paul and Barnabas should goe vp to Hierusalem vnto the Apostles and* ELDERS, *about this question. Act.* 15. And againe, *They vvere receiued of the* * *congregation and of the Apostles and* ELDERS. Againe, *The Apostles & Elders came together to reason of this matter.* Againe, *Then pleased it the Apostles and Elders vvith the vvhole cōgregation to send &c.* Againe, *The Apostles and Elders and brethren send greating &c.* Againe, *They deliuered them the decrees for to keepe, that vvere ordained of the Apostles and* ELDERS. If in al these places they had translated *Priests* (as in deede they should haue done according to the Greeke vvord) it had then disaduantaged them this much, that men vvould haue thought, both the dignitie of Priests to be great, & also their authoritie in Councels, as being here ioyned vvith the Apostles, to be greatly reuerenced & obeied. To keepe the people from all such holy and reuerent cogitatiōs of Priests, they put *Elders*, a name vvherevvith our holy Christian forefathers eares vvere neuer acquainted, in that sense.

πρεσβυτέρους. Presbyterοα.

* The later Bibles read Church.

Act. 16.

5 But let vs goe forvvard. Vve haue heard often & of old time, of making of Priests: and of late yeres also, of making Ministers: but did ye euer heare in al England of making

king Elders? Yet by theſe mens tranſlations it hath been in England a phraſe of Scripture this thirtie yere: but it muſt needes be very ſtrãge, that this making of elders hath not al this vvhile been practiſed & knovvẽ, no not among them ſelues in any of their churches vvithin the realme of England.

Tit. 1. To Titus they make the Apoſtle ſay thus, *For this cauſe left I thee in Creta, that thou ſhouldeſt ordaine* ELDERS *in euery citie, &c.* Againe of Paul

τοὺς πρεσβυτέρους. Presbyteros. and Barnabas: *Vvhen they had ordained Elders by election, in euery* congregation.* Act. 14. If they had

* Bib. an. 1562. ſaid plainely as it is in the Greeke, & as our forefathers vvere vvont to ſpeake, and the truth is: *Titus vvas leaft in Creta to ordaine Prieſts in euery citie*: and, *Paul and Barnabas made Prieſts in euery Church*: then the people vvould haue vnderſtood them: they know ſuch ſpeaches of old, and it had been their ioy and comfort to heare it ſpecified in holy Scriptures. Novv they are told another thing, in ſuch nevvneſſe of ſpeaches and vvordes, of Elders to be made in euery citie & congregation, and yet not one citie nor cõgregation to haue any Elders in all England, that vve knovv not vvhat is prophane noueltie of

1 Tim. 6. vvordes, vvhich the Apoſtle vvilleth to be auoided, if this be not an exceding profane noueltie.

6 That it is noueltie to all Engliſh Chriſtian eares, it is euident. And it is alſo profane

fane, because they do so English the Greeke vvord of *ordaining* (for of the vvord *Presbyter* vve vvill speake more anone) as if they should trãslate Demosthenes, or the lawes of Athens concerning their choosing of Magistrates, vvhich vvas by giuing voices vvith liftĩg vp their hands. so do they force this vvord here, to induce the peoples election, & yet in their churches in Englãd the people elect not ministers, but their bishop. vvhereas the holy Scripture saith, they ordained to the people: and vvhatsoeuer force the vvord hath, it is here spoken of the Apostles, and pertaineth not to the people, and therfore in the place to Titus it is another vvord vvhich cannot be forced further, then to ordaine & appoint. And they might knovv (if malice and Heresie vvould suffer them to see and confesse it) that the holy Scriptures, and fathers, and Ecclesiastical custome, hath dravven this & the like wordes from their profane & common signification, to a more peculiar and Ecclesiastical speache: as Episcopus, an *ouerseer* in Tullie, is a *Bishop* in the nevv Testament.

χειροτονεῖν Act. 14.

χειροτονήσαντες αὐτοῖς.

καταστῆσαι. Tit. 1.

7 And concerning χειροτονία vvhich vve novv speake of, S. Hierom telleth them (in c. 58. Esai.) that it signifieth *Clericorum ordinationem*, that is, *geuing of holy orders*, *vvhich is done*

not

Greg. Naziã. in titul. Ser. 1. 4. 5. μετὰ τῶ τοῦ πρεσβυτερίου χειροτονίαν. and, ἐπίσκοπος ἐχειροτονήθη.

Ignat. ep. 10. saith of Bishops, βαπτίζουσι, ἱερουργοῦσι, χειροτονοῦσι, χειροθετοῦσι.

χειροτονία. ἐπίθεσις τῶν χειρῶν

not onely by praier of the voice, but by imposition of the hand: according to S. Paul vnto Timothee, Manus citò nemini imposueris. Impose or *put hands quickly on no man.* that is, be not hastie or easie to giue holy orders. Where these great etymologistes, that so straine the original nature of this vvord to profane stretching forth the hand in elections, may learne an other Ecclesiastical etymologie thereof, as proper and as vvel deduced of the vvord as the other, to vvit, *putting forth the hand* to giue orders: & so they shal finde it is al one with that vvhich the Apostle calleth imposition of hands, *1 Tim. 4. 2 Tim. 1*: and consequently, for, *ordaining Elders by election*, they should haue said, *ordaining* or *making Priests by imposition of hands*: as els vvhere S. Paul, 1 Tim. 5. and the Actes of the Apostles (Act. 6. and 13.) do speake in the ordaining of the seuen Deacons and of SS. Paul and Barnabas.

8 But they are so profane and secular, that they translate the Greeke vvord πρεσβύτερος in al the nevv Testament, as if it had the old profane signification still, & vvere indifferent to signifie the auncients of the Ievves, the Senatours of Rome, the elders of Lacedemonia, and the Christian Clergie. in so much that they say, Paul *sent to Ephesus, and called the Elders of the Church*: Act. 20, and yet they vvere such as had their flockes, & cure of

τοὺς πρεσβυτέρους

of soules, as followveth in the same place. They make S. Paul speake thus to Timothee, *Neglect not the gift* (so they had rather say then *grace*, lest holy orders should be a Sacrament) *giuen thee vvith the laying on of the hands of the Eldership.* or, *by the authoritie of the Eldership.* 1 Tim. 4. Vvhat is this companie of Eldership? Somevvhat they vvould say like to the Apostles word, but they vvil not speake plainely, lest the vvorld might heare out of the Scriptures, that Timothee vvas made Priest or Bishop euen as the vse is in the Catholike Church at this day. let the 4 Councel of Carthage speake for both partes indifferently, and tell vs the Apostles meaning, *A Priest vvhen he taketh his orders, the Bishop blessing him and holding his hand vpon his head, let all the Priests also that are present, hold their hands by the Bishops hand vpon his head.* So doe our Priests at this day, vvhen a bishop maketh priests: & this is the laying on of the hands of the companie of Priests, vvhich S. Paul speaketh of, and vvhich they translate, *the companie of the Eldership.* Onely their former translation of 1562 in this place (by vvhat chance or consideration vve knovve not) let fall out of the penne, *by the authoritie of Priesthod.*

χάρισμα

Bib. 1579. 1577.

τοῦ πρεσβυτερίου. Presbyterij.

ca. 3 in the yere 436. Vvhere S. Augustine vvas present and subscribed.

9 Othervvise in all their English Bibles all the belles ring one note as, *The Elders that rule vvell, are vvorthie of double honour.* And, *Against*

an Elder receiue no accusation, but vnder tvvo or three vvitnesses. 1 Tim. 5. And, *If any be diseased among you, let him call for the Elders of the Church, and let them pray ouer him, and anoynt him vvith oile, &c.* Iacob. 5. Vvhereas S. Chrisostom out of this place proueth the high dignitie of Priests in remitting sinnes, in his booke entitled, *of Priesthod*, vnles they vvill translate that title also, *of Eldership*. Againe they make S. Peter say thus: *The Elders vvhich are among you, I exhort vvhich am also an Elder, feede ye Christes flocke, as much as lyeth in you, &c.* 1 Pet. 5.

τοὺς πρεσβυτέρους τῆς ἐκκλησίας.

lib. 3. de Sacerdotio.

περὶ ἱερωσύνης.

10 Vvhere if they vvill tell vs (as also in certaine other places) that our Latin translation hath *Seniores* and *maiores natu*: vve tel them, as heretofore vve haue told them, that this is nothing to them, vvho professe to translate the Greeke. Againe vve say that if they meant no vvorse then the old Latin translatour did, they vvould be as indifferét as he, to haue said sometime Priests and Priesthod, vvhen he hath the vvordes *Presbyteros* and *Presbyterium*: as vve are indifferent in our translation, saying Seniors and Auncients, vvhen vve finde it so in our Latin: being vvell assured that by sundrie vvordes he meant but one thing, as in Greeke it is but one, and as both Erasmus, and also Beza him self alvvaies translate it, keeping the name *Presbyter* and *Presbyteri*: of vvhó by reason they should haue learned, rather

S. Hierom readeth, *Presbyteros ego compresbyter*, Ep. 85. ad Euagr. & in 1 ad Gal: prouing the dignitie of Priests. and yet in 4 Gal. he readeth according to the vulgar Latin text, *Seniores in vobis rogo consenior & ipse.* Vvhereby it is euidét, that *Senior* here & in the Actes is a Priest, & not cótrarie, *Presbyter*, an elder.

rather then of our Latin tráſlatour, vvhom othervviſe they cõdemne. And if they ſay, they do folovv them, and not him, becauſe they tráſlate not *Senior* and *maior natu*, but the vvord *Preſbyter* or πρεσβύτερος, an Elder, in al places: vve tell them, and herein vve conuent their cõſcience, that they do it to take avvay the external Prieſthod of the nevv Teſtament, & to ſuppreſſe the name Prieſt, againſt the Eccleſiaſtical, and (as novv ſince Chriſt) very proper and vſual ſignification thereof, in the nevv Teſtament, councels, & fathers, in al common vvriting and ſpeaking: ſpecially the Latin *Preſbyter*, vvhich grevve to this ſignification out of the Greeke in the foreſaid places of holy Scripture.

11 In ſo much that immediatly in the firſt Canons and Councels of the Apoſtles and their ſucceſſors, nothing is more common then this diſtinction of Eccleſiaſtical degrees and names, *Si Epiſcopus, vel Presbyter, vel Diaconus &c. If any Biſhop, or Prieſt, or Deacon* do this or that. Vvhich if the Proteſtants or Caluiniſts vvil tranſlate after their maner thus, *If a Biſhop, or Elder, or Deacon &c*: they do againſt them ſelues, vvhich make *Presbyter* or *Elder* a common name to all Eccleſiaſtical perſons: & not a peculiar degree, next vnto a Biſhop. So that either they muſt con-

See can. Apoſt. Conc. 1 Nic. Epiſtol. Ignat. Conc. Carth. 4.

Beza in 1 Pet. 5.

demne al antiquitie for placing *Presbyter* in the second degree after a Bishop, or they must translate it Priest as vve doe, or they must make *Elder* to be their second degree, and so put Minister out of place.

12 And here vve must aske them, hovv this name Minister came to be a degree distinct from Deacon, vvhereas by their ovvne rule of trãslation, Deacon is nothing els but a minister: and vvhy keepe they the old & vsual Ecclesiastical name of Deacon in translating *Diaconus*, and not the name of *Priest*, in translating *Presbyter*? doth not *Priest* come of *Presbyter* as certainely and as agreably as Deacon of *Diaconus*? doth not also the french and Italian, vvord for Priest come directly from the same? vvill you alvvaies folovv fansie and not reason, do vvhat you list, translate as you list, and not as the truth is, and that in the holy Scriptures, vvhich you boast and vaunt so much of? Because your selues haue them vvhom you call Bishops, the name Bishop is in your English Bibles, vvhich othervvise by your ovvne rule of trãslation, should be called an Ouerseer or Superintendent: likevvise Deacon you are content to vse as an Ecclesiastical vvord so vsed in antiquitie, because you also haue those vvhom you call Deacons: Onely Priests must be turned contemptu-

Margin notes: διάκονος Diaconus. — 1 Tim. 3. Bib. 1577. 1579. — Prebstre. Prete.

ously

ously out of the text of the holy Scriptures, and Elders put in their place, because you haue no Priests, nor vvil none of them, and because that is in cõtrouersie betvvene vs. & as for Elders, you haue none permitted in England, for feare of ouerthrovving your Bishops office & the Queenes supreme gouernemẽt in all spiritual things & causes. Is not this to folovv the humour of your heresie, by Machiauels politike rules vvithout any feare of God?

13 Apostles you say for the most part in your translations (not alvvaies) as vve do, and Prophetes, and Euangelistes, & Angels, and such like, and vvheresoeuer there is no matter of controuersie betvvene you and vs, there you can pleade very grauely for keeping the auncient Ecclesiastical wordes, as your maister Beza for example, beside many other places vvhere he bitterly rebuketh his fellovv Castaleons translation, in one place vvriteth thus: *I cannot in this place dissemble the boldnesse of certaine men, vvhich vvould God it rested vvithin the compasse of vvordes onely. these men therfore concerning the vvord Baptizing, though vsed of sacred vvriters in the mysterie or Sacrament of the nevv Testament, and for so many yeres after, by the secrete consent of al Churches, consecrated to this one Sacrament, so that it is novv grovven into the vulgar speaches almost of al nations, yet they dare presume rashly to change it, and in place thereof to vse the vvord vvashing. delicate men forsooth, vvhich neither are moued vvith the perpetual*

Beza in c. 5. Mat. nu. 25. & c. 10. nu. 2

in 3 ca. Mat. nu. 11.

Baptizo.

Baptisme.

 perpetual

perpetual authoritie of so many ages, nor by the daily custom of the vulgar speache, can be brought to thinke that lavvful for Diuines, vvhich al men graunt to other Maisters and professors of artes: that is, to reteine and hold that as their ovvne, vvhich by long vse and in good faith they haue truely possessed. Neither may they pretend the authoritie of some auncient vvriters, as that Cyprian saith TINGENTES *for* BAPTIZANTES, *and Tertullian in a certaine place calleth* SEQVESTREM *for* MEDIATOREM. *For that vvhich vvas to those auncients as it vvere nevv, to vs is old: and euen then, that the self same vvordes vvhich vve novv vse, vvere familiar to the Church, it is euident, because it is very seldom that they speake othervvise. but these men by this noueltie seeke after vaine glorie, &c.*

Baptizo. Mediator.

14 He speaketh against Castaleon, vvho in his nevv Latin translation of the Bible, changed al Ecclesiastical vvordes into profane and Heathenish, as *Angelos* in to *genios*, *Prophetas* into *Fatidicos*, *Templum* into *fanum*, and so forth. But that vvhich he did for folish affectation of finenesse and stile, do not our English Caluinists the very same vvhen they list, for furthering their Heresies? Vvhen the holy Scripture saith idols according as Christians haue alvvaies vnderstood it for false goddes, they come and tell vs out of Homer & the Lexicos, that it may signifie an image, & therfore so they translate it. do they not the like in the Greeke vvord that by Ecclesiastical vse signifieth, *penance*, and *doing penance*, vvhen they argue out of Plutarche, and by the profane sense

εἴδωλον. Confut. of the Reas. fo. 35. μετάνοια. μετανοεῖν.

ſenſe thereof, that it is nothing els but chãging of the minde or amendment of life? Vvhereas in the Greeke Church, *Pœnitentes*, that is, they that vvere in the courſe of penance, and excluded from the Church as *Catechumeni*, and *Energumeni*, till they had accompliſhed their penance, the very ſame are called in the Greeke οἱ ἐν μετανοίᾳ ὄντες.

Dionyſ. Ec. Hier. c. 3.

15 They therfore leauing this Eccleſiaſtical ſignification, & tranſlating it according to Plutarche, do they not much like to Caſtaleo? Do they not the ſame, againſt the famous and auncient diſtinction of *Latrîa* and *Dulîa*, vvhen they tell vs out of Euſtathius vpon Homer, and Ariſtophanes the Grammarian, that theſe tvvo are al one? Vvhereas vve proue out of S. Auguſtine in many places, the ſecond Councel of Nice, Venerable Bede, & the long cuſtom of the Church, that according to the Eccleſiaſtical ſenſe and vſe deduced out of the Scriptures, they differ very much. Do they not the like in *Myſterium* and *Sacramentum*, vvhich they tranſlate *a Secrete* in the profane ſenſe, vvheras they knovv hovv theſe vvordes are othervviſe taken both in Greeke and Latin, in the Church of God? did they not the like in the vvord *Eccleſia*, vvhen they tranſlated it nothing els but congregation? Do they not the like in χειροτονία, vvhich they

Latrîa. Dulîa. Beza in 4 Mat. nu. 10.

λατρεύω & λατρεία in the Scriptures, almoſt alvvaies vſed for the ſeruice and honour proper to God. *Auguſt. de Ciuit. Dei. li. 10. c. 1.*

Bib. an. 1562.

translate, *ordaining by election*, as it vvas in the profane court of Athens: vvhereas S. Hierom telleth them, that Ecclesiastical vvriters take it for giuing holy orders by imposition of hands? Do they not the like in many other vvordes, vvheresoeuer it serueth their hereticall purpose? And as for profane translation, is there any more profane then Beza him self, that so often in his Annotations reprehendeth the old Translation by the authoritie of Tullie and Terence, Homer and Aristophanes, & the like profane authors? yea so fondly and childishly, that for *Olfactum* vvhich Erasmus vseth as Plinies vvord, he vvill needes say *odoratum*, because it is Tullies vvord.

16 But to returne to our English Translatours: do not they the like to profane Castaleo, and do they not the very same that Beza their Maister so largely reprehendeth, vvhen they translate *Presbyterum*, an Elder? Is it not al one fault to translate so, and to translate, as Castaleo doth *Baptismum, vvashing*? Hath not *Presbyter* been a peculiar and vsual vvord for a Priest, as long as *Baptismus* for the Sacrament of regeneration, which Castaleo altering into a common & profane vvord, is vvorthely reprehended? Vve vvill proue it hath, not for their sake, vvho knovv it vvell ynough, but for the Readers sake, vvhom they abuse, as if they knevv it not.

17 In the first & second Canō of the Apostles vve read thus, *Episcopus a duobus aut tribus Episcopis ordinetur. Presbyter ab vno Episcopo ordinetur. & Diaconus, & alij Clerici.* that is, Let a Bishop be cōsecrated or ordained by tvvo or three Bishops. let *a Priest* be made by one Bishop. See in the 4 Coūcel of Carthage the diuerse maner of cōsecrating Bishops, Priests, Deacōs, &c. Where S. Augustine vvas present & subscribed. Againe, *Si quis Presbyter contemnens Episcopum suum &c. If any Priest contemning his Bishop, make a seueral congregation, and erect a nother altar,* (that is, make a Schisme or Heresie) *let him be deposed.* So did Arius being a Priest against his Bishop Alexander. Againe, *Priests and Deacons let them attempt to do nothing vvithout the Bishop.* The first Councel of Nice saith, *The holy Synode by al meanes forbiddeth, that neither Bishop, nor Priest, nor Deacon &c. haue vvith them any forren vvoman, but the mother, or sister, &c. in vvhom there is no suspicion.* Againe, *It is told the holy Councel, that in certaine places and cities, Deacons giue the Sacraments to Priests. This neither rule nor custom hath deliuered, that they vvhich haue not authoritie to offer the sacrifice, should giue to them that offer, the body of Christ.* The 3 Councel of Carthage vvherein S. Augustine vvas, and to the vvhich he subscribed, decreeth, *That in the Sacraments of the body and bloud of Christ, there be no more offered, then our Lord him self deliuered, that is, bread and vvine mingled vvith vvater.* Vvhich the sixth general Councel of Constantinople repeating and confirming, addeth:

That *Presbyter* hath signified a *Priest*, from the Apostles time, not an *Elder.*

Can. 2.3.4.

Can. Apost. 32.

Can. 40.

Can. 3.

Can. 14.

Can. 24.

εἴ τις οὖν ἐπίσκοπος, ἢ πρεσβύτερος.

If therfore any Bishop or Priest doe not according to the order giuen by the Apostles, mingling vvater vvith vvine, but offer an vnmingled sacrifice, let him be deposed &c. But of these speaches al Councels be full: vvhere vve vvould gladly knovv of these nevv Translatours, hovv *Presbyter* must be translated: either an *Elder*, or a *Priest*

18 Do not al the fathers speake after the same maner, making alvvaies this distinction of Bishop and Priest, as of the first and second degree? S. Ignatius the Apostles scholer doth he not place *Presbyterium* as he calleth it, and *Presbyteros* (Priests, or the Colledge of Priests) next after Bishops, and Deacons in the third place, repeating it no lesse then thrise in one Epistle, & commending the dignitie of all three vnto the people? doth not S. Hierom the very same, saying, *Let vs honour a Bishop, do reuerence to a Priest, rise vp to a Deacon?* And vvhen he saith, that as Aaron and his sonnes and the Leuites vvere in the Temple, so are Bishops, Priests, & Deacons in the Church, for place and degree. And in an other place, speaking of the outrages done by the Vandals and such like, *Bishops vvere taken, Priests slaine, and diuers of other Ecclesiastical orders: Churches ouerthrovven, the altars of Christ made stables for horses, the relikes of Martyrs digged vp. &c.* Vvhen he saith of Nepotian, *fit Clericus, & per solitos gradus Presbyter ordinatur*: he becometh a man of the Clergie, and by the accustomed

Ep. 2. ad Trallianos. τὸ πρεσβυτέριον οἱ πρεσβύτεροι.

Comment. in c. 7. Micheæ.

Ep. 85. ad Euagrium.

Epitaph. Nepotiani c. 9.

ſtomed degrees is made, vvhat? a Prieſt, or an Elder? vvhen he ſaith, *Mihi ante Presbyterum ſedere non licet &c.* doth he meane he could not ſit aboue an Elder, or aboue a Prieſt, him ſelf as then being not Prieſt? Vvhen he, and Vincentius (as S. Epiphanius vvriteth) of reuerence to the degree, vvere hardly induced to be made *Presbyteri:* did they refuſe the Elderſhip? Vvhat vvas the matter that Iohn the B. of Hieruſalem, ſeemed to be ſo much offended vvith Epiphanius and S. Hierom? vvas it not becauſe Epiphanius made Paulianus, S. Hieroms brother, Prieſt vvithin the ſaid Iohns Dioceſe? Ep. 60 apud Hiero. ca. 1. Ep. 1 ad Heliod.

19 Vvhen al antiquitie ſaith, Hieronymus Preſbyter, Cecilius Preſbyter, Ruffinus Preſbyter, Philippus, Iuuencus, Heſychius, Beda, Preſbyteri: and vvhen S. Hierom ſo often in his Cataloge ſaith, Such a man *Presbyter:* is it not for diſtinction of a certaine order, to ſignifie that they vvere Prieſts, and not Biſhops? namely vvhen he ſaith of S. Chryſoſtom, *Ioannes Presbyter Antiochenus*, doth he not meane, he vvas as then but a Prieſt of Antioche? Vvould he haue ſaid ſo, if he had vvritten of him, after he vvas Biſhop of Conſtantinople?

20 But of al other places, vve vvould deſire theſe gay trãſlatours to trãſlate this one place of S. Auguſtine, ſpeaking of him ſelf

a Biſhop

Inter Episto-las Hiero. Ep. 97 in fine.

a Bishop and S. Hierom a Priest: *Quanquā enim secundum honorum vocabula, quæ iam Ecclesiæ vsus obtinuit, Episcopatus Presbyterio maior sit: tamen in multis rebus, Augustinus Hieronymo minor est.* Is not this the English thereof? *For although according to the titles or names of honour, which now by vse of the Church haue preuailed, the degree of Bishop be greater thē Priesthod, yet in many things, Augustine is lesse thē Hierom.* Or, doth it like thē to trāslate it thus, *The degree of Bishop is greater then Eldership &c?* Againe, against Iulian the Heretike vvhen he hath brought many testimonies of the holy Doctors that vvere all Bishops, as of SS. Cyprian, Ambrose, Basil, Nazianzene, Chrysostom: at lenght he cōmeth to S. Hierom vvho vvas no Bishop, and saith: *Nec sanctum Hieronymum, quia Presbyter fuit, contemnendum arbitreris* that is, *Neither must thou think that S. Hierom, because he vvas but a Priest, therfore is to be contemned: vvhose diuine eloquence, hath shined to vs from the East euen to the vvest, like a lampe*, and so forth to his great cōmendation. Here is a plaine distinction of an inferiour degree to a Bishop, for the which the Heretike Iulian did easily contemne him. Is not S. Cyprian full of the like places? is not al antiquitie so full, that vvhiles I proue this, me thinketh I proue nothing els but that snovv is vvhite?

Lib. 1. ca. 2. in fine.

21 In al vvhich places if they vvil translate *Elder*, and yet make the same a common name

name to all Ecclesiastical degrees, as Beza defineth it, let the indifferent Reader consider the absurde cõfusion, or rather the impossibilitie thereof: if not, but they vvill graunt in al these places it signifieth Priest, and so is meant: then vve must beate them vvith Bezaes rod of reprehension against Castaleon: that *vve can not dissemble the boldnes of these mẽ. vvhich vvould God it rested vvithin the custom of wordes onely,* and vvere not important matter, concerning their Heresie. *These men therfore touching the vvord* Priest, *though vsed of sacred vvriters in the mysterie of the nevv Testamẽt, and for so many yeres after by the secrete consent of al Churches, consecrated to this one Sacrament, so that it is novv grovven to be the proper vulgar speach almost of al Nations: yet they dare presume rashly to change it, and in place thereof to vse the vvord Elder. delicate men forsooth* (yea vvorse a great deale, because these do it for heresie & not for delicacie) *vvhich neither are moued vvith the perpetual authoritie of so many ages, nor by the daily custom of the vulgar speach can be brought to thinke that lavvful for* Diuines, *vvhich all men graunt to other Maisters and* Professors *of artes, that is, to reteine and hold that as their ovvne, vvhich* by *long vse and in good faith they haue truely possessed. Neither may they pretend the authoritie of any auncient vvriter* (as that the old Latin Translatour saith *Senior*, and *Seniores*:) *for* ⋆*that vvhich vvas to them as it vvere nevv, to vs is old: and euen then, that the selfsame vvordes vvhich vve novv vse, were more familiar to the Church, it is euident, because it is very seldom that they speake othervvise.*

Annot. in 1 Pet. 5.

Bezaes vvordes in the place aboue alleaged.

Prete Prebstre Priest.

Presbyter for a Priest. *Baptismus* for the Sacrament of Baptisme.

22 Thus vve haue repeated Bezaes vvordes

des againe, onely changing the vvord *Baptisme* into *Priest*, because the case is all one: & so vnvvittingly Beza the successor of Caluin in Geneua, hath giuen plaine sentence against our English Translatours in al such cases, as they go from the cōmon receiued and vsual sense to another profane sense, & out of vse: as namely in this point of Priest and Priesthod. Vvhere vve must needes adde a vvord or tvvo, though vve be to long, because their folly & malice is to to great herein. For vvhereas the very name Priest neuer came into our English tonge but of the Latin *Presbyter* (for therevpon *sacerdos* also vvas so called onely by a consequence) they translate *sacerdos*, Priest, and *Presbyter*, not Priest, but Elder, as vvisely and as reasonably, as if a man should translate *Prætor Londini*, Maire of London: and *Maior Londini*, not *Maire* of London: but Greater of London: or *Academia Oxoniensis*, the Vniuersitie of Oxford: and *Vniuersitas*, *Oxoniensis*, not *the Vniuersitie*, but the Generalitie of Oxford: and such like.

See M. Whitgifts defēce against the Puritans replie. pag. 721 vvhere he affirmeth that this vvord *Priest*, commeth of the vvord *Presbyter*, & not of the vvord *Sacerdos*.

23 Againe, vvhat exceding folly is it, to thinke that by false and profane translation of *Presbyter* into *Elder*, they might take away the external Priesthod of the new Testamēt, vvhereas their ovvne vvord *sacerdos* vvhich they do and must needes translate Priest, is

as

as common and as vsual in all antiquitie, as *Presbyter*: and so much the more, for that it is vsed indifferētly to signifie both Bishops and Priests, which *Presbyter* lightly doth not but in the nevv Testament. as vvhen Constantine the Great said to the Bishops assembled in the Coūcel of Nice, *Deus vos constituit sacerdotes, &c. God hath ordained you priests, and hath giuen you povver to iudge of vs also.* And S. Ambrose, *Vvhen didst thou euer heare, most Clement Prince, that lay men haue iudged Bishops. Shal vve bend by flatterie so farre, that forgetting the right of our Priesthod, vve should yeld vp to others, that vvhich God hath commended to vs?* And therfore doth S. Chrisostō entitle his sixe bookes *De Sacerdotio*, Of Priesthod, concerning the dignitie and calling, not onely of mere Priests, but also of Bishops: & S. Gregorie Nazianzene handling the same argumēt saith, that *they execute Priesthod together vvith* CHRIST. and S. Ignatius saith, *Do nothing vvithout the Bishops, for they are priests, but thou the Deacon of the priests.* And in the Greeke Liturgies or Masses, so often, ὁ ἱερεὺς, *Then the priest saith this, and that*, signifying also the Bishop vvhen he saith Masse: and *S. Denys saith sometime *Archisacerdotem cum sacerdotibus.* the high Priest or Bishop vvith the Priests: vvhereof come the vvordes ἱερατεύειν, ἱερουργεῖν, ἱεράτευμα, ἱερατεία, ἱερουργία, in the auncient Greeke fathers, for the sacred function

Ruffin. li. 1. ca. 2.

Epist. 32. ad Valentinianum Imp.

Iuris Sacerdotalis.

in Apolog. pro sua fug. orat. 1.

χριστῷ συνιερεύειν.

Epist. 10. ad Hieronem.

Sacerdotes.

ἱερεύς.

διάκονος ἱερέων.

ἱεράρχην σὺν τοῖς ἱερεῦσι.

* Ec. Hiera. c. 3.

ction of Priesthod, and executing of the same.

24 If then the Heretikes could possibly haue extinguished priesthod in the vvord *presbyter*, yet you see, it vvould haue remained still in the vvordes *Sacerdos* and *Sacerdotiū*, vvhich them selues translate *Priest* & *Priesthod*: and therfore vve must desire them to translate vs a place or tvvo after their ovvne maner: first S. Augustine speaking thus,

Li. 8. cap 27. De Ciu. Dei. *Quis vnquam audiuit sacerdotem ad altare stantē etiam super reliquias Martyrum, dicere: offero tibi Petre, & Paule, vel Cypriane? Vvho euer heard that a* PRIEST *stāding at the altar, euen ouer the relikes of the Martyrs, said, I offer to thee Peter, & Paul, or Cyprian?* So (vve trovv) they must trāslate it. Againe,

Li. 22 Ciuit. c. 10. *Nos vni Deo & Martyrū & nostro, sacrificiū immolamus, ad quod sacrificium sicut homines Dei, suo loco & ordine nominātur, non tamen à sacerdote inuocantur. Deo quippe, non ipsis sacrificat, quamuis in memoria sacrificet eorum, quia Dei sacerdos est, non illorum. Ipsum verò sacrificium corpus est Christi.* Vve thinke they vvill and must translate it thus: *Vve offer sacrifice to the one onely God both of Martyrs and ours, at the vvhich Sacrifice, as men of God they* (Martyrs) *are named in their place and order: yet are they* * *not inuocated of the priest that sacrificeth. For he sacrificeth to God, & not to them (though he sacrifice in the memorie of them) because he is Gods Priest, and not theirs. And the sacrifice it self is the body of Christ.*

* So as he said before, *I offer to thee Peter*, &c.

25 Likevvise vvhen S. Ambrose saith,

Li. 4. de Sacram. c 4. *The consecration* (of the body of Christ) *vvith vvhat vvordes is it, and by vvhose speache? of our Lord*

Iesu

Iesus. For in the rest that is said, there is praise giuen to God, praier made for the people, for kings, and others: but vvhen it commeth that the venerable sacrament must be consecrated, novv the Priest vseth not his ovvne vvordes, but he vseth the vvordes of Christ. And S. Chrisostom in very many places saith, *The sacred oblation it self, vvhether Peter or Paul, or any meaner Priest vvhatsoeuer offer it, is the very same that Christ gaue to his disciples, and vvhich novv the priests do make or cōsecrate. vvhy so I pray thee? because not men do sanctifie this, but Christ him self, vvhich before consecrated the same.* And againe, *It is not man that maketh the body and bloud of Christ, but he that vvas crucified for vs, Christ: the vvordes are vttered by the Priests mouth, and by Gods povver and grace are the things proposed, consecrated. For this, saith he, is my body. VVith this vvord are the things proposed, consecrated.*

Sacerdos. Ho. 2 in 2 Timoth. *Sacerdos. Sacerdotes* *Sacerdotis*

26 And so by these places, vvhere them selues translate *sacerdos* a Priest, they may learne also hovv to translate *Presbyteros* in S. Hierom saying the very same thing, *that at their praiers, the body and bloud of our Lord is made. and in an other place, that vvith their sacred mouth, they make our Lordes body.* Likevvise vvhen they read S. Ambrose against the Nouatians, that God hath graunted licence *to his Priests* to release and forgiue as vvel great sinnes as litle vvithout exception: and in the Ecclesiastical historie, hovv the Nouatian Heretikes taught that such as vvere fallen into great sinnes, should not aske for remission of the Priest, but of God onely: they may learne hovv to translate *Presbyteros* in S. Hierom

Presbyteri *Sacerdotibus* *à Sacerdote*

rom & in the Ecclesiastical historie, vvhere the one saith thus: *Episcopus & Presbyter, cum peccatorum audierit varietates, scit qui ligandus sit, qui soluendus*: and the other speaketh *de Presbytero Pœnitentiario*, of an extraordinarie Priest that heard confessions and enioyned penance, vvho aftervvard vvas taken avvay, and the people vvent to diuers ghostly fathers as before. And especially S. Chrysostom vvill make them vnderstand what these *Presbyteri* vvere, and hovv they are to be called in English, vvho telleth them in their ovvne vvord, that *Sacerdotes, the Priests of the nevv lavv haue povver not onely to knovv, but to purge the filth of the soule, therfore vvhosoeuer despiseth them, is more vvorthie to be punished then the rebel Dathan and his complices.*

Sozom. li. 7 c. 16. Socrat. li. 5 c. 19.

Li. 3. de Sacerd.

27 Novv then (to conclude this point) seeing vve haue such a cloude of vvitnesses (as the Apostle speaketh) euen from Christs time, that testifie not onely for the name, but for the very principal functions of external Priesthod, in offering the sacrifice of Christs body & bloud, in remitting sinnes, and so forth: vvhat a peeuish, malicious, & impudent corruption is this, for the defacing of the testimonies of the holy Scriptures tending therevnto, to seeke to scratch aduantage of the vvord *Presbyter*, & to make it signifie an Elder, not a Priest: *Presbyterium* Eldership rather then Priesthod: as if other

Hebr. 12.

nevv

nevvfangled cōpanions that vvould forge an Hereſie that there vvere no Apoſtles, ſhould for that purpoſe tranſlate it alwaies *legates*: or that there vvere no Angels, and ſhould tranſlate it alwaies *Meſſengers*: & that Baptiſme vvere but a Iudaical ceremonie, and ſhould tranſlate it *vvaſhing*: vvhich Caſtalio did much more tolerably in his tranſlation then any of theſe ſhould, if he did it onely of curioſitie and folly. And if to take avvay al diſtinction of clergie & laitie the Proteſtants ſhould alvvaies tranſlate *clerum*, *lotte* or *lotterie*, as they do tranſlate it for the ſame purpoſe *pariſh* and *heritage*: might not * Beza him ſelf controull them, ſaing, *that the auncient fathers transferred the name clerus to the College of Eccleſiaſtical Miniſters?*

Clerus.

* In 1 Pet 5. See S. Hierom ad Nepot. de vit. Clericorum ep. 2. c. 5.

28 But alas, the effect of this corruption & hereſie concerning Prieſts, hath it not vvrought vvithin theſe fevv yeres ſuch cōtempt of al Prieſts, that nothing is more odious in our countrie then that name: vvhich before vvas ſo honorable and Venerable, and novv is, among all good men? If miniſterie or Elderſhip vvere grovven to eſtimation in ſteede thereof, ſomevvhat they had to ſay: but that is yet more contemptible, and eſpecially Elders and Elderſhip. for the Queenes Maieſtie & her Coūſellors vvill permit none in gouernement

of any Church in England, and so they haue brought al, to nothing els, but profane laitie. And no maruel of these horrible inconueniences, for as the Sacrifice & Priesthod goe together, and therfore vvere both honorable together: so vvhen they had according to Daniels Prophecie, abolished the daily sacrifice, out of the Church, vvhat remained, but the contempt of Priests and Cleargie and their offices, so far forth, that for the holy Sacrifice sake, Priests are called in great despite, *Massing Priests*, of them that litle consider, or lesse care, vvhat notable holy learned fathers of al ages since Christs time, this their reproche toucheth and concerneth, as by the testimonies before alleaged is manifest, and vvhereof the
Chap. 6. Reader may see a peculiar Chapter in the late Apologie of the English Seminaries.

CHAP. VII.

Heretical translation against PVRGATORIE, LIMBVS PATRVM, CHRISTS DESCENDING INTO HEL.

1 HAVING now discouered their corrupt translations for defacing of the Churches name, and abolishing of Priest and Priesthod: let vs come to another point of verie

tie great importance alſo, and vvhich by the wonted cõſequence or ſequele of error, includeth in it many erroneous branches. Their principal malice then being bent against Purgatorie, that is, against a place vvhere Chriſtian ſoules be purged by ſuffering of temporal paines after this life, for ſurer maintenance of their erroneous denial hereof, they take avvay and denie al third places, ſaying that there vvas neuer from rhe beginning of the vvorld any other place for ſoules after this life, but only tvvo: to vvit, heauen for the bleſſed: & hel for the damned. And ſo it folovveth by their heretical doctrine, that the Patriarches, Prophets, and other good holy men of the old Teſtament, vvent not after their deathes, to the place called *Abrahams boſome*, or *limbus patrum*, but immediatly to heauen: and ſo againe by their erroneous doctrine it folovveth, that the fathers of the old Teſtamẽt vvere in heauen, before our ſauiour Chriſt had ſuffered death for their redemption: and alſo by their erroneous doctrine it folovveth, that our ſauiout Chriſt vvas not the firſt man that aſcended and entred into heauen: and moreouer by their heretical doctrine it folovveth, that our ſauiour Chriſt deſcended not into any ſuch third place, to deliuer the fathers of the old Teſtament out of their priſon, and to bring them triumphătly vvith him into heauen, becauſe by their erroneous doctrine they vvere neuer there: & ſo that article of the Apoſtles Creede concerning our ſauiour Chriſt his deſcending into hel, muſt either be put out by the Caluiniſts, as Beza did in his Confeſſion of his faith printed an.1564, or it hath ſome other meaning, to vvit, either the lying of his body in the graue, or (as Caluine and the purer Caluiniſts his ſchollers vvill haue it) the ſuffering of hel paines and diſtreſſes vpon the Croſſe. Loe the conſequence and coherence of theſe errours and hereſies.

Caluins Inſtitutions li. 2.c.16. Sect. 10. & in his Catechiſme.

2 Theſe novv being the heretical doctrines vvhich they meane to auouch and defend vvhatſoeuer come of it: firſt, they are at a point not to care a ruſh for all the auncient holy Doctors, that vvrite vvith ful conſent to the contrarie (as them ſelues confeſſe, calling it their common errour) ſecondly, they tranſlate the holy ſcriptures in fauour thereof, moſt corruptly & vvilfully, as in Bezaes falſe tranſlation (vvho is Caluins ſucceſſor in Geneua) it is notorious, for he in his nevv Teſtament of the yere 1556. printed by Robertus Stephanus in folio, vvith Annotations, maketh our ſauiour Chriſt ſay thus to his father, *Non derelinques*

Beza in 1 Pet. 3, 19. Caluins Inſtitut. li. 2.c. 16. Sect. 9.

derelinques cadauer meum in sepulchro, *thou shalt not leaue my carcasse in the graue*, *Act.* 2. for that which the Hebrue, & the Greeke, and the Latine, and S. Hierom according to the Hebrue, say: *Nõ derelinques animã meam in inferno*, as plainely as vve say in English, *Thou shalt not leaue my soule in hel.* Thus the Prophet Dauid spake it in Hebrue, *Ps.* 15. thus the Septuaginta vttered it in Greeke, thus the Apostle S. Peter alleageth it, thus the holy Euangelist S. Luke in the Act. of the Apostles, *cap.* 2. recordeth it, and for this, S. Augustine calleth him an infidel that denieth it: yet al this vvould not suffise to make Beza translate it so, because of certaine errours (* as he heretically tearmeth them) vvhich he vvould ful gladly auoid hereby, namely, the Catholike true doctrine of *limbus patrum*, and *Purgatorie*. Vvhat neede vve say more? he translateth *animam*, a *Carcasse*: (so calling our sauiour Christs body, irreuerently, & vvickedly) he translateth *infernum*, graue.

Hiero. in Ps. verso ex Hebræo.

נֶפֶשׁ בְּשְׁאוֹל ψυχὴν εἰς ᾅδου.

*See his Annot. in 2. Act.

3 Neede vve take any great labour to proue this to be a foule corruption, or that it is done purposely, vvhen he confesseth that he thus trãslateth because els it vvould serue the Papists? Vvhich is as much to say, as, the vvord of God if it be truly and sincerely trãslated, maketh in deede for them. For the first part, vve vvill not stand vpon

it, partly because it is of it self most absurd, and they are ashamed of it: partly, because it shall suffise to confute Beza, that tvvo other as famous heretikes as he, Castalio & Flaccus Illyricus vvrite against him in this point, and cõfute him: partly also, because vve speake not here vniuersally of al heretical trãslations, but of the English corruptions specially, & therefore vve may only note here, hovv gladly they also vvould say somevvhat els for, *soule*, euen in the text, if they durst for shame: for in the margent
Bib.an.1579 of that English translation, they say, *or life, or person*: thereby aduertising the Reader, that he may reade thus, if it please him, *Thou shalt not leaue my life in the graue*, or, *Thou shalt not leaue my person*. As though either mans soule or life vvere in the graue, or, *anima*, might be translated *person*, vvhich the self same En-
Act.7.v.14. glish Bible doth not, no not in those places vvhere it is euident that it signifieth the vvhole person. For though this vvord *soule*, by a figure, is sometime taken for the vvhole man, yet euen there they doe not, nor must not traslate it otherwise then soule: because our tonge beareth that figure as vvell as Latine, Greeke, or Hebrue: but here, vvhere it can not signifie the vvhole person, it is vvicked to translate it so.

4 But as for the vvord *graue*, that they put boldly in the text, to signifie that hovv-

ſoeuer you interprete, *ſoule*, or vvhatſoeuer you put for it, it is not meāt according to S. Auguſt. & the faith of the whole Catholike Church, that his ſoule deſcended into Hel, vvhiles his body vvas in the graue: but that his ſoule alſo, was in the graue, hovvſoeuer that is to be vnderſtood. So making it a certaine and reſolute concluſion, that the holy Scripture in this place ſpeaketh not of Chriſts being in Hel, but in the graue: and that according to his ſoule, or life, or perſon, or (as Beza vvill haue it) *His Carcaſſe or body*: and *ſo his ſoule in Hel,* as the holy Scripture ſpeaketh, ſhal be, *his body in the graue,* as Beza plainely ſpeaketh, and the Bezites couertly inſinuate: and vvhite ſhal be blacke, and chaulke ſhal be cheeſe, and euery thing ſhal be any thing that they wil haue it. And al this their euident falſe tranſlation, muſt be to our miſerable deceiued poore ſoules, the holy Scripture and Gods vvord.

See Vigors ſermōs pag. 110. 115. & deinceps.

5 Vvhere vve can not but maruel, vvhy they are afraid to tranſlate the vvordes plainely in this place, *of his ſoule being in Hel*: Vvvhereas in the Creede they admit the vvords, and interprete them, that by ſuffering Hel paines vpon the Croſſe, ſo he deſcended into Hel, and no othervviſe. Vvhy did they not here alſo keepe the vvordes for the credit of their tranſlation, and

afterward (if they would needes) giue them that glose for maintenance of their heresie? This mysterie vve knovv not, and vve vvould gladly learne it of the Puritan Caluinists, vvhose English translation perhaps this is. for, the grosser Caluinists (being not so pure and precise in folovving Caluine as the Puritans be, that haue vvel deserued that name aboue their fellovves) they in

Bib. an. 1561. and 1577.

their other English Bibles haue in this place discharged thē selues of false translatiō, saying plainely, *Thou shalt not leaue my soule in Hel.* But * in vvhat sense they say so, it is very hard to gesse: & perhaps them selues can not tell yet vvhat to make of it, as appeareth by M. Vvhitakers ansvver to F. Campion. And he is novv called a Bishop among them, and proceeded Doctor in Oxford, that could not obtaine his grace to proceede Doctor in Cambridge, because he preached Christes descending into Hel, and the Puritans in their second admonition to the Parliament, pag. 43. crie out against the politike Caluinists, for that in the Creede of the Apostles (made in English meeter & song openly in their Churches in these vvordes: *His spirit did after this descend, into the lovver partes, to them that long in darkenes vvere the true light of their hartes*) they fauour his descending into Hel very much, and so

* See lind. dubit. pa. 19.

Vvhitak. pag. 165.

M. Hues B. of S. Asaph in Vvalles.

conse-

consequently may thereby build *Limbus Patrum*, and *Purgatorie*. And the Puritans in their second replie against M. Whitegifts defense pag. 7. reprehend one of their chefest Caluinistical martyrs for affirming (as they tearme it) a grosse descēding of our Sauiour Christ into Hel. Thus the Puritanes cōfesse plainely their heretical doctrine against Christs descending into Hel.

6 The truth is, hovvsoeuer the politike Caluinists speake, or write in this point more plausibly and couertly to the people, and more agreably to the Article of our faith, then either Caluine or their earnest brethren the Puritans doe, vvhich vvrite and speake as phantastically and madly as they thinke: yet neither doe they beleeue this Article of the Apostles Creede, or interpret it, as the Catholike Church and auncient holy fathers alvvaies haue done, neither can it stand vvith their nevv profession so to doe, or vvith their English translations in other places. It can not stand vvith their profession: for then it vvould folovv that the Patriarches and other iust men of the old Testament vvere in some third place of rest, called *Abrahams bosome*, or *Limbus Patrum*, til our Sauiour Christ descended thither, & deliuered them from thence, vvhich they deny in their doctrine, though they

they sing it in their meeters. Neither can it stand vvith their English translations: because in other places vvhere the holy Scriptures euidently speake of such a place, calling it *Hel* (because that vvas a common name for euery place and state of soules departed, in the old Testamẽt, til our Sauiour Christ by his Resurrection and Ascension had opened heauẽ) there, for *Hel*, they translate *Graue*.

Gen. 37. 7 As vvhen Iacob saith, *Descendam ad filium meum lugens in infernum: I vvil goe dovvne to my sonne into Hel, mourning*: they translate, *I vvil goe dovvne into the graue vnto my sonne, mourning*: as though Iacob thought, that his sonne Ioseph had been buried in a graue, vvhereas Iacob thought, and said immediatly before, as appeareth in the holy Scripture, that a vvilde beast had deuoured him, and so could not be presumed to be in any graue: or as though, if Ioseph had been in a graue, Iacob vvould haue gone dovvne to him into the same graue. For so the vvordes must needes import, if they take graue properly: but if they take graue vnproperly for the state of dead men after this life, vvhy doe they call it *graue*, and not *Hel*, as the vvord is in Hebrue, Greeke, and Latin? No doubt they doe it, to make the ignorãt Reader beleeue that the Patriarch Iacob spake of his body only

שְׁאוֹל ἅδης. Infernus.

only to descend into the graue to Iosephs body: for as concerning Iacobs soule, that vvas by their opinion, to ascẽd immediatly after his death to heauen, and not to descẽd into the graue. But if Iacob vvere to ascend forthvvith in soule, hovv could he say as they translate, *I vvill goe dovvne into the graue vnto my sonne?* As if according to their opinion he should say, My sonnes body is deuoured of a beast, and his soule is gone vp into heauen: vvell, I vvil go dovvne to him into the graue.

8 Gentile Reader, that thou maist the better conceiue these absurdities, and the more detest their guilefull corruptions, vnderstand (as vve began to tell thee before) that in the old Testament, because there vvas yet no ascending into heauen, *the way of the holies* (as the Apostle in his epistle to Hebr. 9. v. 8. the Hebrues speaketh) *being not yet made open*, because our sauiour Christ vvas to * dedi- Hebr. 10. v. 20. cate and beginne the enterãce in his ovvne person, and by his passion to open heauen: therfore (vve say) in the old Testamẽt the common phrase of the holy Scripture is, euen of the best men, as vvel as of others, that dying they vvent dovvne *ad inferos*, or *ad infernum*: to signifie that such vvas the state of the old Testament before our sauiour Christs Resurrection and Ascension, that euery

euery man vvent dovvne, and not vp: descended, and not ascended: by descending I meane not to the graue, vvhich receiued their bodies only: but *ad inferos*, that is, *to hel*, a common receptacle or place for their soules also departed, as wel of those soules that vvere to be in rest, as those that vvere to be in paines & torments. All the soules both good & bad that then died, vvent dovvnevvard, & therfore the place of both sortes vvas called in all the tonges, by a vvord ansvverable to this vvord, *hel*, to signifie a lovver place beneath, not only of tormēts, but also of rest.

9 So vve say in our Creede, that our sauiour Christ him self descended into *hel*, ac-

Epitaph. Nepot. c. 3. cording to his soule: So S. Hierom speaking of the state of the old Testamēt, saith: *Si Abraham, Isaac, Iacob in inferno, quis in cælorum regno* that is, *If Abraham, Isaac, and Iacob vvere in hel, vvho vvas in the kingdom of heauen?* And againe, *Ante Christum, Abraham apud inferos: post Christum latro in Paradiso.* that is, *before the comming of Christ, Abraham vvas in hel: after his comming, the theefe vvas in Paradise.*

Luc. 16. And lest a man might obiect, that Lazarus being in Abrahams bosome, savv the rich glotton a far of in hel, and therfore both Abraham and Lazarus seeme to haue been

See S. Aug. in Psal. 85. v. 13. in heauen: the said holy doctor resolueth it, that Abraham and Lazarus also vvere in hel, but ĩ a place of great rest & refreshing, and therfore very far of from the misera-

ble vvretched glotton that lay in torments.
10 His vvordes be these in effect: If a man vvil say vnto me, that Lazarus vvas seene in Abrahams bosome, and a place of refreshing euen before Christs comming: true it is, but vvhat is that in comparison? *Quid simile infernus & regna cælorum? Vvhat hath hel and heauen like?* As if he should say, Abraham in deede and Lazarus (and consequently many other) vvere in place of rest, but yet in hel, til Christ came, & in such rest, as hath no comparison vvith the ioyes of heauen. And S. Augustine disputing this matter sometime, & doubting whether Abrahams bosom be called hel in the scripture, and vvhether the name of hel be taken at any time in the good part (for of Christes descending into hel, & of a third place where the Patriarches remained vntil Christs cōming, not heauen, but called Abrahams bosom, he doubted not, but was most assured) the same holy doctor in an other place, as being better resolued, doubteth not, vpon these vvordes of the Psalme, *Thou hast deliuered my soule from the lovver hel*, to make this one good sense of this place, that the lovver hel is it, vvherein the damned are tormented: the higher hel is that, vvherein the soules of the iust rested, calling both places by the name of hel.

Epist. 99. ad Euod. & de Gen. ad lit. li. 12. c. 33.

In Psal. 85. v. 13.

11 And

11 And surely of his maruelous humilitie and vvisedom, he vvould haue been much more resolute herein, if he had hard the opinion of S. Hierom, vvhom he often consulted in such questions, and of other fathers, who in this point speake most plainely, that Abrahams bosom or the place vvhere the Patriarkes rested, vvas some part of hel. Tertullian, (*Li.4. aduers. Marcion.*) Saith, *I knovv that the bosome of Abraham vvas no heauenly place, but only the higher hel,* or, *the higher part of hel.* Of which speache of the fathers, rose aftervvard that other name, *limbus patrum*, that is the very brimme or vppermost & outmost part of hel, vvhere the fathers of the old Testament rested. Thus vve see that the Patriarches them selues vvere as then in hel, though they vvere there in a place of rest: in so much that S. Hierom saith againe, *Ante Resurrectionem Christi notus in Iudæa Deus, & ipsi qui nouerant eum, tamen ad inferos trahebantur.* that is, *Before the Resurrection of Christ, God vvas knovvne in Iurie, and they them selues that knevv him, yet vvere dravven vnto hel.* S. Chrysostom vpon that place of Esay, *I vvil breake the brasen gates, and bruse the yron barres in peeces, and vvill open the treasures darkened, &c. So he calleth hel,* saith he, *for although it vvere hel, yet it held the holy soules and pretious vessels, Abraham, Isaac, and Iacob.* Marke that he saith, though it vvere hel, yet there vvere the iust men at that time, til our sauiour Christ

loco citato.

Hom. quod Christus sit Deus to. 5.

ᾅδης. Infernus.

came

came to deliuer them from thence.

12 Therfore did Iacob ſay, *I vvill go dovvne to my ſonne vnto Hel.* And againe he ſaith, *If any misfortune happen to (Beniamin) by the vvay, you ſhal bring my gray head vvith ſorovv vnto Hel,* vvhich is repeated againe tvviſe in the Chapter 44. by vvhich phraſe the holy Scripture vvil ſignifie, not onely death, but alſo the deſcending at that time of al ſorts of ſoules into Hel, both good and bad. And therfore it is ſpoken of al ſortes in the holy Scripture, both of good and of bad. for al vvent then into Hel, but ſome into a place there of reſt, others into other places there of torments. And therfore S. Hierom ſaith, ſpeaking of Hel according to the old Teſtament, *Hel is a place vvherein ſoules are included: either in reſt, or in paines, according to the qualitie of their deſerts.*

Gen. 42.

3 Reg. 2.

in c.13 Oſee.
Aug. in Pſal. 85. v. 13.

13 And in this ſenſe it is alſo often ſaid in the holy Scriptures, that ſuch & ſuch vvere gathered or laid to their fathers, though they vvere buried in diuers places, and died not in the ſame ſtate of ſaluation or damnation: In that ſenſe Samuel being raiſed vp to ſpeake vvith Saul, ſaid, *To morovv thou and thy ſonnes ſhal be vvith me.* that is, dead and in Hel, though not in the ſame place or ſtate there: in this ſenſe al ſuch places of the holy Scripture as haue the vvord *Inferi,* or *Infernus*

The Scriptures ſpeake of an other *Hel*, beſides that of the damned.

corres-

correspondent both to the Greeke and Hebrue, ought to be, and may be most conueniently translated by the vvord, *Hel.* as when it is said, *Thou hast deliuered my soul from the lovver hel.* Ps. 85. v. 13. that is as S. Augustine expoundeth it, Thou hast preserued me from mortal sinnes that vvould haue brought me into the lovver Hel which is for the damned. vvhich place of holy Scripture and the like vvhen they translate *graue*, see hovv miserably it soundeth: *Thou hast deliuered my soul from the lovvest graue.* vvhich they vvould neuer say for very shame, but that they are afraid to say in any place (be the holy Scriptures neuer so plaine) that any soule vvas deliuered or returned from hel, lest thereof it might folovv by and by, that the Patriarches, and our sauiour Christ vvere in such a Hel.

ab inferno inferiori.

Bib. 1579.

14 And that this is their feare, it is euident, because in al other places vvhere it is plaine that the holy Scriptures speake of the Hel of the damned, from vvhence is no returne, there they translate the very same vvord *Hel,* and not graue. As for example, *The vvay of life is on high to the prudent, to auoid from Hel beneath.* loe, here that is translated *Hel beneath,* vvhich before was translated *the lovvest graue.* And againe, *Hel and destruction are before the Lord, hovv much more the hartes of the sonnes of men?* But vvhen

Prouerb. 15. 24.

vvhen in the holy Scriptures there is mention of deliuerie of a ſoul from Hel, then
thus they tranſlate: *God ſhal deliuer my ſoul from* Bib. 1579.
the povver of the graue : for he vvill receiue me. Can De manu inferi.
you tell vvhat they vvould ſay? doth God deliuer them from the graue, or from temporal death, vvhom he receiueth to his mercie? or hath the graue any povver ouer
the ſoul? Againe vvhen they ſay, *Vvhat man* Pſ. 89, 48.
liueth, and ſhal not ſee death? ſhal he deliuer his ſoul from the hand of the graue?

15 If they take *graue* properly, vvhere mans body is buried : it is not true either that euery ſoul, yea or euery body is buried in a graue. But if in al ſuch places, they vvill ſay they meane nothing els but to ſignifie death, & that to go dovvne into the graue, and to die, is al one: vve aſke them vvhy they folovv not the vvordes of the holy Scripture to ſignifie the ſame thing, vvhich call it, going dovvne to *Hel,* not, going dovvne to the *graue?* Here they muſt needes open the myſterie of Antichriſt vvorking in their tranſlations, and ſay, that ſo they ſhould make Hel a common place to all that departed in the old Teſtament, vvhich they vvill not, no not in the moſt important places of our beleefe cõcerning our ſauiour Chriſts deſcending into Hel, & triumphing ouer the ſame. Yea, therfore of

purpose they vvill not, onely for to defeate that part of our Christian Creede.

16 As vvhen the Prophet first, *Osee* 13. & afteruvard the Apostle, 1 *Cor.* 15. in the Greeke,
שאול say thus : *Ero mors tua ô mors, morsus tuus ero inferne. Vbi est, mors, stimulus tuus? Vbi est, inferne, victoria*
ᾅδη. *tua? O death, I vvill be thy death: I vvill be thy sting, ô Hel. Vvhere is, ô death, thy sting? Vvhere is, ô hel, thy vic-*
Bibl. 1579. *torie?* They translate in both places, *O graue,* in stede of, *ô Hel.* What els can be their meaning hereby, but to dravv the Reader from the common sense of our sauiour Christes descending into Hel, and conquering the same, and bringing out the fathers and iust men triumphantly from thence into heauen? Vvhich sense hath allvvaies been the common sense of the Catholike Church
See S. Hier. Comment. in 13. Osee. & holy Doctors, specially vpon this place of the Prophet. And vvhat a kind of speache is this, and out of all tune, to make our sauiour Christ say, *O graue I vvill be thy destruction?* as though he had triumphed ouer the graue, and not ouer Hel: or ouer the graue, that is, ouer death: and so the Prophet should say death tvvise, and Hel not at all.

17 Vvhy, my Maisters, you that are so vvonderful precise translatours, admit that our sauiour Christ descended not into Hel beneath, as you say, yet I thinke you vvill graunt that he triumphed ouer Hel, & vvas conque-

conquerer of the same. Vvhy then did it not please you to suffer the Prophet to say so at the least, rather then that he had conquest onely of death and the graue? You abuse your ignorãt reader very impudently, and your ovvne selues very damnably, not onely in this, but in that you make *graue*, and *death*, al one, and so vvhere the holy Scripture often ioyneth together *death* & *Hel*, as things different and distinct: you make them speake but one thing tvvise, idely and superfluously.

18 But vvill you knovv that you should not confound them, but that *Mors*, & *Infernus*, vvhich are the vvordes of the holy Scripture in al tonges, are distinct: heare vvhat S. Hierom saith, or if you vvil not heare, because you are of them vvhich *haue stopped their eares*, let the indifferẽt Christian Reader harken to this holy Doctor, and great interpreter of the holy Scriptures according to his singular knovvledge in al the learned tonges. Vpon the foresaid place of the Prophet, after he had spoken of our sauiour Christs descẽding into Hel, and ouercomming of death, he addeth: *Betvvene death and Hel this is the difference, that death is that vvhereby the soul is separated from the body: Hel is the place vvhere soules are included, either in rest, or els in paines, according to the qualitie of their deserts. And that death is one thing, and Hel is another: the Psalmist also declareth,* Hierom. in Osee ca. 13.

H ij saying

Psal. 6. *saying:* THERE IS *not in death, that is mindeful of thee, but in Hel vvho shal confesse to thee?* And in an other place. *Let death come vpon them, and let them go dovvne into Hel aliue.* Thus far S, Hierom.

19 By vvhich differences of death and Hel, (vvhereof vve must often aduertise the Reader) are meant tvvo things: death, and the going dovvne of the soule into some receptacle of Hel, in that state of the old Testament, at vvhat time the holy Scriptures vsed this phrase so often. Novv, these impudent trāslators in al these places, translate it *graue*, of purpose to confound it and death together, & to make it but one thing, vvhich S. Hierom shevveth to be different, in the very same sense that vve haue declared.

Bib. 1579.

20 But alas, is it the very nature of the Hebrue, Greeke, or Latin, that forceth them so much to English it *graue*, rather then *Hel?* vve appeale to all Hebricians, Grecians, and Latinists in the vvorld: first, if a man would aske, vvhat is Hebrue, or Greeke, or Latin for *Hel*: vvhether they vvould not ansvver, these three vvordes, as the very proper wordes to signifie it, euen as *Panis* signifieth bread: secondly, if a man vvould aske, vvhat is Hebrue, or Greeke, or Latin for a *graue*: vvhether they vvould ansvver these vvordes, and not three other vvhich they knovv

ᾅδης. שְׁאוֹל *Infernus.*

τάφος. קֶבֶר *Sepulchrum,*

knovv are as proper vvordes for *graue*, as *lac*, is for milke.

21 Yea, note & consider diligently vvhat vve vvill say. let them shevv me out of al the Bible one place, vvhere it is certaine & agreed among all, that it must needes signifie *graue*, let them shevv me in any one such place, that the holy Scripture vseth any of those former three vvordes for graue. As vvhen Abraham bought a place of burial, vvhether he bought *Infernum*: or vvhen it is said the kings of Israel vvere buried in the monuments or sepulchres of their fathers, vvhether it say, *in infernis patrum suorum*. So that not onely Diuines by this obseruation, but Grammarians also and children may easily see, that the proper and natural signification of the said vvordes, is in English *Hel*, and not *graue*. Gen.c.49.

22 And therfore Beza doth strangely abvse his Reader, more then in one place, saying that the Hebrue word doth properly signifie *graue*, being deduced of a verbe that signifieth, to craue or aske, because it craueth alvvaies nevv coarses. as though the graue craued moe then Hel doth, or svvallovved moe, or vvere more hardly satisfied and filled then Hel. for in al such places they translate *graue*. And in one such place they say, *The graue and destruction can neuer be full*. Annot. in Act.2,25.27. & in 1 Cor. 15,55. Bib.1579. Prouer.1,12. 3,15.16. Prou.27,30.

be full. Vvhereas them selues a litle before,
cap.15,11. translate the very same vvordes, *Hel and destruction*: and therfore it might haue pleased them to haue said also, *Hel and destruction can*
Bib.1562. 1577. *neuer be full*, as their pevv-fellovves doe in
Prouerb.1. their translation, & againe, *Vve shal svvalovv*
1 Pet.5. *them vp, like Hel. The Diuel* (vve reade) *goeth about continually like a roaring lion, seeking vvhom he may deuoure*, Vvho is called in the Apocalypse,
Apoc.9,11. *Abaddon*, that is, *destruction*. and so very aptly *Hel* and *destruction* are ioyned together, and are truely said neuer to be filled. Vvhat madnesse and impudencie is it then for
Beza before alleaged. Beza to vvrite thus. *Vvho is ignorant that by the Hebrue vvord, rather is signified a graue, for that it seemeth after a sort to craue alvvaies nevv carcasses?*

23 And againe, concerning our Sauiour Christes descending into Hel, and deliuering the fathers from thence, *it is maruel* saith
Annot. in 2 Act.v,24. Beza, *that the most part of the auncient fathers vvere in this errour, vvhereas vvith the Hebrues the vvord* SHEOL, *signifieth nothing els but* GRAVE. Before, he pleaded vpon the etymologie or nature of the vvord, novv also he pleadeth vpon the authoritie of the Hebrues them selues. If he vvere not knovven to be very impudent and obstinate, vve vvould easily mistrust his skil in the Hebrue, saying that among the Hebrues the vvord signifieth
Nihil aliud. *nothing els but graue.*

24 I vvould gladly knovv, vvhat are those

Heb.

Hebrues? doth not the Hebrue text of the holy Scripture best tell vs the vse of this vvord? Do not them selues translate it *Hel* very often? do not the *septuaginta* alvvaies? If any Hebrue in the vvorld, vvere asked, hovv he vvould turne these vvordes into Hebrue, *Similes estis sepulchris dealbatis: you are like to vvhited graues*: And, *Sepulchrum eius apud vos est: His graue is among you*: vvould any Hebrue I say translate it by this Hebrue vvord vvhich Beza saith among the Hebrues signifieth nothing els but *graue*? Aske your Hebrue Readers in this case, and see vvhat they vvill ansvver.

Sheolim. Sheol,

25 Vvhat are those Hebrues then, that Beza speaketh of? forsooth certaine Ievves or later Rabbines, vvhich, as they do falsely interprete al the holy Scriptures against our Sauiour Christ in other pointes of our beleefe, as against his Incarnatiõ, Death, & Resurrection: so do they also falsely interprete the holy Scriptures against his descending into HEL, vvhich those Ievvish Rabbines deny, because they looke for an other Messias that shal not die at all, and consequently shal not after his death go dovvne into HEL and deliuer the fathers expecting his cõming as our Sauiour Christ did. and therfore those Ievvish Rabbines hold as the HERETIKES doe, that the fathers of the old

The Protestants in interpretation of Scriptures, folovv the late Ievves, rather then the aũciẽt fathers, & Apostolical church.

Testament vvere in heauen before our Sauiour Christs Incarnatiō: & these Rabbines are they vvhich also peruert the Hebrue vvord to the signification of *graue*, in such places of the holy Scriptures as speake either of our Sauiour Christes descending into HEL, or of the fathers going dovvne into HEL, euen in like maner as they peruert other Hebrue vvordes, of the holy Scrip-
Esa. 7 ture as namely, *alma*, to signifie a yong vvoman, not a virgin, against our Sauiours birth of the B. Virgin Marie.

26 And if these later Rabbines be the Hebrues that Beza meaneth, and vvhich these gay English trāslatours folow, vve lament that they ioyne them selues vvith such cōpanions, being the svvorne enemies of our Sauiour Christ. Surely the Christian Hebrues in Rome and els vvhere, vvhich of great Rabbines are become zealous doctors of Christianitie, and therfore honour euery mysterie and article of our Christian faith concerning our Sauiour Christ, they dispute as vehemently against those other Rabbines, as we doe against the Heretikes, and among other things they tell them,
1 Reg. 28. that Saul said, *Raise me vp Samuël*, and that the vvoman said, *I see gods ascending out of the earth.* & *An old man is ascended or come vp.* and that Samuël said, *Vvhy hast thou disquieted me, that I should be raised*

sed vp? and, *To morovv thou and thy sonnes shal be vvith me.* And the booke of Ecclesiasticus saith, Eccl. 46. 23.
that Samuël died, and aftervvard *lifted vp his voice out of the earth, &c.* Al vvhich the holy Scripture would neuer haue thus expressed (vvhether it vvere Samuël in deede or not) if Saul and the Ievves then had beleeued, that their Prophets and Patriarches had been in heauen aboue. And as for the Hebrue vvord, they make it (as euery boy among the Ievves doth vvell knovv) as proper a vvord for *Hel*, as *panis* is for bread. and as vnproper for a graue (though so it may be vsed by a figure of speache) as *Cymba Charontis* is Latin for death.

27 But vvhat speake I of these? do not the greatest and most auncient Rabbines (so to cal them) the *Septuaginta* alvvaies translate the Hebrue vvord, by the Greeke ᾅδης, Geneb. li. 3. de Trin.
vvhich is proprely hel? do not the Talmudistes, and Chaldee paraphrases, and Rabbi Salomon Iarhi, handling these places of the Psalmes, *He vvil deliuer my soule from the hand of Sheol*, interpret it by *Gehinum*, that is, *Gehenna*, *hel?* and yet the Caluinistes bring this place for an example that it signifieth *graue*. likevvise vpon this place, *Let al sinners be turned into* SHEOL: the foresaid Rabbines interpret it by *Gehinum, hel.* In so much that in the Pro- Prouerb. 15.
uerbes and in Iob, it is ioyned vvith *Abaddō*. Iob. 26.

Vvhere

Vvhere Rabbi Leui according to the opinion of the Hebrues, expoundeth *sheol*, to be the lovvest region of the vvorld, a deepe place opposite to heauen, vvhereof it is vvritten, *If I descended into Hel, thou art present*: & so doth Rabbi Abraham expound the same vvord in chap. 2. Ionæ.

28 This being the opinion and interpretation of the Hebrues, See the skil or the honestie of Beza, saying that *sheôl*, vvith the Hebrues signifieth nothing but *graue*. Whereas in deede (to speake skilfully, vprightly, and not contentiously) it may signifie *graue* sometime secondarily, but *Hel*, principally and proprely, as is manifest, for that there is no other vvord so often vsed and so familiar in the Scriptures to signifie Hel, as this, and for that the Septuaginta doe alvvaies interprete it by the Greeke vvord ᾅδης.

29 The vvhich Greeke vvord is so notorious and peculiar for Hel, that the Pagans vse it also for Pluto, vvhom they feigned to be god of hel, and not god of graues: and if they vvould stand vvith vs in this point, vve might beate them with their ovvne kinde of reasoning, out of Poëtes & profane vvriters, and out of all lexicons. Vnles they vvil tel vs (contrarie to their custom) that vve Christians must attend the Ecclesiastical vse of this vvord in the Bible

Bible,and in Chriſtian vvriters,and that in them it ſignifieth graue. For ſo Beza ſeemeth to ſay, that the Greeke Interpreters of the Bible tranſlated the Hebrue vvord aforeſaid by this Greeke vvord, as ſignifying a darke place: vvhereas the Greeke Poëtes vſed it for that vvhich the Latines called *Inferos*, that is, *Hel.* *Vvhich ambiguitie* (ſaith he) *of the vvord, made many erre, affirming Chriſtes deſcending into Hel. So vvas* LIMBVS *builded, vvhereunto aftervvard Purgatorie vvas laid.* Annot. in Act. 2,27.

30 I ſee Beza his vvylines very vvell in this point. for here the man hath vttered al his hart,and the vvhole myſterie of his craftie meaning of this corrupt tranſlation:that to auoide theſe three things, Chriſts deſcending into Hel, *Limbus patrum*, and Purgatorie, he and his companions vvreſt the foreſaid vvordes of the holy Scriptures to the ſignification of graue. But let the indifferẽt chriſtian reader onely conſider Beza his ovvne vvordes in this place,point by point.

31 Firſt he ſaith, that the Greeke Poëtes vvere vvont to vſe the Greeke vvord for Hel: ſecondly, that they vvhich interpreted the Bible out of Hebrue into Greeke, vſed the very ſame vvord for that Hebrue vvord vvhereof vve haue novv diſputed: thirdly,that the aũcient fathers (for of them he ſpeaketh, as a litle before he expreſſeth) ibid. v.24.

vnderſtood

vnderstood the said Greeke vvord for *Hel*, and thereby grevve to those errours (as he impudently affirmeth) of Christes descending into Hel, & of the place in Hel vvhere the fathers rested, expecting the comming of our Sauiour, &c. Vvhereby the Reader doth easily see, that both the profane and also the Ecclesiastical vse of the vvord is for Hel, and not for graue.

Infernus, inferi.

32 And for the Latin vvord, it is the like case for al the vvorld: & if a man vvill aske but his childe that cometh from the Grammar, vvhat is *Infernus*, he vvil say *Hel*, and not *graue*: vvhat is Latin for *graue?* He vvil ansvver *Sepulchrum*, or *monumentum*. but neuer *Infernus*, vnles one of these Caluinisticall Translatours taught him so, to deceiue his father.

33 Novv then, to dravv to a conclusion of this their corruption also in their English translation: vvhereas the Hebrue, and Greeke, and Latin vvordes do most properly and vsually signifie Hel: and both Greeke, and Latin interpreters precisely in euery place vse for the Hebrue vvord, that one Greeke vvord, and that one Latin vvord, vvhich by al custom of speaking & vvriting, signifie Hel: [c] it had been the part of sincere and true meaning translatours, to haue translated it also in English alvvaies by

c If they obiect vnto vs some Catholikes, that translate it, *Sepulchrum*, as they doe: it is a fault in them also, but so far lesse then in the Protestāts, as chaūce medley is in respect of vvilful murby the vvord *Hel*: and aftervvard to haue diſputed of the meaning thereof, vvhether and vvhen it is to be taken for Hel, or graue, or lake, or death, or any ſuch thing. as in one place they haue done it very exactly and indifferently, namely vvhen Ionas ſaith (c 2. v. 2.) out of the vvhales belly, *Out of the belly of Hel, cried I, and thou heardeſt my voice.* ſo al tranſlate it, and vvell, vvhatſoeuer it ſignifie in this place. They thinke that *Hel*, here ſignifieth nothing els but the vvhales belly and the affliction of Ionas, and ſo the vvord may ſignifie by a Metaphorical ſpeach, as vvhen vve ſay in Engliſh, *It is a Hel to liue thus*: and * therfore no doubt they did here tranſlate it ſo, to inſinuate that in other places it might as vvel ſignifie *graue*, as here the vvhales belly. See their marginal annot. Ionæ 2, 2. Bib. 1577.

34 But then they ſhould haue tranſlated it alſo Hel in other places, as they did in this, and aftervvard haue interpreted it graue in their commentaries, and not preſumptuouſly to ſtraiten and limite the vvord of the holy Ghoſt to their priuate ſenſe and interpretation, & to preiudice the auncient and learned holy fathers, vvhich looke far more deepely and ſpiritually into this prophecie, then to Ionas or the vvhale, * our Sauiour him ſelf alſo applying it to his ovvne perſon, and to his being in the hart of Mat. 12.

of the earth three daies and three nightes.
Comment. in 2. Ionæ. And therfore S. Hierom saith, *This belly of Hel, according to the storie is the vvhales belly, but it may much better be referred to the person of Christ, vvhich vnder the name of Dauid, singeth in the Psalme, Thou shalt not leaue my soul in Hel*: (Psal. 15. In inferno.) Vvho vvas in Hel aliue, *and free among the dead.* (Psal. 87.) And that vvhich our Sauiour saith, *The Sonne of man shal be in the hart of the earth,* he doth interprete of his soule in Hel. *for as the hart is in the middes of the body, so is Hel said to be in the middes of the earth.*

35 Thus then presupposing (as vve must) that Ionas speaketh in the person, of our Sauiour Christ, the principal sense is not of the vvhales belly, but of that hel vvhither our Sauiour Christ descended, and from vvhēce he deliuered the fathers of the old Testament, him self ascending into heauen, as their kinge and general capitaine before them, and opening the vvay of heauen vnto them, as is signified in an other prophet: (Mich. 2, 13.) and vvas the first that entred heauen.

36 Against al vvhich truthes and euery point thereof, these translatours are so vvatcheful and vvarie, that vvhere the Apostle saith, (Heb. 10, 20. ἐνεκαίνισε. initiauit.) Christ *began*, and *dedicated* vnto vs the vvay into heauen, they say, in their English translations vvith full consent nothing els but, *He prepared.* Vvhy are they falser here then their Maisters, Caluin, Beza, Illyricus, vvho reade, *Dedicauit?* Is there nothing

thing in the Greeke vvord, but bare preparation? where be these etymologistes now, that can straine and vvring other vvordes to the vttermost aduantage of their heresie, and here are content for the like aduantage, to dissemble the force of this vvord, vvhich by all vse and proprietie signifieth, to make nevv, to begin a thing, to be the first author, to dedicate: as S. Augustine might haue taught them, and their lexicōs, and the Scriptures in many places. This translatiō (no doubt) is not done sincerely and indifferently of them, but for their ovvne deceitfull purpose, as is al the rest. Vvhen S. Paul speaketh of preparation only, they knovv right vvel that he vseth the vsual vvord to prepare: as, *He hath prepared them a citie:* and vvheresoeuer is signified preparation only, let them bring vs one example vvhere it is expressed by the other Greeke vvord, vvhich novv vve speake of.

χειροτονία μετάνοια.

Aug. tract. 48. in Ioan.

Heb. 11, 16. ἡτοίμασε.

37 But it is of more importance, vvhich folovveth, and apparteining altogether to this controuersie. Hebr. 5. v. 7. your translation is thus, in the very English bible that novv is reade in your Churches: *Vvhich in daies of his flesh offered vp praiers vvith strong crying, vnto him that vvas able to saue him from death, & vvas heard in that vvhich he feared.* Is the Greeke here, *In that vvhich he feared?* You knovv that no gram-

Of the yere 1577.

Against Christes descending into Hel.

ἀπὸ τῆς εὐλαβείας.

grammar nor lexicon doth allovv you this trãslation. but either thus, *for reuerence*, or as one of your ovvne Englis h Bibles hath it, *because of his reuerence.*

38 Hovv is it then, that in your later English bibles you chãged your former translatiõ from better to worse? or vvho taught you so to trãslate it? forsooth the Heretike Beza, vvhose translation you folow for the most part in your later bibles, though here, in sense rather then in vvord. And vvho taught Beza? he saith, Caluin vvas the first that euer found out this interpretatiõ. And vvhy? surely for defense of no lesse blasphemie then this, that our Sauiour IESVS Christ vpon the Crosse was horribly afraid of damnation, that he vvas in the very sorovves and torments of the damned, and that this vvas his descending into Hel, and that othervvise he descended not. let the Reader note these nevv teachers vpon this place, and iudge to vvhat vvicked end this translation tendeth.

Ex metu.

Calu. *Catech.* & Institut. li. 2. c. 16.

39 A vvonderful thing: vvhen all antiquitie vvith a general, & full cõsent hath in that place of the holy Scripture read thus, *that Christ vvas heard* (of his father) *for his reuerence* (accordĩg as our Sauiour him self also saith in the raising of Lazarus, and signifieth in his long praier Io. 17:) hovv a blasphemous

Io. 11, 42.

mous and preſumptuous Heretike ſhould be ſo malapert thus to alter it, that *he vvas heard in that vvhich he feared.* that is, that he vvas deliuered from damnation and the eternall paines of Hel, vvhich he vvas ſore afraid of. To the maintenance of which blaſphemie, Beza vvill ſeeme to force the Greeke thus. First (ſaith he) εὐλάϐεια doth not here ſignifie reuerence or pietie, but feare, and ſuch a feare vvhich he calleth *pauorem & conſternationem animi*, that is, dreadfulnes and aſtoniſhment of minde, and other like vvordes, to inſinuate an exceding horrour and feare in our Sauiour Chriſt. for confutation vvherof, vve might eaſily bring the common vſe of this Greeke word in the holy Scriptures to ſignifie not euery feare, but that religious feare vvhich is in the beſt men, ioyned vvith godlines, holines, and deuotion, as vvhen in the Actes they that buried S. Steuen, are called *Viri timorati.* deuout men ſuch as feared God.

ἀπὸ τῆς εὐλαϐείας.

Act 8. ἄνδρες εὐλαϐεῖς.

40 But vve neede not go far, for Beza vvill helpe vs him ſelf, vvho telleth vs in an other place the very ſame. his vvordes be theſe: εὐλάϐεια *ſignificat non quemuis timorem, ſed cum reuerentia potius quàm cum animi trepidatione coniunctum. latini religionem vocant.* that is, εὐλάϐεια *doth not ſignifie euery feare, but that vvhich is ioyned vvith reuerence rather then vvith aſtoniſhment of minde.*

Annot. in Luc. 2. v. 25.

the Latines do call it, religion or religious feare. If this be the true signification of εὐλάβεια, as Beza him self confesseth, vvhy doth he not so translate it in the foresaid place to the Hebrues? Vvhy forsaketh he the old approued Latin translation and general consent of al auncient interpreters, and translateth it, *that feare or astonishement of minde*, , vvhich he saith the vvord doth not signifie?

41 And marke that in his foresaid annotation vpon S. Luke he telleth not a peculiar signification of the Greeke vvord in that place, as though in some other places it might haue an other signification, but he telleth generally vvhat the very nature of the Greeke word is, that is, that it signifieth not euery feare but a feare ioyned vvith reuerence. and he said truely: and they shal hardly giue an instance vvhere it signifieth that feare of astonishment, vvhich both he and they translate in the foresaid place of S. Paul. Such a force hath heresie to leade a man euen contrarie to his ovvne knovvledge, to falsifie Gods holy vvord.

42 Yea Beza saith further to this purpose (much more against his skill in the Greeke tonge, if he had any at all) that ἀπὸ the preposition cannot beare this sense, *For vvhich or in respect vvhereof*. and therfore he trāslateth the Greeke into Latin thus. *Exauditus*

est

eſt ex metu, he vvas heard from feare: not, *for feare*, or, *for his reuerence.* and becauſe *from feare*, is a hard ſpeache and darke, that ſeemeth to be the cauſe vvhy our Engliſh trãſlators ſay, *In that vvhich he feared*, far from Beza in vvord, but aggreably in ſenſe.

43 But for this matter vve ſend them to Flaccus Illyricus a captaine Lutherane, vvho diſputeth this very point againſt the Caluiniſtes: and teacheth them that nothing is more common, then that ſignification of ἀπὸ. For profe vvhereof, vve alſo referre thẽ to theſe places of the holy Scripture. Mat. 13. Luc. 22. and 24. Act 12. Pſal. 87. And Machab. 5, 21. vvhere ἀπὸ vvith a genitiue, and διὰ vvith an accuſatiue, ſignifie al one, vvhich Beza denyeth. Gentle Reader, beare vvith theſe tedious grammatications, fitter to be handled in Latin, but neceſſarie in this caſe alſo, good for them that vnderſtand, & for the reſt an occaſion to aſke of thẽ that haue ſkill in the Greeke tonge, vvhether vve accuſe our aduerſaries iuſtly or no, of falſe tranſlating the holy Scriptures.

Flac. Illyric.

ἀπὸ τῆς χαρᾶς. ἀπὸ τῆς λύπης. ἀπὸ ταλαιπωρίας. ἀπὸ τῆς ὑπερηφανίας. διὰ τὸν μετεωρισμὸν τῆς καρδίας.

44 And vve beſeeche them to giue vs a good reaſon why they profeſſing to folow preciſely the Greeke, do not obſerue trevvly the Greeke points, in ſuch place as concerneth this preſent controuerſie. for the

c.13, 8. place in the Apocalypse which they alleage of our Sauiour Christs suffering frō the beginning (thereby to inferre that the iust men of the old Testament might enter heauen then, as vvel as after his real and actual death) according to the Greeke points saith thus, *Al that dvvel vpon the earth, shal vvorship him* (the beast) *vvhose names haue not been vvritten in the booke of life of the Lambe slaine, from the beginning of the vvorld.* Vvhere it is euident, that the Greeke text saith not, the lambe slaine from the beginning, but that the names of those Antichristian Idolaters vvere not vvritten in Gods eternal booke of predestination from the beginning, as it is also most plaine vvithout al ambiguitie in the 17 Chapter v. 8. If in a place of no controuersie they had not been curious in points of the Greeke, they might haue great reason sometime to alter the same.

45 But if in points of controuersie betvvene vs, they vvil say, diuers pointing is of no importance, they knovv the contrarie by the example of auncient heretikes, vvhich vsed this meane also to serue their false heretical purpose. If they say, our vulgar latine text pointeth it so, let them professe before God and their conscience, that they do it of reuerence to the said auncient latin text, or because it is indifferent, & not for any other cause, & for this one place

vve vvill admit their ansvver.

CHAP. VIII.
Heretical translation concerning IVSTIFICATION.

ABOVT the article of iustification, as it hath many branches, & their errours therein be manifold, so are their English translations accordingly many vvaies false and heretical. First against iustification by good vvorkes and by keeping the commaundements, they suppresse the very name of *iustification* in al such places vvhere the vvord signifieth the commaundements or the Lavv of God, vvhich is both in the old and nevv Testament most common and vsual, namely in the bookes of Moyses, in the Psalme 118. that beginneth thus, *Beati immaculati*: in the Psalme 147.v.19. I Mac.I.v.51.and c.2.v.21. Luc.I.v.6.Ro.2.v.26. In al vvhich places and the like, vvhere the Greeke signifieth *iustices & iustifications* most exactly, according as our vulgar Latin translateth, *iustitias* and *iustificationes*: there the English translations say ioyntly and vvith one consent, *ordinãces*, or, *statutes* For example, Ro.2. *If the vncircumcision keepe the* ORDINANCES *of the Lavv*, shal it not be counted for circumcision? And Luc. 1,6. *They vvere both, righteous before God, vvalking*

δικαιώματα

τὰ δικαιώματα.

δίκαιοι.

καὶ δικαι-ώμασι. *in al the commaundements and* ORDINANCES *of the Lord, blamelesse.* Vvhy translate you it *ordinaces*, and auoid the terme, *iustifications*? is it because you vvould folovv the Greeke? I beseeche you is not δίκαιος, iust, δικαιοῦσθαι, to be iustified, δικαιώματα, iustifications or iustices? In the old Testament you might perhaps pretend, that you folovv the Hebrue vvvord, חקים and therfore there you translate, *statutes*, or, *ordinances*. But euen there also, are not the Seuentie Greeke interpreters sufficient to teach you the signification of the Hebrue vvord: vvho alvvaies interprete it, δικαιώματα, in English, iustifications?

2 But be it, that you may cõtroule them in the Hebrue, vvhich none but fooles vvil graunt vnto you: in the nevv Testament vvhat pretense haue you? do you there also translate the Hebrue vvord, or rather the Greeke? the Greeke vndoubtedly you should translate. what reason then can you haue vvhy you doe not? none other surely then that vvhich Beza giueth for him self, saying, that he reiected the vvord, *iustificatiõs* (notvvithstanding it expressed the Greeke, *vvord for vvord*, notvvithstanding the Seuentie Greeke interpreters vsed it *to signifie the vvhole Lavv*, and in Latin it be commonly translated, *iustificationes*) notvvithstanding al Annot. in 1 Luc. this, for this only cause (saith he) did I reiecte

iecte it, to auoid the cauillatiōs that might be made by this vvord, against iustification by faith. As if he should say, This vvord truely translated according to the Greeke, might minister great occasion to proue by so many places of Scripture, that mans iustification is not by faith only, but also by keeping the lavv, and obseruing the commaundements, vvhich therfore are called according to the Greeke and Latin, *iustifications*, because they concurre to iustification, and make a man iust, as by S. Lukes vvordes also is vvel signified, vvhich haue this allusion, that they vvere both iust, because they walked in al the iustifications of our Lord. Vvhich they of purpose suppresse by other vvordes.

3 And hereof also it riseth, that vvhen he cānot possibly auoid the vvord in his trās-lation (as Apoc. 19, 8. *Bissinum enim iustificationes sunt sanctorum, The silke is the iustifications of Sainctes:*) there he helpeth the matter with this commentarie, That *iustifications*, are *those good vvorkes vvhich be the testimonies of a liuely faith.* But our English translatours haue an other vvay to auoid the vvord euen in their trāslatiō. For they say here, *the righteousnes of Sainctes:* because they could not say, *ordinances of Sainctes:* and they vvould not say, *iustificatiōs of sainctes:* knovving very vvel (by Bezaes ovvne cō-

τὰ δικαιώματα.

Beza Annot. in Apoc. 19.

mentarie) that this vvord includeth the good vvorkes of sainctes: vvhich vvorkes if they should in translating call their iustifications, it vvould goe sore against iustification by only faith. Therfore doe they trãslate in steede thereof, *ordinances*, &, *statutes*, vvhere they can, vvhich are termes furthest of from iustification: and vvhere they can not, there they say, *righteousnes*, making it also the plural number, vvhereas the more proper Greeke vvord for righteousnes is εὐθύτης (Dan. 6, 22.) vvhich there some of thẽ translate *vngiltinesse*: because they vvil not translate exactly, if you vvould hire them.

4 And therfore as for, *iustice*, and, *iustifications*, they say *righteousnes*: so for, *iust*, they translate, *righteous*. and by this meanes, *Ioseph vvas a righteous man*, rather then a iust man: and Zacharie & Elisabeth *vvere both righteous before God*, rather then iust: because vvhen a man is called iust, it soundeth that he is so in deede, and not by imputation only: as a vvise man, is vnderstood to be vvise in deede, and not only so imputed. Therfore do they more gladly and more often say, *righteous men*, rather then, *iust men*, and vvhen they do say, *iust men*, as sometime they doe lest they might seeme vvilful inexcusably: there they vnderstand, iust by imputation, and not in deede, as is to be seen in Bezaes

Bib. of the yere 1577. most approued.
Mat. 1, 19.
Luc. 1, 6.

Anno-

Annotatiõs vpon the Epistle to the Romanes. Note also that they put the vvord, *iust*, vvhen faith is ioyned vvithal. as Ro. 1. *The iust shal liue by faith.* to signifie that iustification is by faith. But if vvorkes be ioyned vvithal, and keeping the commaundemẽts, as in the place alleaged Luc. 1. ther they say, *righteous*, to suppresse iustification by vvorkes.

5 And certaine it is, if there vvere no sinister meaning, they vvould in no place auoid to say, iust, iustice, iustification, where both the Greeke and Latin are so, vvord for vvord. as for example 2 Tim. 4, 8. In al their bibles, *Henceforth there is laid vp for me a crovvne of* RIGHTEOVSNES, *vvhich the Lord the* RIGHTEOVS *iudge shal* GIVE *me at that day.* And againe 2 Thess. 1. *Reioyce in tribulations vvhich is a token of the* RIGHTEOVS IVDGEMENT *of God, that you may be counted vvorthie of the kingdom of God for vvhich ye suffer. For it is a* RIGHTEOVS THING *vvith God, to recompense tribulation to them that trouble you: and to you that are troubled, rest vvith vs, in the reuelation of the Lord* IESVS *from heauen.* And againe Hebr. 6, 10. *God is not* VNRIGHTEOVS *to forget your good vvorke and labour, &c.* These are very pregnant places to discouer their false purpose in concealing the vvord, *iustice*, in al their bibles. For if they vvil say, that iustice is not an vsual English vvord in this sense, and therfore they say, *righteousnes*: yet I trovv, *iust*, and, *vniust*, are vsual and vvel knovven.

τῆς δικαιοσύνης.

ὁ δίκαιος κριτὴς ἀποδώσει &c.

τῆς δικαίας κρίσεως.

δίκαιον ἐστι iustum est.

οὐ γὰρ ἄδικος.

Non enim iniustus est Deus.

knovven. Vvhy then vvould they not ſay at the leaſt, in the places alleaged, *God the* IVST *iudge, A token of the* IVST IVDGEMENT *of God, It is* A IVST *thing vvith God, God is not* VNIVST *to forget, &c?* Vvhy is it not at the leaſt in one of their Engliſh Bibles, being ſo both in Greeke and Latin?

The ſcriptures moſt euident for *iuſtification by vvorkes,* againſt *only faith.*

6 Vnderſtand gentle Reader, and marke vvel, that if S. Paules vvordes vvere truely tranſlated thus, *A crovvne of* IVSTICE *is laid vp for me, vvhich our Lord the* IVST *iudge vvil* RENDER *vnto me at that day*, and ſo in the other places: it vvould inferre, that men are iuſtly crowned in heauen for their good workes vpon earth, and that it is Gods *iuſtice* ſo to doe, & that he vvil do ſo becauſe he is *a iuſt iudge*, & becauſe he vvil ſhevv his IVST IVDGEMENT, and he vvil not forget ſo to doe, becauſe he is not *vniuſt*: as the auncient fathers (namely the Greeke doctors S. Chryſoſtom, Theodorete, & Oecumenius vpon theſe places) do interpret and expound. in ſo much that Oecumenius ſaith thus vpon the foreſaid place to the Theſſalonians, ὅρα ὅτι &c. *See here, that to ſuffer for Chriſt procureth the kingdom of heauen according to* IVST IVDGEMENT, *and not according to grace.* Vvhich leſt the Aduerſarie might take in the vvorſe part, as though it vvere only Gods iuſtice or iuſt iudgement, and not his fauour or grace alſo, S. Auguſtine excellently

Pſal. 57. Si vtique eſt fructus iuſto, vtique eſt Deus iudicans eos in terra.

κατὰ δικαιοκρισίαν, καὶ οὐ κατὰ χάριν.

lently declareth hovvv it is both the one and the other: to vvit, his grace and fauour and mercie, in making vs by his grace to liue and beleeue vvel, and so to be vvorthy of heauen: his iustice and iust iudgement, to render and repay for those vvorkes vvhich him self vvrought in vs, life euerlasting. Vvhich he expresseth thus: *Hovv should he render or repay as a iust iudge, vnles he had giuen it as a merciful father?* Vvhere S. Augustine vrgeth the vvordes of *repaying* as due, and of being A IVST IVDGE therfore. both vvhich the said translatours corrupt, not only saying, *righteous iudge,* for, *iust iudge*: but, that he vvil *giue* a crovvne, vvhich is of a thing not due, for that vvhich is in the Greeke, *He vvil render or repay*: vvhich is of a thing due and deserued, & hath relation to vvorkes going before, for the vvhich the crovvne is repaied. He said not (saith Theophylacte vpon this place) *he vvil giue*, but, *he vvil render or repay*, as a certaine dette. for he being iust, vvil define & limite the revvard according to the labours. the crovvne therfore is due dette, because of the iudges iustice. So saith he.

Aug. de gra. & lib. arb. ca. 6.

ἀποδώσει.

7 Vvhich speaches being most true as being the expresse vvordes of holy Scripture, yet vve knovv hovv odiously the Aduersaries may & doe misconster them to the

ignorant,

ignorant, as though vve chalenged heauen by our ovvne vvorkes, and as though vve made God bound to vs. Vvhich vve do not, God forbid. but because he hath pre-
Eph.2, v.10. pared good vvorkes for vs (as the Apostle saith) to vvalke in them, and doth by his grace cause vs to doe them, and hath promised life euerlasting for them, and telleth vs in al his holy Scriptures, that to doe them is the vvay to heauen: therfore not presuming vpon our ovvne vvorkes as our ovvne or as of our selues, but vpon the good vvorkes vvrought through Gods grace by vs his seely instruments, vve haue
Hebr.10. great confidence (as the Apostle speaketh) and are assured that these vvorkes proceding of his grace, be so acceptable to him, that they are esteemed and be vvorthie and meritorious of the kingdom of heauen. Against which truth, let vs see further, their heretical corruptions.

CHAP. IX.

Heretical translation against MERITES *or* MERITORIOVS WORKES *and the* REWARD *for the same.*

When

WHEN they translate (Ro. 8,18) thus, *I am certainely persuaded, that the afflictions of this time,* ARE NOT WORTHIE OF THE GLORIE *vvhich shal be shevved vpon vs:* do they not meane to signifie to the reader, & must it not needes so sound in his eares, that the tribulations of this life, be they neuer so great, though suffered for Christ, yet do not merite nor deserue the heauenly glorie? but in the Greeke it is far otherwise. I vvil not stand vpon their first vvordes, *I am certainely persuaded,* vvhich is a far greater asseueration then the Apostle vseth, and I maruel hovv they could so translate that Greeke word, but that they vvere disposed, not only to translate the Apostles vvordes falsely against meritorious vvorkes, but also to auouch and affirme the same lustely, vvith much more vehemencie of vvordes then the Apostle speaketh. vvel, let vs pardon them this fault, & examine the vvordes folovving. Vvhere the Greeke saith not, as they translate vvith ful consent in al their English Bibles, *The afflictions are not vvorthie of the glorie &c.* but thus, *The afflictions of this time are not equal, correspondent, or cōparable to the glorie to come.* * because the afflictions are short, the glorie is eternal: the afflictions smal and fevv in comparison, the glorie great and abboundant aboue measure.

Bib. 1577.

λογίζομαι. I suppose.

οὐκ ἄξια πρὸς τὴν μέλλουσαν δόξαν. Non sunt condignæ ad futuram gloriam.

* S. Chrys. vpon this place.

2 This

2 This is the Greeke phrase & the Apostles meaning, vvhich vve neede not greatly to proue, because their ovvne Doctors Caluin and Beza do so interpret it, & therfore vvonder it vvere that the Geneua English bibles also should forsake their Maisters, and folovv the errour of the other English bibles, but that they thought the more voices the better. In the meane time the people seeth no other translation, & thinketh it is the Apostles very vvordes. But Beza him self telleth them the contrarie, translating thus: *Statuo minimè esse paria quæ presenti tempore perpetimur, futuræ gloriæ nobis reuelandæ.* that is, *I am of this opinion, that the things vvhich vve suffer in this present time, are not equal to the glorie that shal be reuealed to vs.* And in his commentarie, thus, *S. Paules discourse and matter handled in this place, declare, that he speaketh not of the valure or price of the afflictions vvhich vve suffer for Christ, but rather by comparing their qualitie and quantitie vvith life euerlasting, he gathereth that vve shal be infinitly more happie vvith Christ, then vve are miserable here. Therfore did he vse the* * *Greeke vvord rightly and properly, vvhich the Grammarians say is spoken of such things, as being poised or vveighed, are found of one vveight.* Thus far Beza.

* ἄξια.

3 If then a comparison only be signified, vvhy do they not so trãslate it in English, that it may be taken for a comparison in our English phrase? For they knovv very vvel that if a man should say in English, accor-

according as they tranſlate, Good vvorkes are *not vvorthie* of heauen, this man is *not vvorthie* of my fauour, he is *not vvorthie* of ſuch a liuing, of ſo great praiſes: euery Engliſh man vnderſtandeth it thus, that they *deſerue not* heauen, and that ſuch a man *deſirueth not* this or that. Euen ſo muſt the reader needes take it in this place, and they muſt needes haue intēded that he ſhould ſo take it. For though he Greeke phraſe may ſignifie a compariſon, being ſo vttered, yet not the Engliſh. and if it might, yet obſcurely and ambiguouſly: and if it might, yet here they do falſely tranſlate ſo, becauſe here the Greeke phraſe is othervviſe, and therfore ſhould othervviſe be Engliſhed. For it is not, ἄξια τῆς δόξης, vvhich is, as they trāſlate, *vvorthy of the glorie*: but, ἄξια πρὸς τὴν δόξαν, which cānot be ſo trāſlated. For if it might, then theſe Greeke phraſes vvere al one, and might be vſed indifferently. And then I muſt deſire them to turne me this into Greeke, *He is not vvorthie of thankes.* and if they turne it by the Apoſtles phraſe in this place οὐκ ἄξιός ἐστι πρὸς τὴν χάριτα, to al Grecians they ſhal be ridiculous. And yet this is as vvel turned out of Engliſh into Greeke, as they haue turned the other out of Greeke into Engliſh.

Prou. 3. ἄξιον αὐτῆς

4 Marie, if they vvould exppreſſe a compariſon

parison of equalitie or inequalitie betwene thing & thing, thē this is the proper Greeke phrase thereof, and much more proper for

The Greeke ἄξιος, signifieth a comparison.

this purpose, thē by ἄξιος, & a genitiue case. Which notvvithstanding is often so vsed in the Scriptures, by vvay of cōparison. as Prouerb. 3. concerning the praise of vvisedom.

πᾶν τίμιον οὐκ ἄξιον αὐτῆς ἐστι.

כָּל־ חֲפָצִים לֹא יִשְׁווּ־ בָהּ

Vvhere S. Augustine to expresse the comparison, readeth thus, *Omne pretiosum non est illi dignum*: and S. Hierom according to the Hebrue thus, *omnia quę desiderantur nō valent huic cōparari.* or, *adæquari.* and Ecclci 26, vve haue the very like speache proceding of the said Greeke vvord ἄξιος *Omnis ponderatio non est digna continentis animæ.* Vvhich the English Bibles translate thus, *There is no vveight to be compared vnto a minde that can rule it self.* or, *vvith a continent minde.*

5 And if ἄξιος vvith a genitiue case signifie a comparison, and them selues so translate

ἄξια πρὸς τὴν δόξαν

it in al their Bibles, should not ἄξιος in the Apostles phrase much more be so trāslated? I appeale to their ovvne cōsciences. Againe if here in Ecclicus they say not according

ἄξιος ἐγκρατοῦς ψυχῆς.

to the Greeke vvordes, *There is no vveight vvorthie of a continent minde*, because they vvould by an English phrase expresse the comparison: is it not more then euident, that vvhen they translate the Apostle by the very same vvordes, *Vvorthie of the glorie &c*: they knovv

knovv it can not, and they meane it ſhould not ſignifie a compariſon? I can not ſufficiently expreſſe, but only to the learned and ſkilful reader, their partial and heretical dealing. Briefely I ſay, they tranſlate, οὐκ ἄξιος ἐγκρατοῦς ψυχῆς, *Not to be compared vvith a continent minde*, being in Greeke word for word *Not vvorthie of a continent minde*: and contrarievviſe they tranſlate in S. Paul, οὐκ ἄξια πρὸς τὴν μέλλουσαν δόξαν, *Not vvorthie of the glorie to come*, being in the Greeke, *Not to be cōpared to the glorie to come.* according to the very like Latin phraſe by *dignus* Eccl. 6. *Amico fideli nulla eſt comparatio, & non eſt* DIGNA *ponderatio auri & argenti* CONTRA BONITATEM FIDEI, that is, according to their ovvne tranſlation, *A faithful frende hath no peere, vveight of gold & ſiluer is not to be compared to the goodnes of his faith.*

6 Novv if they vvil ſay, though their tranſlation of S. Paules vvordes be not ſo exact and commodious, yet the ſenſe and meaning is al one (for if theſe preſent afflictions be not equal or comparable to the glorie to come, then neither are they worthie of it, nor can deſerue or merite it) let the Chriſtian reader marke the difference. Firſt their Beza and Caluin telleth them that the Apoſtle ſpeaketh of the one, and not of the other. Secōdly, the paſſions & afflictions that Chriſt our Sauiour ſuffered al

Hovv good vvorkes merite life euerlaſting, though one incomparably excede the other.

his life, vvere not comparable to the eternal glorie vvhich he obtained thereby: yet did he thereby deserue and merite eternal glorie, not only for him self but for al the vvorld: yea by the least affliction he suffered, did he deserue al this. vnles you vvil deny also that he merited and deserued his glorie, vvhich your opinion a man might

Heb. 2, 9. in the new Testament of the yere 1580. & Bib. 1579.

very vvel gather by * some of your false translations, but that you vvould thinke vs to suspicious, vvhich perhaps vve vvil examine hereafter. Thirdly, the present pleasure of aduoutrie during a mans life, is not comparable to the eternal torments of hel fire: and yet it doth merite and deserue the the same. Fourthly, the Apostle by making an incomparable difference of the glorie to come vvith the afflictiōs of this time, doth

περιρέπει μειζόνως.

(as S. Chrisostom saith) exhort them the more vehemently and moue them to sustaine al things the more vvillingly: but if he said as they translate, The afflictions are not vvorthie of heauen, you are neuer the neerer heauen for them, only beleeue: this had not been to exhort them, but to discourage them. Fifthly, the Apostle vvhen he

2 Cor. 4. v. 17.

vvil els vvhere encourage them to suffer, saith plainely, *Our tribulation vvhich presently is for a moment and light*, WORKETH *aboue measure exceedingly, an eternal vveight of glorie in vs.*

κατεργάζεται.

7 See you not a compariſon betvvene ſhort and eternal, light tribulation, & exceding vveightie glorie: and yet that one alſo *vvorketh* the other, that is, cauſeth, purchaſeth, and deſerueth the other? for, like as the litle ſeede being not cõparable to the great tree, yet cauſeth it and bringeth it forth: ſo our tribulatiõs & good vvorkes othervviſe incomparable to eternal glorie, by the vertue of Gods grace vvorking in vs, worketh, purchaſeth, and cauſeth the ſaid glorie. for ſo they knovv very wel the Greeke vvorde importeth: though here alſo they tranſlate it moſt falſely, *prepareth*. Bib. an. 1577.

See this Greeke word 2 Cor. 7. thriſe. Vvhere thẽ ſelues tranſlate it, *cauſeth, Worketh* v.10,11.

8 Laſtly, for moſt manifeſt euidence, that theſe preſent tribulations and other good vvorkes are meritorious & vvorthie of the ioyes to come, though not cõparable to the ſame: you ſhal heare the holy Doctors ſay both in one paſſage or ſentence. S. Cyprian thus: *O vvhat maner of day ſhal come, my brethren, vvhen our Lord ſhal recount the* MERITES *of euery one, and pay vs the revvard or ſtipend of faith and deuotion? Ep.56.* here are merites & the revvard for the ſame. It folovveth in the ſaid Doctor, *Vvhat glorie ſhal it be, and hovv great ioy, to be admitted to ſee God, ſo to be honoured that thou receiue the ioy of eternal life with Chriſt thy Lord* GOD, *to receiue there that vvhich neither eie hath ſeen, nor eare hath heard, nor hath aſcended into the hart of man. for, that vve ſhal receiue greater things, then here either vve doe, or ſuffer, the Apoſtle* pronounceth, ſaying, *The paſſions of this time are*

ep. 56. nu. 3.

Singulorum merita.

not condigne or cōparable to the glorie to come, Here vve see that the stipend or revvard of the merites aforesaid, are incōparably greater then the said merites.

Ser. 37. de Sanctis. *præmia meritorum.*

9 Likevvise S. Augustine: *The exceding goodnes of God hath prouided this, that the labours should soone be ended, but the revvardes of the* MERITES *should endure vvithout end: the Apostle testifying,* THE PASSIONS OF THIS TIME ARE NOT COMPARABLE &c. *For vve shal receiue greater blisse, then are the afflictions of al passions vvhatsoeuer.* Thus vve see plainely, that short tribulations are true merites of endles glorie, though not comparable to the same: vvhich truth you impugne by your false and heretical translation. But let vs see further your dealing in the self same controuersie, to make it plainer that you bend your translations against it, more then the text of the Scripture doth permit you.

ἀξίους ἑαυτοῦ. dignos se. ἐπείρασεν εὗρεν.

10 In the booke of vvisedom, vvhere there is honorable mention of the merites of Saincts and their revvardes in heauen, the holy Scripture saith thus: *God hath proued them, and findeth them* MEETE FOR HIMSELF. To omit here that you vse the present tense, vvhereas in the Greeke they are preter tenses (God knovveth vvhy, only this vve knovv, that it is no true nor sincere trāslation) but to vvincke at smaller faultes, vvhy

vvhy say you here in al your Bibles, that God findeth his Saincts and holy seruants *meete for him self*, and not, *vvorthie of him self*? See your partialitie, and be ashamed.

11 In the Apostles places before examined, you said negatiuely, that the afflictions of this time vvere NOT WORTHIE OF the glorie to come, the Greeke not bearing that trāslation: but here, vvhen you should say affirmatiuely, and that vvord for vvord after the Greeke, that God found them WORTHIE OF HIM SELF, there you say, MEETE FOR HIM SELF, auoiding the terme, *vvorthie*, because merite is included therein. So that vvhen you vvil in your translation deny merites, then *condignæ ad*, signifieth, *vvorthie of*: vvhen you should in your trāslation affirme merites, then *Dignus* vvith an ablatiue case doth not signifie, *vvorthie of*. No maruel if such vvilfulnes vvil not see the vvord *merite*, or that vvhich is equiualent thereto, in al the Scripture. for vvhen you do see it, and should translate it, you suppresse it by an other vvord. But this is a case vvorthie of examination, vvhether the Scripture haue the vvord, *merite*, or the equiualēt thereof. for vve vvil force them euen by their ovvne translations, to confesse that it is found there, and that they should translate it accordingly

ἀξίους ἑαυτοῦ.

Condignæ ad gloriam.

dignos se.

Merite of good vvorkes plainely proued by the Scriptures.

often vvhen they doe not, yea, that if vve did not see it in the vulgar Latin translatiõ, yet they must needes see it and finde it in the Greeke.

12 First vvhen they translate the foresaid place thus, *The afflictions of this time are not vvorthie of the glorie to come*: they meane this, *deserue not the glorie to come*, for to that purpose they do so translate it, as hath been declared. Againe, vvhen it is said, *The vvorkeman is vvorthie of his hire or vvages*: Vvhat is meant, but that he deserueth his vvages? And more plainely Tob. 9. they translate thus: *Brother Azarias, if I should giue my self to be thy seruant, I shal not* DESERVE *thy prouidence.* And such like. If then in these places, both the Greeke & the Latin signifie, *to be vvorthie of*, or, *not to be vvorthie of, to deserue*, or, *not to deserue*: then they must allovv vs the same signification and vertue of the same vvordes in other like places. Namely Apoc. 5. of our Sauiours merites, thus: *The lambe that vvas killed,* IS VVORTHIE *to receiue povver, and riches, &c.* Vvhat is that to say, but, DESERVETH *to receiue?* For so I trust they vvil allovv vs to say of our Sauiour, that he in deede deserued. Againe, of the damned, thus: *Thou hast giuen them bloud to drinke, for they* ARE VVORTHIE. or, THEY HAVE DESERVED. is it not al one? lastly of the elect, thus: *They shal vvalke vvith me in vvhite, because*

οὐκ ἄξια.

ἄξιος τοῦ μισθοῦ. *dignus mercede sua.*

Non ero condignus prouidentiæ.

ἄξιός ἐστιν

Apoc. 16. ἄξιοι γάρ εἰσι.

because they are vvorthie, Apoc. 3. that is, because *they deserue it.* and so in the place before by them corrupted, *God found them vvorthie of him:* that is, such as *deserued* to be vvith him in eternal glorie. Thus by their ovvne translation of ἄξιος and *dignus*, are plainely deduced, vvorthines, desert, and merite of saincts, out of the Scriptures.

δι ἄξιοί εἰσιν, *Digni sunt.* ἀξίους ἑαυτοῦ, *Dignos se.*

13 But to procede one steppe further, vve proue it also to be in the Scriptures, thus. Them selues translate thus Heb. 10, 29. *Of hovv much sorer punishement shal he be vvorthie, vvhich treadeth vnder foote the sonne of God?* though one of their Bibles of the yere 1562, very falsely and corruptly leaueth out the vvordes, *vvorthie of*, saying thus, *Hovv much sorer shal he be punished &c*: Fearing no doubt by translating the Greeke vvord sincerely, this consequence that novv I shal inferre. to vvit, If the Greeke vvord here, by their ovvne trãslation, signifie *to be vvorthie of*, or, *to deserue*, being spoken of paines and punishement deserued: then must they graunt vs the same vvord so to signifie els vvhere in the nevv Testament, vvhen it is spoken of deseruing heauen and the kingdom of God. as in these places. Luc. 21. *Vvatch therfore, al times praying, that you* MAY BE VVORTHIE *to stand before the sonne of man.* and c. 20. THEY THAT ARE VVORTHIE *to attaine to that vvorld & to the resurrection from the dead, neither marie, nor are maried.*

ἀξιωθῆναι & καταξιωθῆναι signifie deserue.

πόσῳ χείρονος ἀξιωθήσεται τιμωρίας.

ἵνα καταξιωθῆτε σταθῆναι.

οἱ καταξιωθέντες.

εἰς τὸ καταξιωθῆναι ὑμᾶς τῆς βασιλείας.

& 2 Theſſ.1. *That you may* BE VVORTHIE *of the kingdom of God, for vvhich alſo ye ſuffer.*

14 Thus you ſhould tranſlate in al theſe places, according to your tranſlation of the former place to the Hebrues: or at the leaſt-vviſe you ſhould haue this ſenſe and meaning, as the old vvulgar Latin hath, tranſlating in al theſe places, *counted vvorthie*, but meaning vvorthie in deede: as vvhen it is ſaid, Abraham was reputed iuſt, it is meant, he vvas iuſt in deede. If you alſo haue this meaning in your tranſlations, vvhich here folovv the vulgar Latin: then vve appeale to your ſelues, vvhether, to be counted vvorthie, and to be vvorthie, & to deſerue, and to merite, be not al one: and ſo here alſo *Merite* is deduced. But if you meane according to your hereſie, to ſignifie by tráſlating, *counted vvorthie*, that they are not in deede vvorthie: then your purpoſe is heretical, and tranſlation falſe and repugnant to your tranſlating the ſame vvord in other places, as is declared, and novv further vve vvil declare.

Qui digni habebuntur. Vt digni habeamini.

ἀξιῶσαι to make worthie, ἀξιωθῆναι to be made, or to be worthie.

15 They vvhom God doth make vvorthie, they are truely and in deede vvorthie: are they not? but by your ovvne tranſlation of the ſame vvord in the actiue voice, God doth make them vvorthie. therfore in the paſſiue voice it muſt alſo ſignifie to

be

be made or to be in deede vvorthie. For example, 2 Theſſ. 1, 11. You tranſlate thus, *vve alſo pray for you*, THAT OVR GOD MAY MAKE YOV VVORTHIE *of this calling.* According to vvhich tranſlation, vvhy did you not alſo in the ſelf ſame chapter a litle before tranſlate thus: *That you* MAY BE MADE VVORTHIE (and ſo be vvorthie) *of the kingdom of God, for vvhich alſo you ſuffer?* You knovv the caſe is like in both places. & in the Greeke doctors you ſpecially ſhould knovv (by your oſtẽtation of reading them in Greeke) that they according to this vſe of holy Scripture, very often vſe alſo this vvord both actiuely & paſſiuely, *to make vvorthie*, & *to be made*, or, *to be vvorthie.* See the Greeke Liturgies.

ἵνα ὑμᾶς ἀξιώσῃ τῆς κλήσεως.

εἰς τὸ καταξιωθῆναι ὑμᾶς τῆς βασιλείας.

ἀξιῶσαι. ἀξιωθῆναι.

16 Vvhich S. Chryſoſtom, to put al out of doubt, explicateth thus in other vvordes, *That he make vs vvorthie of the kingdom of heauen. Ser. 1. de orando Deo.* And vpon the epiſtle to Titus c. 3. in the ſame ſenſe paſſiuely, *God graunt vve may al* BE MADE VVORTHIE (or be vvorthie) *of the good things promiſed to them that loue him.* And in an other place of the ſaid doctor it muſt needes ſignifie, to be vvorthie. as vvhen he ſaith, *In Coloſ. 1. No man liueth ſuch a trade of life, that he is vvorthie of the kingdom, but al is his gift.* For to ſay thus, *No man ſo liueth that he can be counted vvorthie of the kingdom of heauen:* is falſe,

ἵνα ἡμᾶς ἀξίους ἀπεργάσηται τῆς βασιλείας.

ἀξιωθῆναι.

ὥστε βασιλείας ἀξιωθῆναι.

is against the Protestants ovvne opinion, vvhich say they are counted vvorthie, that are not. Againe, to say, *No man so liueth that he can be made vvorthie*: is false, because God can make the worst man worthie. It remaineth then to say, *No man so liueth that he is vvorthie.* Vvhich a litle before he declareth thus, *No man by his ovvne proper merites obtaineth the kingdom of heauen.* that is, as his ovvne, and of him self vvithout the grace of God. And yet vve must shevv further out of the Scriptures, that God maketh vs vvorthie, and so vve are in deede vvorthie, and here also vve must conuince you of false and partial interpretation.

ἀπὸ καλορθωμάτων οἰκείων.

17 The Greeke vvord ἱκανός (I pray you) vvhat doth it signifie? you must ansvver that it signifieth not onely, *meete*, but also, *vvorthie.* for so Beza teacheth you, & so you translate Mat. 3,11. & c. 8, 8. & 1 Cor. 15, 9. *I am not vvorthie*, in al three places. And vvhy (I pray you) did you not likevvise folovv the old Latin interpreter one steppe further, saying, *Giuing thankes to God the father* THAT HATH MADE VS WORTHIE, but translating rather thus, *Vvhich hath made vs meete to be partakers of the inheritance of the saincts in light.* Here vvas the place vvhere you should haue shevved your sinceritie, and haue said that God maketh vs vvorthie of heauenly blisse.

οὐκ εἰμὶ ἱκανός.

τῷ ἱκανώσαντι ὑμᾶς εἰς τὴν μερίδα. Col. 1. v. 12.

blisse. because you know if *ἱκανὸς* be *vvorthy*, then *ἱκανῶσαι* is *to make vvorthie*. But you are like to Beza your Maister, vvho (as though al interpretation of vvordes vvere at his commaundement) saith, here and here and so forth *I haue folovved the old Latin interpreter*, translating it, *vvorthie*: but in such and such a place (meaning this for one) *I chose rather to say*, MEETE. but that both he and you should here also haue translated, *vvorthie*, the Greeke fathers shal teach you, if vve be not vvorthie, or able to controule so mightie Grecians, as you pretend to be vvhen you crovve vpon your ovvne dunghil, otherwise in your translations shevving smal skil, or great malice.

Annot. in 3. Mat. No. Test. 1556.

Idoneum dicere malui.

18 The Greeke fathers (I say) interprete the Apostles vvord here, thus: *κατηξίωσεν ἡμᾶς, καὶ ἐχαρίσατο ἡμᾶς ἱκανοὺς γενέσθαι*. that is, hath made vs vvorthie, and giuen vs the grace to be vvorthie. and S. Basil in orat. Liturg. making both Greeke vvordes al one, saith, THOV HAST MADE VS WORTHIE *to be ministers of thy holy altar.* and anon after, MAKE VS WORTHIE *for this ministerie.* And S. Chrisost. vpon the Apostles place, *God doth not only giue vs societie vvith the Saincts, but maketh vs also vvorthie to receiue so great dignitie.* And here is a goodly consideration of the goodnes of God tovvard vs, that

Oecum. in Caten.

καταξιώσας ἡμᾶς.

ἱκάνωσον ἡμᾶς.

that doth in deede by his grace make vs vvorthie of so great things, vvho othervvise are most vnvvorthie, vile, and abiect. Vvhich making of vs vvorthie, is expressed by the said Greeke vvordes, more then by the Latin, *mereri*, because it declareth whence our merite and vvorthines procedeth. to vvit, of God. both vvhich S. Chrysostom expresseth excellently thus: *Vvhen he brought in Publicans to the kingdom of heauen, he defamed not the kingdom of heauen, but magnified it also vvith great honours, shevving that there is such a Lord of the kingdom of heauen, vvhich hath made euen vnvvorthie persons to be so much better, that they should deserue euen the glorie of that dignitie.* And Oecumenius saith, *that it is Gods glorie*, *TO MAKE HIS SERVANTS WORTHIE *of such good things: and that it is their glorie*, *TO HAVE BEEN MADE WORTHIE *of such things.* in 2, Thess. 1.

Ho. de Cruce & latrone.

Vt etiam illius dignitatis gloriam mererentur.

*ἀξιῶσαι.

*ἠξιῶσθαι.

19 Thus vve see hovv the holy Scripture vseth equiualent vvordes to signifie, *merite*, vvhich you suppresse as much as you can. So likevvise vve might tel you of other vvordes and phrases that do plainely import and signifie *merite*. as vvhen it is said Ecclesiastici 16. *Euery man shal finde according to his vvorkes.* Budee both your Maister and ours in the Greeke tongue, telleth vs that the Greeke vvord εὑρέσθαι (to finde) is proprely to receiue for that vvhich a man hath giuen or laboured. & to requite you vvith some profane authoritie, because you delight

κτ' τὰ ἔργα αὐτοῦ εὑρήσει.

λαβεῖν ἀνθ' ὧν τις ἔδωκεν ἢ ἐποίησεν.

much in that kinde) the vvhole oration of Demosthenes πρὸς λεπτίνην, vvil tel you the same. Novv, to receiue for that vvhich a man hath laboured or vvrought, vvhat doth it els presuppose, but merite & desert? It is a common phrase of the Scripture, that God vvil iudge and revvard or repay according to euery mans vvorkes. doth not this include merite & demerite of vvorkes? but I vvot not hovv, nor vvherfore, in this case you translate sometime, *deedes*, for *vvorkes*, saying, *Vvho vvil revvard euery man according to his deedes.* and againe, *You see then hovv that of deedes a man is iustified, and not of faith only.*

εὑρεῖν ἀλήθειαν.

Ecclsi 16. Psal. 61. Apoc. 22.

κατὰ τὰ ἔργα αὐτοῦ. ἐξ ἔργων.

20 I knovv you vvil tel vs that you vse to say *deedes* or *vvorkes* indifferently, as also you may say, that you put no difference betvvene *iust* and *righteous*, *meete* and *vvorthie*, but vse both indifferently. To the ignorant this is a faire ansvver, and shal soone persuade them: but they that see further, must needes suspect you, til you giue a good reason of your doing. For, the controuersie being of faith and *vvorkes*, of *iustice* and *iustification* by vvorkes, of the *vvorthines* or value of vvorkes: vvhy do you not precisely keepe these termes pertaining to the controuersie, the Greeke wordes being alwaies pregnant in that significatiõ? Vvhy should you once translate the Greeke ἔργα, *deedes*, rather

rather then, *vvorkes*. You knovv it is proprely, *vvorkes*, as πράξεις, *deedes*. It vvere very good in matters of cõtrouersie to be precise. Beza maketh it a great fault in the old vulgar Latin translator, that he expresseth one Greeke vvord in Latin diuers vvaies. You choppe & Change significations here and there as you list, and you thinke you satisfie the reader maruelous vvel, if sometime you say *idol*, and not alvvaies, *images*: sometime *iust*, and not alvvaies *righteous*: & if in other places you say vvorkes, or if one Bible hath vvorkes, vvhere an other hath deedes, you thinke this is very vvel and vvil ansvver al the matter sufficiently. God and your conscience be iudge herein, and let the wise reader consider it deepely. The least thing that vve demaund the reason of, rather then charge you vvithal, is, vvhy your Church bible saith in the places before alleaged, *The righteous iudgement of God, vvhich vvil revvard euery man according to his deedes.* and, *man is iustified by deedes, and not by faith only.* Vvhereas yov knovv the Greeke is more pregnant for vs then so, and the matter of controuersie vvould better appeare on our side, if you said thus: *The* IVST *iudgement of God, vvhich vvel revvard euery man according to his* VVORKES. and, *Man is iustified by vvorkes, and not by faith only.*

Prefat. in no. Test. 1556.

δικαιοκρισία. ἔργα. ἐξ ἔργων.

21 But vvil you not yet see merite and merito-

meritorious vvorkes in the Scripture? I maruel your ſkil in the Greeke teacheth you nothing in this point. S. Iohn ſaith: *Looke to your ſelues, that you loſe not the things which you haue vvrought, but that you may receiue a full revvard.* Me thinketh, in theſe wordes the equiualẽt of merite is eaſily ſeen of any mã that is not wilfully blinde. but you ſhould ſee further then the cõmon ſort. for you know that the Greeke here ſignifieth, not only that which vve worke, but that which we worke for. as in the Greeke phraſe of vvorking for a mãs liuing, & as you tranſlate Io. 6. v. 27. LABOVR NOT FOR THE MEATE *that periſheth*, but *for that meate vvhich endureth vnto life euerlaſting.* Such * labourers God hired to vvorke in his vineyard, and [c] *the vvorkeman is vvorthie of his hire.* So that the Apoſtle in the former vvordes exhorteth to perſeuẽrãce, that vve loſe not the revvard or pay, for vvhich vve vvorke, and vvhich by vvorking vve merite and deſerue.

2. Epiſt. v. 8.
ἃ εἰργάσασθε.
ἐργάζεσθαι τὸν βίον.
ἐργάζεσθε τὴν βρῶσιν.
* ἐργάτας Mat. 20.
ἐργάτης Luc. 10.

22 Againe Beza telleth vs, that ἀντιμισθία ſignifieth *mercedem quæ meritis reſpondet*, that is, a revvard anſvverable to the merites. and vve finde many vvordes in the Scripture like vnto this, μισθὸς, ἀπόδοσις, * μισθαποδοσία, μισθαποδότης, Vvhich are on Gods part, vvho is the revvarder and recõpenſer. and on our part vve haue (as the Apoſtle ſaith, Hebr. 10. & 4) *great confidence. cõfidence* (ſaith Photius a notable

Annot. in Ro. c. 1. v. 27
ἀντιμισθία.
* Hebr. 2. & 11.
παρρησία.

notable Greeke father) *of our vvorkes, confidence of our faith, of our tentations, of our patience. &c.* Yea vve haue ἀνταπόδοσις & ἀντάμειψις in the Scripture, vvhich must needes signifie as much as Bezaes ἀντιμισθία. By the one, is said, *In keeping thy commaundements is great revvard.* Againe, *You shal receiue* THE RETRIBVTION *of inheritance.* Col. 3. v. 24. And 2 Thessal. 1. v. 6. Gods repaying iust and retribution of Hel or Heauen for good and euil desertes, is expressed by the same vvord. & by the other, is said, *I haue inclined my hart to keepe thy iustifications* (or commaundements) alvvaies FOR REWARD.

τὴν ἀπὸ τῶν ἔργων, &c. Phot. apud Oecu. in Hebr. 10. Ps. 18. & 118. ἀνταπόδοσις πολλή. ἀνταποδοῦναι. διʼ ἀντάμειψιν.

23 But al this vvil not suffise you. for vvheresoeuer you can possibly you vvil haue an euasion. and therfore in this later place you runne to the ambiguitie of the Hebrue vvord, and translate thus: *I haue applied my hart to fulfil thy statutes alvvaies,* EVEN VNTO THE END. Alas my masters, are not the Seuentie Greeke interpreters sufficient to determine the ambiguitie of this vvord? is not S. Hierom, in his translation according to the Hebrue? are not al the auncient fathers both Greeke and Latin? It is ambiguous (say you) and therfore you take your libertie. You doe so in deede, and that like Princes. for in an other place, vvhere the Greeke hath determined, you folovv it vvith al your hart, saying, *fall dovvne before his fotestoole*

עֵקֶב

ὅτι ἅγιος ἐστι

footeſtoole, becauſe he is holy: vvhereas the ambiguitie of the Hebrue, vvould haue borne you to ſay, as in the vulgar Latin, *becauſe it is holy.* and ſo it maketh for holines of places, vvhich you can not abide.

קדוש הוא

24 But you vſe (you ſay) the ambiguitie of the Hebrue. Take heede that your libertie in taking al aduantages, againſt the common and approued interpretation of the vvhole Church, be not very ſuſpicious. for if it do ſignifie alſo revvard, as (you knovv) it doth very commonly, and your ſelf ſo tranſlate it (Pſal.18, v.11) vvhen you can not chooſe: and if the Septuaginta do here ſo tranſlate it in Greeke, and * S. Hierom in his Latin tranſlation according to the Hebrue, and the auncient fathers in their commentaries: vvhat vpſtart nevv Maiſters are you that ſet al theſe to ſchoole againe, and teach the vvorld a nevv tranſlation? If you vvil ſay, you folovv our ovvne great Hebrician, Sanctes Pagninus. vvhy did you folovv him in his tranſlation, rather then in his Lexicon called Theſaurus, vvhere he interpreteth it as the vvhole Church did before him? Vvhy did you folovv him (or Benedictus Arias either) in this place, and do not folovv them in the ſelf ſame caſe, a litle before tranſlating that very Hebrue vvord vvhich is in this place, *propter retributionem*

* Propter æternam retributioné. ſcz vitę ęternæ, vt eam merear percipere. *in cō-ment.*

Pſalm.118. v.112.

butionem , for revvard ? So that you folovv
עֵקֶב nothing, neither iudgemẽt nor, learning in Hebrue or Greeke, but only your ovvne errour and Heresie, vvhich is, that vve may not do vvel in respect of revvard, or, for revvard. and therfore because the holy Prophet Dauid said of him self the cõtrarie, that he did bend his vvhole hart to keepe Gods cõmaundements *for revvard*, you make him say an other thing.

25 And to this purpose perhaps it is (for other cause I can not gesse) that you make such a maruelous transposition of vvordes in your transliation (Mat. 19.) saying thus: *Vvhen the Sonne of man shal sit in the throne of his maiestie, ye that haue folovved me in the regeneratiõ, shal sit also vpõ tvvelue seates.* Whereas the order of these vvordes both in Greeke and Latin, is this: *You that haue folovved me, in the regeneration, vvhen the Sonne of man shal sit in his maiestie, you also shal sit vpon tvvelue seates.* To folovv Christ in the regeneration, is not easily vnderstood vvhat it should meane: but to sit vvith Christ in the regeneration, that is, in the resurrection, vpon 12 seates, this is familiar and euery mans interpretation, and concerneth the great revvard that they shal then haue, vvhich here folovv Christ as the Apostles did.

No. Test. 1580. 26 The like transposition of vvordes is in some of your Bibles (Hebr. 2. v. 9.) thus.

Vve

Vve see IESVS *crovvned vvith glorie and honour, vvhich vvas a litle inferior to the Angels, through the suffring of death.* Vvhereas both in Greeke and Latin, the order of the vvordes is thus: *Him that was made a litle inferior to Angels, vve see* IESVS, *through the passion of death, crovvned vvith honour and glorie.* In this later, the Apostle saith, that Christ vvas crovvned for his suffring death, and so by his death merited his glorie. but by your translation, he saith that Christ vvas made inferior to Angels by his suffring death, that is (saith Beza) *For to suffer death*: and taking it so, that he vvas made inferior to Angels, that he might die, then the other sense is cleane excluded, that for suffering death he vvas crovvned vvith glorie: & this is one place among other, wherby it may very vvel be gathered that ⋆ some of you thinke that Christ him self did not merite his ovvne glorie and exaltation. So obstinatly are you set against merites and meritorious vvorkes. To the vvhich purpose also you take avvay mans free vvil, as hauing no habilitie to vvorke tovvard his ovvne saluation.

Vt mori posset.

See Caluin in epist. ad Philip.

CHAP. X.

Heretical translation against FREE VVIL.

1 AGAINST free vvil your corruptions be these. Io. 1, 12.
ἐξουσίαν. vvhere it is said, *As many as receiued him, he gaue them povver to be*
No. Test, 1580. *made the sonnes of God:* some of
your translations say, he gaue them *prerogatiue* to be the sonnes of God. Beza, *dignitie.*
Vvho protesteth that vvhereas in other
places often he trāslated this Greeke vvord,
povver and *authoritie*, here he refused both, in
deede against free vvil, vvhich he saith the
Sophistes vvould proue out of this place,
Vt liceret filios Dei fieri reprehending Erasmus for folovving them
in his translation. But vvhereas the Greeke
vvord is indifferent to signifie *dignitie*, or *libertie*, he that vvil translate either of these,
restraineth the sense of the holy Ghost and
determineth it to his ovvne fansie. If you
may translate, *dignitie*: may not vve as vvel
trāslate it, *libertie?* yes surely. For you knovv
it signifieth the one as vvel as the other
both in profane and Diuine vvriters. and
you can vvel call to minde αὐτεξούσιος, and
τὸ αὐτεξούσιον, vvhence they are deriued, and
that the Apostle calleth a mans libertie of
1 Cor. 7, 37. his ovvne vvill, ἐξουσίαν περὶ τοῦ ἰδίου θελήμα-
τος. Novv then if *potestas* in Latin, and *povver*
in English, be vvordes also indifferent to
signifie both dignitie and libertie, translate
so in the name of God, and leaue the text
of

of the Scripture indifferent as vve doe: and for the ſenſe vvhether of the tvvo it doth here rather ſignifie, or vvhether it doth not ſignifie both (as no doubt it doth, & the fathers ſo expound it) let that be examined othervviſe. It is a common fault vvith you and intolerable, by your tranſlation to abridge the ſenſe of the holy Ghoſt to one particular vnderſtāding, and to defeate the expoſition of ſo many fathers, that expoūd it in an other ſenſe and ſignification. As is plaine in this example alſo folovving.

2 The Apoſtle (1 Cor. 15, 10.) ſaith thus: *I, laboured more aboundantly then al they: yet not I, but the grace of God vvith me.* Vvhich may haue this ſenſe, *not I, but the grace of God which is with me,* as S. Hierom ſometime expoūdeth it: or this, *not I, but the grace of God vvhich laboured vvith me.* & by this later is moſt euidētly ſignified, that the grace of God and the Apoſtle, both laboured together, and not only grace, as though the Apoſtle had done nothing, like vnto a blocke, forced only: but that the grace of God did ſo concurre as the principal agent vvith al his labours, that his free vvil vvrought vvithal. Againſt vvhich truth & moſt approued interpretatiō of this place, you trāſlate according to the former ſenſe only, making it the very text, & ſo excludīg al other ſenſes and commentaries, as your

ἡ χάρις τοῦ θεοῦ ἡ σὺν ἐμοί.

Maiſters Caluin & Beza taught you, vvho ſhould not haue taught you if you vvere vviſe, to doe that vvhich neither they nor you can iuſtifie. They reprehend firſt the vulgar Latin interpreter for neglecting the Greeke article, and ſecondly them that by occaſiō thereof, would by this place proue free vvil. by vvhich their cōmentarie they do plainely declare their intent and purpoſe in their tranſlation, to be directly againſt free vvil.

ἡ χάρις ἡ σὺν ἐμοί.

3 But concerning the Greeke article omitted in tranſlation, if they vvere but Grammarians in both tongues, they might knovv that the Greeke article many times can not be expreſſed in Latin, and that this is one felicitie & prerogatiue of the Greeke phraſe aboue the Latin, to ſpeake more briefely, commodiouſly, and ſignificantly, by the article. Vvhat neede vve goe to Terence and Homer, as they are vvont? Is not the Scripture ful of ſuch ſpeaches? *Iacobus Zebedæi, Iacobus Alphæi, Iudas* Iacobi, *Maria Cleophæ*, and the like. Are not al theſe ſincerely trāſlated into Latin, though the Greeke article be not expreſſed? Can you expreſſe the article, but you muſt adde more then the article, and ſo adde to the text, as you doe very boldly in ſuch ſpeaches through out the nevv Teſtament, yea you doe it vvhen there

there is no article in the Greeke: as Io.5,36. (vvitnes)
and 1 ep.Io.2,2. Yea ſometime of an here- (ſinnes.)
tical purpoſe: as Eph.3. *By vvhom vve haue bold-* Bib.1562.
neſſe and entrance vvith the confidence vvhich is by the
faith of him, or, *in him*, as it is in other your bi- No.Teſt. 1580.
bles. You ſay, *confidence vvhich is by faith*, as
though there vvere no confidence by workes: you knovv the Greeke beareth not
that tranſlation, vnles there vvere an article ἐν πεποιθή-
after, *confidence*, vvhich is not, but you adde σει, διὰ τῆς
it to the text heretically. as alſo Beza doth πίστεως.
the like (Ro. 8,2.) and your Geneua En-
gliſh Teſtamēts after him, for the hereſie of
imputatiue iuſtice: as in his Annotations
he plainely deduceth, ſaying confidently,
I doubt not but a Greeke article muſt be vnderſtood, τοῦ πνεύ-
and therfore (forſoth) put into the text ματος (τοῦ)
alſo. He doth the ſame in S. Iames 2, v. 20: ἡ πίστις (ἡ).
ſtill debating the caſe in his Annotations
vvhy he doth ſo, and vvhen he hath concluded in his fanſie, that this or that is the
ſenſe, he putteth it ſo in the text, and tranſlateth accordingly. Nō maruel now, if they
reprehend the vulgar Latin interpreter for
not tranſlating the Greeke article in the
place vvhich vve began to treate of, vvhen
they finde articles lacking in the Greeke
text it ſelf, and boldly adde them for their
purpoſe in their tranſlation. Vvhereas the
vulgar Latin interpretation is in al theſe

 places

places so sincere, that it neither addeth nor diminisheth, nor goeth one iote from the Greeke.

Non ego, sed gratia Dei mecum.

4 But you vvil say in the place to the Corinthians, there is a Greeke article, and therfore there you doe vvel to expresse it. I ansvver, first, the article may then be expressed in translation, vvhen there can be but one sense of the same: secondly, that not only it may, but it must be expressed, vvhen vve can not othervvise giue the sense of the place. as Mat. 1, 6. *Ex ea quæ fuit Vriæ.* Vvhere you see the vulgar interpreter omitteth it not, but knovveth the force & signification thereof very vvel. mary in the place of S. Paul vvhich vve novv speake of, vvhere the sense is doubtful, & the Latin expresseth the Greeke sufficiētly othervvise, he leaueth it also doubtful and indifferent, nor abridging it as you do, saying, *the grace of God vvhich is vvith me:* nor as Caluin, *gratia quæ mihi aderat:* nor as Illyricus, *gratia quæ mihi adest.* Vvhich tvvo later are more absurde then yours, because they omit and neglect altogether the force of the preposition, *cum,* vvhich you expresse saying, *with me.* but because you say, *which is vvith me:* you meane heretically as they doe, to take away the Apostles cooperation and labouring together vvith the grace of God, by his free

ἐκ τῆς τοῦ Οὐρίου.

ἡ χάρις ἡ σὺν ἐμοί.

σὺν ἐμοί.

free vvil: vvhich is by the article and the prepoſition moſt euidently ſignified.

5 And here I appeale to al that haue ſkil in Greeke ſpeaches and Phraſes, vvhether the Apoſtles vvordes in Greeke, ſound not thus: I *laboured more abound antly then al they: yet not I, but the grace of God (that laboured) vvith me.* Vnderſtanding not the participle of *Sum,* but of the verbe going before. as in the like caſe vvhen our Sauiour ſaith, *It is not you that ſpeake, but the holy Ghoſt that ſpeaketh in you.* If he had ſpoken ſhort thus, *but the holy Ghoſt in you,* you perhaps vvould tranſlate as you doe here, *the holy Ghoſt* WHICH IS IN YOV. but you ſee the verbe going before is rather repeated, *Not you ſpeake, but the holy Ghoſt* THAT SPEAKETH IN YOV. Euen ſo, *Not I laboured, but the grace of God labouring vvith me,* or, WHICH LABOVRED WITH ME. So praieth the vviſe man Sap. 9, 10. Send vviſedom out of thy holy heauens, that ſhe may be vvith me, *and labour vvith me* as your ſelues tranſlate. Bib. 1577.

ἐκοπίασα: οὐκ ἐγὼ δὲ, ἀλλ' ἡ χάρις τοῦ θεοῦ ἡ σὺν ἐμοί (συγκοπιάσασα, συνεργουμένη &c.) τὸ πνεῦμα τὸ ἐν ὑμῖν.

Et mecum laboret.

6 And ſo the Apoſtle calleth him ſelf and his felovv preachers, *Gods coadiutors,* collabourers, or ſuch as labour and vvorke vvith God, vvhich alſo you falſely tranſlate, *Gods labourers,* to take avvay al cooperation, and in ſome of your Bibles moſt foliſhly and peeuiſhly, as though you had ſvvorne not to tranſlate the Greeke, *Vve together are*

θεοῦ συνεργοί, S. Auguſtine, *Cooperarij,* & 2 Cor. 6, 1. συνεργοῦντες δὲ.

Gods

συγκληρο-νόμοι χρι-στοῦ.

Gods labourers. as vvel might you translate (Ro. 8, 17) that *vve together be Christs heires:* for that, vvhich the Apostle saith *coheires*, or *ioynt heires vvith him*: the phrase and speach (as you know) in Greeke being al one. So doth Beza most falsely translate, *Vna viuificauit nos per Christum*, for that vvhich is plaine in the Greeke, *He hath quickened vs together vvith Christ*, Vvhere the English Bezites leaue also the Greeke, and folovv our vulgar Latin translation rather then Beza, vvho goeth so vvide from the Greeke, that for shame they dare not folovv him. Fie vpon such hypocrisie & pretensed honour of God, that you vvil not speake in the same termes that the holy Scripture speaketh, but rather vvil teach the holy Ghost hovv to speake, in not translating as he speaketh. As though these phrases of Scripture, men are Gods coadiutors, covvorkers with his grace, raised vvith Christ, coheirs vvith him, compartakers of glorie vvith him, vvere al spoken to the dishonour of God and Christ, & as though these being the speaches of the holy Ghost him self, needed your reformation in your English trãslatiõs. Otherwise if you meane vvel, and vvould say as vve say, that whatsoeuer good vve doe, vve doe it by Gods grace, and yet vvorke the same by our free wil together vvith Gods grace as the mouer and

Eph. 2. v. 5.

The English translators are ashamed of their Maister.

and helper and directer of our vvil: vvhy do you not translate in the foresaid place of S. Paul accordingly?

7 You say moreouer in some of your Bibles thus: *So lieth it not then in a mãs vvill or running, but in the mercie of God.* Vvhatsoeuer you meane, you knovv this translation is very dissolute and vvide from the Apostles vvordes, and not true in sense. for saluation is in vvilling and running: according to that famous saying of S. Augustine, *He that made thee vvithout thee, vvil not iustifie thee vvithout thee*: that is, against thy vvil, or, vnles thou be vvilling. and the Apostle saith, *No man is crovvned, vnles he fight lavvfully.* and againe, *So runne* THAT YOV MAY *obtaine.* and againe, *The doers of the Lavv shal be iustified.* And our Sauiour, *If thou vvilt enter into life, keepe the commaundements.* Vve see then that it is in vvilling, and running, & doing: but to vvil, or runne, or doe, are not of man, but of GODS mercie. and so the Apostle speaketh, *It is not of the vviller, nor runner, but of God that hath mercie.* And it is much to be marueled, vvhy you said not, *It lieth not in the vviller, nor in the runner*: vvhich is neere to the Apostles vvordes, but so far of, *in a mans vvill and running.*

Bib. 1562. οὐ θέλοντος, τρέχοντος, ἀλλ' ἐλεοῦντος.

Aug. Serm. 15 de verb. Apostoli.

2 Timoth. 2.
1 Cor. 9.
Rom. 2.
Mat. 19.

8 Againe, touching cõtinencie & the chast single life, you translate thus: *Al men can not receiue this saying.* Mat. 19. v. 11. Novv you vvot vvel,

οὐ πάντες χωροῦσι.

Maruelous strang translation. vvel, that our Sauiour saith not, *Al men can not*, but, *al men doe not* receiue it: and that therfore, (as S. Augustine saith) because al vvil
De grat. & lib. arb. c. 4. not. But when our Sauiour aftervvard saith, *He that* CAN *receiue it, let him receiue it*: he addeth
ὁ δυνάμενος χωρεῖν, χωρείτω. an other Greeke vvord to expresse that sense. vvhereas by your fond translation he might haue said, ὁ χωρῶν χωρείτω. and againe by your translation, you should translate these his later vvordes thus: *He that can or is able to receiue it, let him be able to receiue it.* For so you translate χωρεῖν before, as though it vvere al one vvith δύνασθαι χωρεῖν. Do you not see your follie, & falshod, & boldnes, to make the reader beleeue that our Sauiour should say, Euery man can not liue chast, it is impossible for them, and therfore no man should vovv chastitie, because he knovveth not vvhether he can liue so or no?

Bibl. 1579. 9 Againe in some of your Bibles (Gen. 4. v. 7.) where God saith plainely, that Cain should receiue according as he did vvel or euil, because sinne vvas subiect vnto him, and he had the rule and dominion thereof, euidently declaring his free vvill: you translate it thus, *If thou doest vvel, shalt thou not be accepted? and if thou doest not vvel, sinne lieth at the doore: and also vnto thee* HIS *desire shal be subiect, and thou shalt rule ouer* HIM. By vvhich relatiues falsely put in the masculine gender, you, exclude

clude the true antecedent *sinne*, and referre them to Abel Cains brother. as though God had said, not that sinne should be in his dominiõ or subiect vnto him, but his brother Abel. But that this is most false and absurd, vve proue many vvaies. First S. Augustine saith directly the contrarie: *Tu dominaberis illius: nunquid Fratris? absit. cuius igitur nisi peccati. Thou shalt rule* (saith he) *ouer vvhat? Ouer thy brother? Not so. ouer vvhat then but sinne?* S. Hierom also explicateth this place thus: *Because thou hast free vvill, I vvarne thee that sinne haue not dominion ouer thee, but thou ouer sinne.* Moreouer the text it self, if nothing els, is sufficient to conuince this absurditie. For vvhere this vvord, *sinne*, goeth immediatly before in the same sentence, and not one vvord of Abel his brother in that speache of God to Cain, hovv is it possible, or vvhat coherence can there be in saying as you translate, *sinne lieth at the doore, and thou shalt haue dominion ouer him*, that is, *thy brother*. but if vve say thus, *Sinne lieth at the doore, and thou shalt haue dominion thereof*: it hath this direct & plaine sense, If thou doest ill, sinne lieth at the doore ready to condemne thee, because it is in thee to ouerrule it.

Li. 15. c. 7. de Ciuit. Dei.

Quæst. Heb. in Genes.

10 Novv if against the coherence of the text, and exposition of the holy Doctors and of the vvhole Church of God, you pretend

tend the Hebrue grammar forſooth, as not bearing ſuch conſtruction: not to trouble the common reader that can not iudge of theſe things, and yet fully to ſatisfie euery man euen of common vnderſtanding, vve requeſt here the Aduerſaries them ſelues to tel vs truely according to their knovvledge and ſkill, vvhether the Hebrue conſtruction or point of grammar be not al one in theſe vvordes, *Sinne* LIETH *at the doore*: & in theſe, *the deſire* THEREOF *ſhal be ſubiect to thee,* & *thou ſhalt rule ouer* IT. If they ſay (as they muſt needes) that the Hebrue conſtruction or Syntaxis is al one, then vvil it folovv that the Hebrue beareth the one as vvel as the other: & therfore vvhen the ſelf ſame tranſlation of theirs maketh no ſcruple of Grammar in the former, but tranſlate as vve doe, *Sinne lieth at the doore*: a blinde man may ſee that in the later vvordes alſo, the Hebrue is but a fooliſh pretence, and that the true cauſe of tranſlating them othervviſe, procedeth of an heretical humor, to obſcure and deface this ſo plaine and euident Scripture for mans free vvill.

חַטָּאת רֹבֵץ. אֵלֶיךָ תְּשׁוּקָתוֹ תִּמְשָׁל־בּוֹ.

11 And as for the Hebrue grammar in this point, vvere it not for troubling the reader, vve could tel them that the vvord, *ſinne*, in Hebrue is not here of the fœminine gender (as they ſuppoſe) but of the maſcu-

line

line. so saith S. Hierom expresly vpon this place, vvho had as much knovvledge in the Hebrue tongue as al these nevv Doctors. Aben Ezra also the great Rabbine, in his Hebrue commẽtaries vpon this text, saith, it is a mere forgerie and fiction to referre the masculine relatiue othervvise then to the vvord, *sinne*: vvhich, though els vvhere it be the feminine gender, yet here it is a masculine, according to that rule of the Grammarians, that the doubtful gender must be discerned by the verbe, adiectiue, pronovvne, or participle ioyned vvith the same: as the said Hebrue doctor doth in the vvord, *paradise*, Gen. 2. vvhich there by the pronovvnes he pronounceth to be a feminine, though els vvhere a masculine. Lastly, if the vvord, *sinne*, vvere here and alvvaies onely a feminine, & neuer a masculine: yet they haue litle skil in the Hebrue tongue, that thinke it strange to matche masculines and feminines together in very good and grammatical constructiõ. Vvherof they may see a vvhole chapter in Sanctes Pagninus vvith this title, *Fœminea masculeis iuncta.* that is, Feminines ioyned vvith masculines.

q. Hebr. in Genes.

Quinquarboreus.

12 Novv for the last refuge, if they vvil say al this needed not, because in other their bibles it is as vve vvould haue it: vve

tel

tel them, they muſt iuſtifie and make good al their tranſlations, becauſe the people readeth al, and is abuſed by al, and al come forth vvith priuiledge, printed by the Q. printer &c. If they vvil not, let them confeſſe the faultes, and call them in, and tell vs vvhich tranſlation or trãſlations they vvill ſtand vnto. In the meane time they muſt be content to heare of al indifferently, as there ſhal be cauſe and occaſion to touche them.

No. Teſt. 1580.

13 Againe they tranſlate in ſome of their Bibles againſt free vvill, thus, *Chriſt, vvhen vve vvere yet* OF NO STRENGTH, *died for the vngodly.* Ro. 5. v. 6. The Apoſtles vvord doth not ſignifie that vve had no ſtrenght, but that vve vvere vveake, feeble, infirme. Man vvas vvounded in free vvil by the ſinne of Adam (as he that in the Goſpel vvent dovvne from Hieruſalem to Iericho, vvhich is a parable of this thing) he vvas not ſlaine altogether. but I ſtand not here, or in any place to diſpute the controuerſie, that is done els vvhere. This onely I ſay, becauſe *they falſely hold that free vvill vvas altogether loſt by Adams ſinne, therfore they tranſlate accordingly, *Vvhen vve had no ſtrength.* But the Greeke vvord is vvel knovven both in profane authors and Eccleſiaſtical, and ſpecially in the nevv Teſtament it ſelf, through

ὄντων ἡμῶν ἀσθενῶν.

Luc. 10.

*Vvhitakers pag. 18.

through out, to ſignifie nothing els, but, vveake, feeble, ſicke, infirme. looke me through the nevv Teſtamẽt, vvhereſoeuer, infirmitie, feeblenes, languiſhing, and the like are ſpoken of, there is found this Greeke vvord to expreſſe it. Vvhat Grecian knovveth not (be he but ſimply acquainted vvith phraſes and nature of vvordes) vvhat ἀσθενεῖν, and ἀσθενῶς ἔχειν, doe ſignifie. Vvhen the Apoſtle ſaith, *Quis infirmatur, & ego non vror? Vvho is vveake and infirme, and I am not much greiued?* ſhal vve tranſlate, *vvho is of no ſtrength*, &c. or let them giue vs an inſtance, vvhere it is certaine that this vvord muſt needes ſignifie, *of no ſtrength*. Vvil they pretend the etymologie of the vvord? a ridiculous and abſurd euaſion. vve aſke them of ῥώμη, a vvord of the very ſame ſignificatiõ, vvhich being compounded in like maner as the other, vvhat doth it ſignifie? any thing els but infirmitie and feeblenes? Yea it is ſo far from ſignifying, *no ſtrength*, that the greateſt Grecians ſay, it is not ſpoken propre ly of him that for vveakenes keepeth his bedde, vvhich is νοσεῖν, but of him that is il diſpoſed and diſtempered in body. Yet the etymologie is al one vvith that word vvhich theſe men vvil haue to ſignifie him that hath no ſtrength. And if they vvil needes vrge the etymologie, vve tel them, that σθένος & ῥώμη ſignifie

Multi inter vos infirmi ſũt &c. 1 Cor. 11. v. 30.

Cùm infirmor, tum potens ſum. 2 Cor. 12. v. 10. & alibi.

2 Cor. 11, 29

σθένος and ἀ priuatiuũ. ἄῤῥωςος. ἀῤῥωςεῖν. ἀῤῥωςία.

Lexicon magnum Baſileæ.

περὶ τοῦ καχεκτοῦντος τῷ σώματι.

signifie, *robur*, that is, great strength such as is in the strongest and stoutest champions. and so the etymologie may take place, to signifie a man of no great strength, not, of no strength. But M. Vvhitaker putteth vs in good hope, they vvill not stand vpon etymologies.

pag. 209.

14 Vvhen they haue bereaued and spoiled a man of his free vvill, & left him vvithout al strength, they goe so far in this point, that * they say, the regenerate them selues haue not free vvil and abilitie, no not by and vvith the grace of God, to keepe the commaundements. To this purpose they translate (Io. 5, 3) thus: *His commaundements are not greuous*. rather then thus, *His commaundements are not heauie*. for in saying, *they are not heauie*, it vvould folovv, they might be kept & obserued: but in saying, *they are not greuous*, that may be true, were they neuer so heauie or impossible, through patience. As vvhen a man can not doe as he vvould, yet it greeueth him not, being patient and vvise, because he is content to doe as he can, and is able. Therfore doe they choose to translate, that the commaundements are not greuous, vvhere the Apostle saith rather, they are not heauie. much more agreably to our Sauiours vvordes, *My burden is light* : and to the wordes of God by Moyses, Deu. 30. *This commaunde-*

Beza in Annot. Ro. 2, 27.

Mādata eius grauia non sunt. αἱ ἐντολαὶ βαρεῖαι οὐκ εἰσί.

maundement vvhich I commaund thee this day, is not aboue thee (that is, beyond thy reache) *but the vvord is very neere thee, in thy mouth and in thy hart, that thou maiest doe it*: and to the cõmon signification of the Greeke vvord, vvhich is, *heauie*. Beza vvould say somevvhat in his commentarie, hovv the commaundements are heauie or light, but his conclusion is against free vvill, and that there can be no perfection in this life, inueighing against them that would proue it out of this place: vvhich is as much to say (but he is ashamed to speake plainely) that vve can not keepe the cõmaundements: vvhich the holy Doctors haue long since condemned & abhorred as most absurd, that God should commaũd that, vnder paine of dãnation, which is impossible to be done.

οὐκ ὑπέρογκός ἐστι. לֹא נִפְלֵאת מִמְּךָ βαρύς.

15 Thus hauing taken avvay free vvil to doe good, and possibilitie to keepe the cõmaundements, and al merite or valure and efficacie of good vvorkes, their next conclusion is, that vve haue no true iustice or righteousnes in vs, but an imputatiue iustice, that is, Christs iustice imputed to vs, be vve neuer so foule and filthie in our soules, so that vve beleeue only, and by faith apprehend Christs iustice. For this purpose they corrupt the Scriptures in their English bibles, thus.

CHAP XI.

Heretical translation for IMPVTATIVE IVSTICE, *against true inherent iustice.*

1 ONE place might suffise, in steede of many, vvhere Beza doth protest, that his adding or alteration of the text, is, specially against
Annot. in Rom. 5, 18. *the execrable errour of inherent iustice*, vvhich (he saith) is to be auoided as nothing more. His false translation, thus our English Bezites and Caluinists folovv in their Bibles.
Rom. 5. *Likevvise then as by the offense of one*, the fault came *on al men to condemnation: so by the iustifying of one*, the benefite abounded, *tovvard al men to the iustification of life*. Vvhere there are added to the text of the Apostle, sixe vvordes: and the same so vvilfully and voluntarily, that by the three first, they make the Apostle say, sinne came on al men by Adam, and they vvere made sinners in deede: by the three later, they make him say, not that iustice or righteousnes came likevvise on al men by Christ, to make them iust in deede, but that the benefite of Christs iustice abounded tovvards them, as being imputed forsooth vnto them. Vvhereas, if they Would needes adde to the text (vvhich yet is intolerable, so much, and in so doubtful a case) they should

should at the least haue made the case equal, as the Apostle him self teacheth them to doe, in the very next sentence, saying thus, *For as by one mans disobedience many vvere made sinners, so by the obedience of one shal many also be made righteous.* so they translate, rather then, *be made iust.* For they are the lothest men in the vvorld to say that vve are made iust, for feare of iustice inherent in vs, though the Scripture be neuer so plaine. as here vve see the Apostle maketh the case like, that vve are made iust by Christ, as vve vvere made sinners by Adam.

2 And it is a vvorld to see, hovv Beza shifteth from one significatiõ of the vvord *iustified*, or, *made iust*, to an other. Sometime to be iustified, is to be pronoũced quitte from al sinne, or declared iust before Gods iudgement seate: & so he trãslateth it in the text Act. 13. v. 39. and as though his guilty conscience vvere afraid of a blovv, he saith he fleeth not the terme of iustifying or iustification, because he vseth it in other places. He doth so in deede, but then his commentarie supplieth the turne: as Ro. 2. v. 13. *Not the hearers of the Lavv are* RIGHTEOVS *before God* (so they delight to trãslate, rather then, IVST *before God*) *but the doers of the Lavv shal be* IVSTIFIED. that is (saith Beza) *shal be pronounced iust.* The Apostle must needes say by

δικαιωθῆναι. absolui. δικαιοῦται. absoluitur.

Iusti pronũtiabuntur.

 the

the coherence and consequence of his vvordes, not the hearers are iust, but the doers shal be iust or iustified. Beza vvil in no case haue it so, but either in text or commentarie make the Apostle say as him self imagineth. Yet in an other place he protesteth very solemnely, that to be iustified, is not, to be pronounced or accounted iust, but rather to be iust in deede: and that, he proueth out of S. Paul, Ro. 5. v. 19. vvho maketh it al one, *to be iustified*, &, *to be made iust.* and againe by this reason, that it should be manifestly repugnant to Gods iustice, to account him for iust, that is not iust, and therfore that mã in deede is made iust. Thus Beza. Vvould you not thinke, he vvere come to be of our opinion? but he reuolteth againe, & interpreteth al these goodly vvordes in his old sense, saying, *Not that any qualitie is invvardly giuen vnto vs, of vvhich vve are named iust: but because the iustice of Christ is imputed to vs by faith freely.* By faith then at the least vve are truely iustified. Not so neither, but *faith* (saith he) *is an instrument vvherevvith vve apprehẽd Christ our iustice.* So that vve haue no more iustice in vs, then vve haue glorie: for glorie also vve apprehend by faith.

Annot. Ro. 3. v. 20.

δικαιοῦσθαι δίκαιον καθίστασθαι.

Non quasi nobis indatur qualitas.

Annot. in Ro. 4. v. 2.

Pro iustitia. εἰς δικαιοσύνην.

3 For this purpose both he and the English Bibles translate thus: *Abraham beleeued God, and it vvas reputed to him* FOR IVSTICE

Ro. 4.

Ro. 4 v. 3. & 9 Vvhere he interpreteth, *for iustice*, to be nothing els but, *in the steede & place of iustice*: so also taking avvay true inherent iustice euen from Abraham him self. But to admit their translation (vvhich notvvithstanding in their sense is most false) must it needes signifie, not true inherent iustice, because the Scripture saith, it vvas reputed for iustice? Doe such speaches import, that it is not so in deede, but is onely reputed so? Then if vve say, This shal be reputed to thee for sinne: for a great benefite, and so forth: it should signifie, it is no sinne in deede, nor great benefite. But let them call to minde, that the Scripture vseth to speake of sinne & of iustice alike. *It shal be sinne in thee*, or, *vnto thee*, as they translate Bibl. 1577: or as S. Hierom translateth, *It shal be reputed to thee for sinne*: Deut. c. 23 & 24. and (as them selues translate) *it shal be righteousnes vnto thee, before the Lord thy God.* & againe Deut. c 6. *This shal be our righteousnes before the Lord our God, if vve keepe al the commaundements, as he hath commaunded vs.* If then iustice only be reputed, sinne also is only reputed: if sinne be in vs in deede, iustice is in vs in deede.

Vice & loco

Reputabitur tibi in peccatum.

הָיָה בְךָ חֵטְא

ἔσαι ἐν σοὶ ἁμαρτία.

צְדָקָה תִּהְיֶה לָּנוּ

4 Againe the Greeke fathers make it plaine, *that to be reputed vnto iustice*, is to be true iustice in deede, interpreting S. Paules vvordes in Greeke, thus: *Abraham obtained iustice*,

Oecum. in caten. Photius.

δικαιοσύνην εὗρε.

 stice,

τοῦτο γὰρ ἐς τὸ, ἐλογίσθη αὐτῷ εἰς δικαιοσύνην. τοῦ πίστιν, ὅτι ἐδικαιώθη.

stice, Abraham vvas iustified. for that is, say they, *It vvas reputed him to iustice.* Doth not S. Iames say the like, (c. 2. v. 23) testifying, that in that Abraham vvas iustified by faith and vvorkes, the Scripture vvas fulfilled, that saith, *It vvas reputed him to iustice?* Gen. 15. v. 6. In vvhich vvordes of Genesis, vvhere these vvordes vvere first vvritten by Moyses, in the Hebrue there is not, *for iustice*, or, *in steede of iustice,* (vvhich Beza pleadeth vpon, by the Hebrue phrase) but thus, *He* (God) *reputed it vnto him, iustice.* though here also the English Bibles adde, *for.* vvhich, precisely transla-ting the Hebrue they should not doe, specially vvhen they meane it vvas so counted or reputed for iustice, that it was not iustice in deede.

וַיַּחְשְׁבֶהָ לּוֹ צְדָקָה

5 But as for either the Hebrue or Greeke vvord, that is here vsed, to *repute* or *account*, they are then vsed, vvhen it must needes signifie, that the thing is so in deede, and not onely so reputed. as, Psal. 118. octonario SAMEC. *I haue reputed or accounted al the sinners of the earth, preuaricators* or *transgressors. præuaricantes reputaui.* So did the Septuaginta take the Hebrue vvord and reade it. And S. Paul, *So let a man repute* or *account vs as the Ministers of Christ.* Let them goe now & say, that neither they, vvere sinners in deede, nor these, Christs ministers in deede, because they vvere reputed for such. let them say the children of the

ἐλογισάμην

חִשַּׁבְתִּי

ἡμᾶς λογιζέσθω. 1 Cor. 4.

the promis were not the ſeede of Abraham, λογίζεται
becauſe the Apoſtle ſaith, Ro. 9. v. 8. *they* εἰς σπέρμα.
are reputed for the ſeede. But hovvſoeuer it be, the Proteſtants vvil haue it ſo to be taken, at the leaſt in the matter of iuſtification.

6 Againe, vvhere S. Paul ſaith, 2 Cor. 5. *That vve might be made the iuſtice of God in him:* they in their firſt tranſlations, intolerably corrupt it thus. *That vve by his meanes ſhould be* Bib. 1562.
that righteouſnes, vvhich BEFORE GOD IS δικαιοσύνη
ALLOWED. Who taught them to trāſlate θεοῦ ἐν
ſo diſſolutely, *Iuſtitia Dei, the righteouſnes vvhich*
before God is allovved? did not their errour and αὐτῷ.
hereſie, vvhich is, that God reputeth and accounteth vs for iuſt, though vve be in deede moſt foule ſinners, and that our iuſtice being none at al in vs, yet is allovved and accepted before him for iuſtice and righteouſnes?

7 Againe to this purpoſe: they make S. 1 Eph. v. 6.
Paul ſay that God *hath made vs accepted,* or *freely accepted* in his beloued ſonne as they make the Angel in S. Luke ſay to our Lady, *Haile*
freely beloued: to take avvay al grace inherent ἐχαρίτωσε.
& reſidēt in the B. Virgin, or in vs: vvhereas the Apoſtles vvord ſignifieth, that vve are truely made gratious or grateful & acceptable, that is to ſay, that our ſoul is invvardly endued & beautified vvith grace & the vertues proceding thereof, & conſequently is holy in deede before the ſight of God, & not

only so accepted or reputed, as they imagin. If they knovv not the true signification of the Greeke vvord, & if their heresie vvil suffer them to learne it, let them heare S. Chrysostom not only a famous Greeke Doctor, but an excellent interpreter of al S. Paules epistles: vvho in this place putteth such force and significancie in the Greeke vvord, that he saith thus by an allusion and

χαρίσαϑαι. distinction of vvordes: *He said not*, VVHICH

χαριτῶσαι. HE FREELY GAVE VS, *but*, WHEREIN HE MADE VS GRATEFVL, *that is, not onely deliuered vs from sinnes, but also made vs beloued and amiable, made our soule beautiful, grateful, such as the Angels and Archangels are desirous to see, and such as himself is in loue vvithal, according to that in the Psalme*, THE KING SHAL DESIRE, *or* BE IN LOVE WITH THY BEAVTIE. So S. Chrysostom & after him Theophylacte, vvho vvith many mo vvordes & similitudes explicate this Greeke vvord and this making of the soule gratious and beautiful invvardly, truly, and inherently.

8 And I vvould gladly knovv of the Aduersaries, if the like Greeke vvordes be not of that forme and nature, to signifie so

ἀξιῶσαι. much as, *to make vvorthy, to make meete*: and

ἱκανῶσαι. vvhether he vvhom God maketh vvorthie, or meete, or grateful, iust, and holy, be not so in very deede, but by acceptation only.

χαριτῶσαι. if not in deede, then God maketh him no better

better then he vvas before, but only accepteth him for better: if he be so in deede, then the Apostles vvord signifieth not, to make accepted, but to make such an one as being by GODS grace sanctified and iustified, is vvorthie to be accepted, for such puritie, vertue, and iustice as is in him.

9 Againe, for this purpose (Dan. 6,22.) they vvil not translate according to Chaldee, Greeke, and Latin, *Iustice vvas found in me.* but they alter it thus, *My iustice vvas found out.* & other of them, *My vnguiltinesse vvas found out.* to dravv it from inherent iustice, vvhich vvas in Daniel.

εὐθύτης εὑρέθη ἐν ἐμοί. זָכוּ הִשְׁ- תְּכַחַת לִי.

10 Againe, it must needes be a spot of the same infection, that they translate thus, *As David* DESCRIBETH *the blessednes of the man vnto vvhom God imputeth righteousnes.* Ro. 4,6. as though imputed righteousnes vvere the *description* of blessednes. They knovv the Greeke doth not signifie, *to describe.* I vvould once see them precise in folovving the Greeke and the Hebrue. if not, vve must looke to their fingers.

λέγει τὸν μακαρισμὸν τοῦ ἀνθρώπου.

CHAP. XII.

Heretical translation for SPECIAL FAITH, *vaine securitie, and* ONLY FAITH.

AL other meanes of saluation being thus taken avvay, their only & extreme refuge is, Only faith, and the same, not the Christian faith of the articles of the Creede and such like, but a special faith and confidence, whereby euery man must assuredly beleeue, that him self is the sonne of God, and one of the elect and predestinate to saluation. If he be not by faith as sure of this as of Christs Incarnation, he shal neuer be saued.

2 For this heresie, they force the Greeke to expresse the very vvord of assurance and certaintie, thus: *Let vs dravv nigh vvith a true*

ἐν πληροφορίᾳ πίστεως

hart, IN ASSVRANCE OF FAITH. Heb. 10. v. 22. and Beza, *certa persuasione fidei*, that is, *vvith a certaine and assured persuasion of faith*: interpreting him self more at large in an other place, that he meaneth thereby such a persuasion and so effectual, as by vvhich vve knovv assuredly vvithout al doubt, that nothing can separate vs from God. Vvhich their heretical meaning maketh their translation the lesse tolerable, because they neither expresse the Greeke precisely, nor intend the true sense of the Apostle. they expresse not the Greeke, vvhich signifieth properly the fulnes and complement of any thing, and therfore the Apostle ioyneth it sometime vvith

Annot. in 1 Luc. v. 1.

vvith faith, els vvhere (*Hebr. 6. v. 11.*) vvith hope, vvith knovvledge, or ([a] *Col. 2. v. 2.*) vnderstanding, to signifie the fulnes of al three, as the vulgar Latin interpreter most sincerely (b *Ro. 4. v. 21.*) alvvaies translateth it: and to Timothee, (c *2 Tim. 4.*) he vseth it to signifie the ful accomplishment and execution of his ministerie in euery point. Where a man may vvonder that Beza to mainteine his conceiued signification of this vvord, translateth here also accordingly, thus: *Ministerij tui plenam fidem facito*: but their more currant church English Bibles are content to say vvith the vulgar Latin interpreter, *fulfil thy ministerie*: or, *fulfil thine office to the vtmost.* and the Greeke fathers do finde no other interpretation. Thus, vvhen the Greeke signifieth fulnes of faith, rather then assurance or certaine persuasion, they translate not the Greeke precisely. Againe in the sense they erre much more, applying the foresaid wordes to the certaine and assured faith that euery man ought to haue (as they say) of his ovvne saluation. Vvhereas the Greeke fathers expound it of the ful and assured faith that euery faithful man must haue of al such things in heauen as he seeth not, namely that Christ is ascended thither, &c. adding further and prouing out of the Apostles vvordes next folovving, that the Protest.

πληροφορίαν τῆς ἐλπίδος.
[a] πληροφορίας τῆς συνέσεως.
b πληροφορηθεὶς, *Plenissime sciēs.*
c πληροφόρησον.
Ministerium tuum imple.
An. 1577.
an. 1562.

Ignat. Ep. Smyrn.
Ἐκκλησίᾳ Θεοῦ πάσης πεπληροφορημένη ἐν πίστει καὶ ἀγάπῃ.
ἐν πληροφορίᾳ πίστεως.
Chrys. Theodoret.
Theophyl. vpon Ro. 10

Chryso. ho. 19. in c. 10. ad Hebr. Protestants * only faith is not sufficient, be it neuer so special or assured.

3 Yet do these termes please them exceedingly, in so much that for *the chosen gift of faith,* Sap. 3, 14. they translate, THE SPECIAL *gift of faith*: and Ro. 8, 38. *I am sure,* that nothing can separate vs from the loue of God. as though the Apostle vvere certaine and assured not only of his ovvne saluation, but of other mens. For to this sense they do so translate here, vvhereas in * other places out of cōtrouersie, they translate the same vvord as they should do, *I am persuaded. they are persuaded* &c. For vvho knovveth not that πείθομαι importeth onely a probable persuasion? They vvil say that, *I am sure,* and *I am persuaded*, is al one. Being vvel meant, they may in deede signifie alike, as the vulgar Latin interpreter doth commonly trāslate it, but in this place of controuersie, vvhether the Apostle vvere sure of his saluation or no, vvhich you say he vvas, yea vvithout reuelation, vve say he vvas not: here vvhy vvould you translate, I *am sure,* & not as in other places, *I am persuaded,* but in fauour of your errour, by insinuating the termes of *sure,* & *assurance,* and such like: as elsvvhere you neglect the termes of iust and iustification. In vvhich your *secrete things of dishonesties and craftines* (as the Apostle calleth it)

Marginal notes: τῆς πίστεως χάρις ἐκλεκτή, Fidei donum electum. πέπεισμαι. Bib. 1577. Luc. 20, 6. Ro. 15, 14. Hebr. 6, 9. 2 Cor. 4.

it) vve can not alvvaies vse demõstrations to cõuince you: but yet euen in these things vve talke vvith your conscience, and leaue the consideration thereof to the vvise reader.

4 You hold also in this kinde of controuersie, that a man must assure him self that his sinnes be forgiuen. but in the booke of Ecclesiasticus c. 5. v. 5. vve reade thus, *Of thy sinne forgiuen, be not without feare.* or (as it is in the Greeke) *Of forgiuenes and propitiation be not vvithout feare, to heape sinne vpon sinnes.* Vvhich you translate fallsely thus: *Because thy sinne is forgiuen thee, be not therfore vvithout feare.* Is that περὶ ἐξιλασμοῦ, *because thy sinne is forgiuen thee?* You knovv it is not. but that vve should be afraid of the very forgiuenes thereof, whether our sinne be forgiuen or no, or rather, vvhether our sinne shal be forgiuen or no, if vve heape one sinne vpon an other. Vvhich seemeth to be the truest sense of the place, by the vvordes folovving. as though he should say, Be not bold vpon forgiuenesse to heape sinne vpon sinne, as though God vvil easily forgiue &c.

περὶ ἐξιλασμοῦ μὴ ἄφοβος γίνου, προσθεῖναι ἁμαρτίαν ἐφ' ἁμαρτίαις.

5 I touched before vpon an other occasion, hovv you adde to the text, making the Apostle say thus, Eph. 3. *By vvhom vve haue boldnes and entrance vvith* THE CONFIDENCE VVHICH IS *by the faith of him* or (as in an other bible

Bib. 1562.

Bib. 1577. Bible, vvhich is al one) *in the confidence by faith*
ἐν πεποιθή- *of him.* The learned and skilful among you
σει, διὰ τῆς in the Greeke tongue, know that this trans-
πίστεως αὐ- lation is false for tvvo causes. the one is,
τοῦ. because the Greeke in that case should be
thus, ἐν τῇ πεποιθήσει τῇ διὰ τῆς πίστεως αὐτοῦ an
other cause is, the point after πεποιθήσει. so
that the very simple and sincere translation
is this, *vve haue affiance and accesse vvith confidence, by the faith of him.* euen as els where it is said, we
1 Io. 3. haue confidence, if our hart reprehend vs
not: vve haue confidence by keeping the
commaundements, by tribulations and af-
Hebr. 10. flictions and al good vvorkes. hope also
2 Cor. 3. giueth vs great confidence. Against al
vvhich, your translation is preiudicial, limiting & defining our confidence tovvard
God, to be faith, as though vve had no confidence by vvorkes, or othervvise.

6 For this confidence by faith onely, Beza translateth so vvilfully and peruersely, that either you vvere ashamed to folovv him, or you lacked a cōmodious English vvord correspondent to his Latin. *If I haue al faith* (saith the Apostle) *and haue not charitie, I am*
πᾶσαν πί- *nothing. totam fidem,* (saith Beza) I had rather
στιν. translate, then, *omnem fidem, because the Apostle*
1 Cor. 13. *meaneth not al kinde of faith,* to vvit, *the faith that iusti-*
Annot. in *fieth:* but he meaneth that if a man haue the
No. Test. 1556. faith of Christs omnipotencie, or of any

other

other article of the Creede, or of al vvholy and entierly and perfectly, that is nothing vvithout charitie. This is Bezas *tota fides, vvhole faith*, thinking by this tranſlation to exempt from the Apoſtles vvordes their ſpecial iuſtifying faith, & vvreſtling to that purpoſe in his annotations againſt Pighius & other Catholike Doctors. Whereas euery man of ſmal ſkill may ſee, that the Apoſtle nameth al faith, as he doth al knowledge & al myſteries: comprehẽding al ſortes of the one & of the other: al kind of knovvledge, al kinde of myſteries, al faith vvhatſoeuer, Chriſtian, Catholike, hiſtorical, or ſpecial, vvhich tvvo later, are Heretical termes nevvly deuiſed.

πᾶσαν τὴν γνῶσιν. πάντα μυστήρια. πᾶσαν τὴν πίστιν.

7 And I vvould haue any of the Bezites giue me a ſufficient reaſon, vvhy he tranſlated, *totam fidem*, and not alſo, *totam ſcientiam*: vndoubtedly there is no cauſe, but the hereſie of ſpecial and onely faith. And againe, vvhy he tranſlateth Iaco. 2, 22. *Thou ſeeſt, that faith vvas* (adminiſtra) *a helper of his vvorkes*: and expoundeth it thus, *faith vvas an efficient cauſe and fruiteful of good vvorkes.* Whereas the Apoſtles vvordes be plaine, that *faith vvrought together vvith* his vvorkes, yea and that his faith vvas by vvorkes made perfecte. This is impudent handling of Scripture, to make vvorkes the fruite only and effect of faith, vvhich is your hereſie.

συνήργει. ἐτελειώθη.

8 Vvhich heresie also must needes be the
cause, that, to suppresse the excellencie of
charitie (which the Apostle giueth it aboue
faith or any other gift vvhatsoeuer, in these
vvordes, *And yet I shevv you a more excellent vvay*
1 *Cor.* 12. *v.* 31.) he in one edition of the nevv
καὶ ἔτι καθ' ὑπερβολὴν ὁδὸν ὑμῖν δείκνυμι. Testament (*in the yere* 1556.) translateth thus,
Behold moreouer also I shevv you a vvay most diligently.
Vvhat cold stuffe is this, and hovv impertinent? In an other edition (an. 1565.) he
mended it thus: *And besides I shevv you a vvay to*
excellencie. In neither of both expressing the
comparison of preeminence & excellencie
that charitie hath in the Apostles vvordes,
and in al the chapter folovving. Vvherein
you did wel (for your credite) not to folow
him (no not your Bezites them selues) but
to translate after our vulgar Latin interpreter, as it hath alvvaies been read and vnderstood in the Church.

9 Luther vvas so impudent in this case,
that, because the Apostle spake not plainely ynough for only faith, he thrust (only)
Luther. to. 2 fol. 405. edi. Witteb. an. 1551. into the text of his translation, * as him self
vvitnesseth. You durst not hitherto pre-
sume so far in this question of only faith
Act. 9, 22. Bib. 1577. 1 Pet. 1, 25. 2 Par. 36, 8. 2 Cor. 5, 21. 1 Pet 2, 13. in the Bib. 1562. though * in other controuersies you haue
done the like, as is shevved in their places.
But I vvil aske you a smaller matter, which
in vvordes and shevv you may perhaps
easily

easily ansvver, but in your conscience there vvil remaine a gnavving vvorme. In so many places of the Gospel, vvhere our Sauiour requireth the peoples faith, vvhen he healed them of corporal diseases only, why do you so gladly translate thus, *Thy faith hath saued thee*: rather then thus, *thy faith hath healed thee*, or, *made the vvhole?* is it not, by ioyning these vvordes together, to make it sound in English eares, that faith saueth or iustifieth a man? in so much that Beza noteth in the margent thus, *fides saluat*: that is, *faith saueth*. & your Geneua Bibles, in that place vvhere it can not be taken for faith that iustifieth, because it is not the parties faith, but her fathers that Christ required, there also translate thus, *Beleeue only, and she shal be saued.* Vvhich translation, though very false and impertinēt for iustifying faith, as you seeme to acknovvledge by translating it other-vvise in your other Bibles: yet in deede you must needes mainteine & hold it for good, whiles you allenge this place for only faith, as is euident in your vvritings.

Mar. 10, 52. Luc. 18, 42. & c. 8. v. 48.

Luc. 8, 50.

See Goughs sermon and Tomsons answer to the L. Abbot of vvestmester.

10 This then you see is a fallacie, vvhen faith only is required to the health of the body, as in many such places (though not in al) there by translation to make it sound a iustifying faith, as though faith only were required to the health of the soule. Whereas

that faith vvas of Christs omnipotécie only
Annot. in 1 Cor. 13, 2. & povver, vvhich Beza confesseth may be in the diuels them selues, and is far from the faith that iustifieth. If you say, the Greeke signifieth as you translate: it doth so in deede, but it signifieth also very commonly to be healed corporally, as (by your ovvne
Bib. 1577. translation) in these places. Marc. 5. v. 28. Marc. 6. v. 56. Luc. 8. v. 36. & v. 51. Where you translate, *I shal be vvhole. They vvere healed. He vvas healed. She shal be made vvhole.* And vvhy do you here trãslate so? because you knovv, *to be saued,* importeth rather an other thing, to vvit, saluation of the soule: and therfore vvhen faith is ioyned withal, you translate rather, *saued,* then *healed* (though the place be meant of bodily health only) to insinuate by al meanes your iustification by only faith.

CHAP. XIII.

Heretical translation against PENANCE *and* SATISFACTION.

VPON the heresie of onely faith iustifying and sauing a man, folovveth the denial of al penãce & satisfaction for sinnes. Vvhich Beza so abhorreth, (*Annot, in Mat. 3. v. 2.*) that
μετάνοια. he maketh protestation, that he auoideth
μετανοεῖτε. these termes, *Pœnitentia,* and, *Pœnitentiam agere,* of purpose: and that he vvill alvvaies vse for them in translating the Greeke vvordes

resipiscentia,

reſipiſcentia, and, *reſipiſcere*. Vvhich he doth obſerue perhaps, but that ſometimes he is vvorſe then his promis, tranſlating moſt falſely and heretically for *reſipiſcentia*, *reſipiſcentes*: ſo that your Engliſh Bezites them ſelues are aſhamed to tranſlate after him. Vvho othervviſe folovv his rule for the moſt part, tranſlating *reſipiſcentia*, *amendement of life*: & *reſipiſcite*, *amend your liues*. & the other Engliſh bibles vvhen they tranſlat beſt, ſay, *repentance*, & *repent*: but none of them all once haue the vvordes, *penance*, and, *doe penance*. Vvhich in moſt places is the very true tranſlation, according to the very circũſtance of the text, and vſe of the Greeke vvord in the Greeke Church, and the auncient Latin tranſlation thereof and al the fathers reading thereof, and their expoſitions of the ſame. Vvhich foure pointes I thinke not amis, briefely to proue, that the reader may ſee the vſe and ſignification of theſe vvordes, vvhich they of purpoſe vvill not expreſſe, to auoid the termes of, *penance*, and, *doing penance*.

Act. 26, 20 in No. Teſt. an.1556. and in his later tranſlation 1565.

Mat 3. v. 8. Luc. 3. v. 8.

μετανοεῖν, Agere pœnitentiam.

2 Firſt, that the circumſtance of the text doth giue it ſo to ſignifie, vve read in Saint Mathevv, c. 11. v. 21. *If in Tyre and Sidon had been vvrought the miracles that haue been vvrought in you, they had done penance in hearecloth or ſackecloth and aſhes long agoe.* And in S. Luc. c. 10. v. 13. *they had done penance, ſitting in ſackecloth and aſhes.* I beſeeche

That *μετανοεῖν* is to doe penãce. *μετενόησαν ἂν* pœnitentiã egiſſent.

you, these circumstances of sackcloth and ashes adioyned, doe they signifie penance and affliction of the body, or only amēdement of life, as you vvould haue the vvord to signifie? S. Basil saith, *in Ps. 29. Sack-*
εἰς μετά-
cloth maketh for penance. For the fathers in old time sit-
νοιαν.
ting in sackcloth and ashes, did penance. Vnles you
μετενόησαν.
vvil translate S. Basil also after your fashiō, vvhom you can not any vvay translate, but the sense must needes be, *penāce*, & *doing penāce.*
Againe S. Paul saith, *You vvere made sorie to pe-*
2 Co. 7, 9.
nance, or, *to repentance*, say vvhich you vvill: and *The sorovv vvhich is according to God, vvorketh penāce*, or, *repentance vnto saluation.* Is not sorovv and bitter mourning & affliction, partes of penance? Did the incestuous man vvhom S.
1 Cor. 5.
Paul excommunicated, and afteruvard absolued him because of his exceding sorovv
2 Cor. 2.
and teares, for feare lest he might be ouervvhelmed vvith sorovv, did he I say chāge his minde only or amend his life, as you translate the Greeke vvord, and interpret repentance? did he not penance also for his
Mat. 3.
fault, enioyned of the Apostle? vvhen S.
Luc. 3.
Iohn the Baptist saith, & S. Paul exhorteth
Act. 26.
the like, *Doe fruites vvorthie of penance*, or as you translate, *meete for repentance*: Doe they not plainely signifie penitential vvorkes, or the vvorkes of penance? vvhich is the very cause vvhy Beza rather translated in those

places;

places, *Doe the fruites meete for them that amend their liues.* or, giue vs some other good cause ô ye Bezites, vvhy your maister doth so fouly falsifie his translation.

Fructus dignos iis qui resipuerint. καρποὺς ἀξίους τῆς μετανοίας.

3 Secondly, for the signification of this Greeke vvord in al the Greeke Church, and Greeke fathers, euen from S. Denys the Areopagite S. Paules scholer, vvho must needes deduce it from the Scriptures, and learne it of the Apostles: it is most euident, that they vse this vvord for that penance vvhich vvas done in the primitiue Church according to the penitẽtial canons, vvherof al antiquitie of Councels and fathers is ful. in so much that S. Denys reckening vp the three sortes of persons that vvere excluded from seeing and participating of the diuine mysteries of Christes body and bloud, to vvit, Catechumens, Pœnitents, and the possessed of il spirites: for, Pœnitents, he saith in the Greeke, *οἱ ἐν μετανοίᾳ ὄντες.* that is, such as vvere in their course of penance, or had not yet done their ful penance. Vvhich penance S. Augustine declareth thus: (Ho. 27. inter 50 ho. and ep. 108.) *Est pœnitentia grauior. &c. There is a more greuous and more mournefúl penance, vvhereby proprely they are called in the Church, that are Pœnitentes: remoued also from partaking the sacramẽt of the altar.* And the Greeke Ecclesiastical historie thus: *In the Church of Rome there is a manifest and knovvn place for the*

Ec. Hier. c. 3. in principio.

Pœnitentes. οἱ μετανοοῦντες. οἱ ἐν μετανοίᾳ ὄντες.

Sozom. li. 7. c. 16.

τῶν μετανοούντων.

See S. Hier. in epitaph. Fabiolæ.

POENITENTS.*& in it they stād sorovvful, & as it vvere mourning, & vvhen the sacrifice is ended, being not made partakers thereof, vvith vveeping and lamentation they cast them selues flat on the ground. then the Bishop vveeping also vvith compassion lifteth them vp, and after a certaine time enioyned, absolueth thē frō their* penāce. *This, the Priests,* or, *Bishops of Rome keepe from the very beginning euen vntil our time.*

Li. 5. c. 19.

4 In these vvordes & other in the same chapter, & in Socrates Greeke historie likevvise whē they speake of *Pœnitents*, that confessed and lamented their sinnes, that vvere enioyned penance for the same, & did it: I vvould demaund of our English Græcians, in vvhat Greeke vvordes they expresse al this. Do they it not in the vvordes vvhich vve novv speake of, & vvhich therfore are proued most euidētly to signifie penāce & doing penāce? Againe, vvhen the most aūcient Coūcel of Laodicea *can. 2*, saith, *That the time of penāce should be giuen to offenders according to the proportion of the fault*: and againe, *can. 9. That such shal not communicate til a certaine time, but after they haue done penance and confessed their fault, then to be receiued*: and againe *Can. 19. After the Catechumens are gone out, that praier be made of the Penitents, or them that are in doing penance*: And vvhen the first Councel of Nice saith, *can. 12.* about shortening or prolonging the daies of penance, *that they must vvel examine their purpose and maner of doing penance.* that is, vvith what alacritie of minde, teares, patience, humilitie, good vvorkes, they accomplished the same, and accordingly to deale

κατὰ τὴν ἀναλογίαν τοῦ πταίσματος, καιροῦ μετανοίας δοθέντος.

τῶν ἐν μετανοίᾳ.

τὴν προαίρεσιν καὶ τὸ εἶδος τῆς μετανοίας.

deale more mercifully vvith them, as is there expressed in the councel: vvhen S. Basil, *Can. 1. ad Amphiloch.* speaketh after the same sort: vvhen S. Chrysostom calleth the sackcloth and fasting of the Niniuites for certaine daies, *tot dierum pœnitentiam, so many daies penance*: in al these places, I would gladly knovv of our English Grecians, vvhether these speaches of penance and doing penance, are not expressed by the said Greeke vvordes, vvhich they vvil in no case so to signifie.

5 Or, I vvould also aske them, vvhether in these places they vvil translate, *repentance*, and, *amendement of life*, vvhere there is mentioned a prescript time of satisfaction for their fault by such and such penal meanes: vvhether there be any prescript times of repentance or amendement of life, to continue so long, and no longer: if not, then must it needes be translated, *penance*, and, *doing penance*, vvhich is longer or shorter according to the fault and the maner of doing the same. I may repent in a moment, and amend my life at one instant, and this repentance and amendement ought to continue for euer. but the holy Councels and fathers speake of a thing to be done for certaine yeres or daies, and to be released at the Bishops discretion: this therfore is penance, and not

repent.

repentance only or amendemēt of life, and is expressed by the foresaid Greeke wordes, as also by*an other equiualent therevnto.

*ὑποπίπτειν.

6 I omit that this very phrase, *to doe penance*, is vvord for word expressed thus in Greeke, ποιεῖν μετάνοιαν. And Ausonius the Xp̄ian Poëte (vvhom I may as vvel alleage once, and vse it not, as they do Virgil, Terence, and the like very often) vseth this Greeke vvord so euidētly in this sense, that Beza saith, he did it for his verse sake, because an other vvord vvould not stand so vvel in the verse. But the reader (I trust) seeth the vse and signification of these Greeke vvordes by the testimonie of the Greeke fathers them selues, most auncient and approued.

Litur. Chrys. in rubricis, pag. 69. 104.

Metanoea.

Annot. in 3 Mat. v. 2.

7 Thirdly, that the auncient Latin Interpreter doth commonly so translate these vvordes through out the nevv Testament, that needeth no proofe, neither vvil I stand vpon it (though it be greater authoritie then they haue any to the cōtrarie) because the Aduersaries knovv it and mislike it, and for that and other like pointes it is belike, that one of them saith it is the vvorst translation of al, vvhereas Beza his Maister saith it is the best of al. so vvel they agree in iudgement, the Maister and the man.

μετανοεῖν Pœnitētiam agere.

Discou. of Sand. Rocke pag. 147. Præfat. in No. Test. an. 1556.

8 I come to the fourth proofe, vvhich is, that al the Latin Church and the glorious

Doctors

Doctors thereof haue alvvaies read as the
vulgar Latin interpreter tranſlateth theſe
vvordes, and expound the ſame of penance,
and doing penance. To name one or tvvo
for an example, S. Auguſtines place is very Ep. 108.
notable, vvhich therfore I ſet dovvne, and
may be tranſlated thus: *Men doe penance before* Agunt homines pœnitentiam.
Baptiſme, of their former ſinnes, yet ſo that they be alſo
baptized, Peter ſaying thus, DOE YE PENANCE, Act. 2.
AND LET EVERY ONE BE BAPTIZED. *Men alſo*
doe penance, if after Baptiſme they do ſo ſinne, that they
deſerue to be excommunicated and reconciled againe, as in
al Churches they doe vvhich be called, POENITENTES. Sicut agunt qui Pœnitẽtes appellantur.
For of ſuch penance ſpake S. Paul, 2 Cor. 12, 21. *ſaying,*
THAT I LAMENT NOT MANY OF THEM
WHICH BEFORE HAVE SINNED, AND
HAVE NOT DONE PENANCE FOR THEIR
VNCLEANNESSE. *Vve haue alſo in the Actes, that* Act. 8, 18.
Simon Magus being baptized, vvas admoniſhed by Peter
TO DOE PENANCE *for his greuous ſinne. There* Vt ageret pœnitentiã.
is alſo in maner a daily Penance of the good and humble
beleeuers, in vvhich vve knocke our breaſtes, ſaying,
FORGIVE VS OVR DETTES. *For theſe* (venial
and daily offenſes) *faſtes and almes and praiers are* Quotidianã agere pœnitentiam.
vvatchfully vſed, and humbling our ſoules vve ceaſe not
after a ſort to doe daily penance.

9 In theſe vvordes of S. Auguſtine it is plaine that he ſpeaketh of painful or penitential vvorkes for ſatisfaction of ſinnes, that is, penance: againe, that there are three kindes of the ſame, one before Baptiſme, an other after Baptiſme for great offenſes, greater and longer: the other daily for common

mon and litle venial faultes vvhich the best men also cõmit in this fraile nature. againe, that the tvvo former are signified & spoken of in the three places of Scripture by him alleaged. Where vve see, that he readeth altogether as the vulgar interpreter translateth, and expoundeth al three places of penance for sinne, & so approueth that signification of the Greeke vvord. Yea in saying that for venial sinnes vve knocke our breast, fast, giue almes, and pray, and so cease not *Quotidianam agere pœnitentiam*: vvhat doth he meane but daily penance and satisfaction? Reade also S. Cyprian (beside other places) epist. 52. num. 6. Vvhere his citatiós of Scripture are according to the old Latin interpreter, and his exposition according, of doing penance, and making satisfaction for sinnes committed. But I neede not procede further in alleaging either S. Cyprian or other auncient fathers for this purpose, because the Aduersaries graũt it. Hovvbeit in vvhat termes they graunt it, and hovv malapertly they accuse al the auncient fathers at once for the same, it shal not be amis here to put dovvne their vvordes.

10 Vvhereas the reuerend, godly, and learned Father, Edmund Campion, had obiected in his booke, the Protestants accusation of S. Cyprian for the matter of penance

nance: the good man that anſvvereth for both vniuerſities, ſaith thus to that point: *But vvhereas Magdeburgenſes* (Lutheran vvriters of that citie) *complaine that he depraued the doctrine of repentance, they do not feine or forge this crime againſt him, but vtter or diſcloſe it. For al men vnderſtand that it vvas to true. Neither vvas this Cyprians fault alone, that he vvrote of repentance many things incommodiouſly and vnvviſely, but al the moſt holy fathers almoſt at that time vvere in the ſame errour. For vvhiles thy deſired to reſtraine mens manners by ſeuere lavves, they made the greateſt part of repentance to conſiſt in certaine external diſcipline of life, vvhich them ſelues preſcribed. In that they puniſhed vice ſeuerely, they vvere to be borne vvithal: but that by this meanes they thought to pay the paines due for ſinnes, and to ſatisfie Gods iuſtice, and to procure to them ſelues aſſured impunitie, remiſſion, and iuſtice, therin they derogated not a litle from Chriſts death, attributed to much to their ovvne inuentions, & finally depraued repentance.* Thus far the Anſvverer.

Vvhitak. pa. 97. cont. ration. Edm. Camp.

Doctrinam pœnitentiæ.

De pœnitentia.

Imprudéter.

Pœnitentiæ.

11 Marke hovv he accuſeth the fathers in general of no leſſe crime, then taking avvay from Chriſt the merites of his Paſſion, attributing it to their ovvne penance and diſcipline. Vvhich if they did, I maruel he ſhould call them in this very place vvhere he beginneth to charge them vvith ſuch a crime, *ſanctiſſimos patres*, moſt holy fathers. The truth is, he might as vvel charge S. Paul vvith the ſame, vvhen he ſaith, vve ſhal *Be the heires of God, and coheires vvith Chriſt, yet ſo, if vve ſuffer vvith him, that vve may alſo be glorified vvith him.* S. Paul ſaith, our ſuffering alſo vvith Rom. 8.

Chriſt

Christ, is necessarie to saluation: Maister vvhitakers saith, it is a derogatiō to Christs suffering. Christ fasted for vs, therfore our fasting maketh nothing to saluation. He praied for vs, vvas scourged, and died for vs: therfore our praier, scourging, and emprisonment, yea & death it self for his sake, make nothing to life euerlasting, and if vve should thinke it doth, vve derogate from Christs Passion. Alas, is this the diuinitie of England novv a daies? to make the simple beleeue that the auncient fathers and holy men of the primitiue Church by their seuere life and voluntarie penance for their sinnes and for the loue of Christ, did therin derogate from Christes merites and Passions?

12 I may not stand vpon this point, neither neede I. the principal matter is proued by the Aduersaries cōfession, that the holy Doctors spake, vvrote, and thought of penance and doing penance as vve doe, in the same termes both Greeke and Latin: and vvith Catholikes it is alvvaies a good argument, and vve desire no better proofe, then this, The Protestants graunt, al the aūcient fathers vvere of our opinion, and they say it vvas their errour. For, the first part being true, it is madnesse to dispute, vvhether al the aūciént fathers erred, or rather the nevv

Protestants

Proteſtants. as it is more then madneſſe to thinke that Luther alone might ſee the truth more then a thouſand Auguſtines, a thouſand Cyprians, a thouſand Churches. Vvhich not vvithſtanding the palpable abſurditie thereof, yet M. Whitakers auoucheth it very ſolemnely. pag. 101.

13 And yet againe (that the reader may ſee hovv they play faſt and looſe at their pleaſure) this is the man that vvhen he hath giuen vs al the fathers on our ſide not only in the matter of penance, but alſo * in inuocation of Sainctes, and in diuers other errours, as he calleth them: the very ſame man (I ſay) in the very next leaues almoſt, reneuveth M. Iuels old bragge, that vve haue not one cleere ſentence for vs of any one father vvithin ſixe hundred yeres after Chriſt, and againe, that the ſame faith reigneth novv in England, vvhich theſe fathers profeſſed. Vvhat faith, M. vvhitakers? not their faith concerning penance, or inuocation of Sainćts (as your ſelf confeſſe) or other ſuch like errours of theirs as you terme them. Vvhy are you ſo forgetful or rather ſo impudent to ſpeake contraries in ſo litle a roome? Such ſimple anſvvering vvil not ſerue your aduerſaries learned booke, vvhich you in vaine goe about by fooliſh Rhetorike to diſgrace, vvhen the vvorld

Pag. 109. Pag. 101. pag. 114 117.

vvorld seeth you are driuen to the vvall, & either can say nothing, or do say that, vvhich confuteth it self vvith the euident absurditie thereof.

14 But to leaue M. Whitakers (vvho is a simple cōpanion, to sit in iudgemēt vpon al the aunciēt Doctors, & to condemne them of heinous errour in the matter of penāce) I trust the reader seeth by the former discourse, the vsual Ecclesiastical signification, and consequently both the true and false
μετάνοια. translation of the foresaid Greeke vvordes.
μετανοεῖν. Not that they must or may alvvaies be trāslated, *penance*, or, *doing penance*. For in the Scri-
μετανοεῖν. ptures God is said *Pœnitentiam agere*, vvho can not be said to doe penance, no more then he can be said to amend his life, as the Protestants commonly translate this vvord. Therfore I conclude, that this vvord being spoken of God in the Scriptures, is no more preiudice against our translation of doing penance, then it is against theirs, of amendement of life. Likevvise vvhen it is
μετανοοῦν- spoken of the reprobate & damned in hel:
τες. Sap. 5. vvho as they can not doe penance proprely, so much lesse amend their liues.
Pœnitētiam agentes.

15 Moreouer, it is purposely against penance, that they translate amisse, both in
Esd.c.9. Daniel & Esdras, vvhose voluntarie mour-
Dan.10. ning, fasting, afflicting of them selues for their

their owne sinnes and the peoples, is notoriously set forth in their bookes. There
they make the Angel say thus to Daniel. v. 12.
From the first day that thou didst set thine hart TO Bib. 1579.
HVMBLE *thy self*. Vvhat is this humbling
him self? can vve gather any penance thereby? none at al. but if they had said accor- κακωθῆναι
ding to the Hebrue, Greeke, and Latin, *from* vt te affligeres.
the first day that thou didst set thine hart TO AFFLICT
thy self, vve should easily conceiue vvorkes לְהִתְעַנּוֹת
of penance, and it vvould include Daniels mourning, fasting from flesh, vvine, and other meates, abstaining from ointments, the space of the daies, mentioned in the beginning of the same chapter.

16 Againe, in al their bibles of the yeres
1562. 1577. 1579. they make Esdras c. 9, 5. ἀπὸ τῆς ταπεινώσεώς
after his exceding great penance, say onely
this, *About the euening sacrifice I arose vp from my* μου.
HEAVINESSE. neither translating the He- מִתַּעֲנִיתִי
brue, vvhich is the same vvord that in Daniel, nor the Greeke, vvhich signifieth affliction and humiliation.

17 Againe, in the prophet Malachie (c. 3, 14.) they translate thus: *Ye haue said, It is but vaine to serue God, and vvhat profite is it that vve haue kept his commaundements and vvalked* HVMBLY *before his face?* Vvhat is this same, *humbly?* vvhen vve say in English, *he goeth humbly*: vve imagine or conceiue no more but this, that he is an humble man and behaueth him self

humbly. but they knovv very vvel, the Prophete speaketh of an other thing: and if it had pleased them to haue translated the
קֹדֵר Hebrue vvord fully and significantly in the sense of the holy Ghost, they might haue learned by cōference of other places where the same Hebrue vvord is vsed, that it signifieth such heauines, sadnes, sorovvfulnes, and affliction, as men expresse by blacke mourning garmēts, the nature of the vvord importing blacknes, darkenes, lovvring, & the like. Vvhich is far more then vvalking humbly, and vvhich is vvholy suppressed by so translating. See the Psalme 34. v. 14.
πενθῶν καὶ σκυθρωπάζων. Ps. 37. v. 7. Ps. 41. v. 10. Vvhere the Prophet vseth many vvordes & speaches to expresse sorovvful penance: and for that vvhich in
קֹדֵר Latin is alvvaies, *contristatus*, in Greeke a vvord more significant, in Hebrue it is the
קְדֹרַנִּית same kind of vvord that they translate, *humbly*. Vvhereas in deede this vvord hath no signification of humilitie proprely, no not of that humilitie I meane vvhich is rather to be called humiliation or affliction,
κακωθῆναι, ταπεινωθῆναι. as the Greeke words implie. But it signifieth proprely the very maner, countenance, gesture, habite of a pensife or forlorne man: and if they vvil say, that they so translate it in other places, the more is their fault, that knovving the nature of the vvord, they

they vvil notvvithſtanding ſuppreſſe the force and ſignification thereof in any one place, & ſo tranſlate it, that the reader muſt needes take it in an other ſenſe, and can not poſſibly conceiue that vvhich the vvord imporceth. for, *to vvalke humbly,* ſoundeth in al Engliſh eares, the vertue of humility, vvhich this vvord doth neuer ſignifie, and not humilitie or humiliation by affliction, vvhich it may ſignifie, though ſecondarely and by deduction onely.

18 Againe, vvhat is it els but againſt penance & ſatisfaction, that they deface theſe vſual and knovven vvordes of Daniel to the king, *Redime eleemoſynis peccata tua*, *Redeeme thy ſinnes vvith almes*: altering and tranſlating it thus, *Breake of thy ſinnes by righteouſnes*. Firſt, the Greeke is againſt them, vvhich is vvord for vvord according to the vulgar and cõmon reading: Secõdly, the Chaldee word vvhich they tranſlate, *breake of*, by Munſters ovvne iudgemẽt *in lexico Chald.* ſignifieth rather and more principally, *to redeeme*. Thirdly, the other vvord vvhich they trãſlate, *righteouſnes*, in the Scriptures ſignifieth alſo, *eleemoſynam*, as the Greeke interpreters tranſlate it *Deut.* 6. & 24. and it is moſt plaine in S. Matthevv, vvhere our Sauiour ſaith (Mat. 6. v. 1) *Bevvare you doe not your iuſtice before men*. Vvhich is in other greeke copies, *your almes*. And S. Au-

Dan. 4, 24.

ἐν ἐλεεμοσύναις λύτρωσαι.

בִּצְדָקָה

פְּרָק

δικαιοσύνην.

ἐλεεμοσύνην.

in Ps.49.v.5 gustine proueth it by the very text. for (saith he) *as though a man might aske, vvhat iustice? he addeth,* WHEN THOV DOEST AN ALMES DEEDE. *He signified therfore that almes are the workes*
Psal.111. *of iustice.* And in the Psal. they are made one, *He distributed, he gaue to the poore, his iustice remaineth for euer and euer.* Vvhich Beza translateth, *his beneficence or liberalitie remaineth &c.* Againe, S. Hierom a sufficient Doctor to tel the signification of the Hebrue or Chaldee vvordes, both translateth it so, and expoundeth it so in his commentarie. Moreouer, the vvordes that immediatly folovv in Daniel, interprete it so vnto vs, *And thy iniquities*
Annot. in Mat.6.v.1. *vvith mercies to the poore.* Lastly, Beza him self saith, *that by the name of iustice vvith the Hebrues, is also signified beneficence or beneficialnes to the poore, yea and that in this place of Daniel it is specially*
2 Cor.9. *taken for almes.* So that vve see there is no impediment neither in the Chaldee nor Greeke, vvhy they might not haue said, as the Church of God alvvaies hath said, *Redeeme thy sinnes vvith almes, and thy iniquities vvith mercies to the poore.* but their Heresie vvill not suffer them to speake after the Catholike maner, that almes and merciful deedes are a redemption, ransom, and satisfaction for sinnes.

19 And vvhat a miserable humor is it in these cases, to flie as far as they can from the aũcient receiued speache of holy Scripture,

that

that hath ſo many yeres ſounded in al faithful eares, and to inuent nevv termes and phraſes, when the original text both Greeke and Hebrue fauoureth the one as much, or more, then the other. as, that they chooſe to ſay in the Epiſtle to Titus (vvhere the Apoſtle exceedingly exhorteth to good vvorkes) *mainteine good vvorkes*, and, *ſhevv forth good vvorkes*, rather then according to the auncient Latin tranſlation, *bonis operibus præeſſe*, *to be cheefe and principal in doing good vvorkes*, vvhich is the very true and vſual ſignification of the Greeke vvord, and implieth a vertuous emulation among good men, vvho ſhal doe moſt good vvorkes or excel in that kinde. But they that looke to be ſaued by faith onely, no maruel if neither their doings nor tranſlations tend to any ſuch excellencie.

προΐστασθαι καλῶν ἔργων.

CHAP. XIIII.

Heretical tranſlation againſt the holy SACRAMENTS, *namely* BAPTISME *and* CONFESSION.

AN other ſequele of their only faith is, that the Sacraments alſo helpe nothing tovvard our ſaluation, and therfore they partely take them cleane avvay, partly depriue them of 1 al grace, vertue, and efficacie, making them poore & beggarly elements, either vvorse, or no better then those of the old Lavv.

σφραγὶς.

2 For this purpose Beza is not content to speake as the Apostle doth, (*Ro.* 4. *v.* 11.) that circumcision vvas a seale of the iustice of faith, but because he thinketh that, to small a terme for the dignitie of circumcision, as him self confesseth, *be gladly auoideth it* (I vse his ovvne wordes) & for the Novvne putteth the Verbe, so dissolutely and presumptuously, that the English Bezites them selues here also dare not folovv him in trāslation, though in opinion they agree. The cause of his vvilful translation he declareth in his Annotations vpon the same place, to vvit, the dignitie of circumcision, equal vvith any Sacrament of the nevv Testament. His vvordes be these. *Vvhat* (saith he) *could be spoken more magnifical of any Sacrament? therfore they that put a real difference betvvene the Sacraments of the old Testament and ours, neuer seeme to haue knovven hovv far Christs office extendeth.* Vvhich he saith, not to magnifie the old, but to disgrace the nevv.

libens refugi. quod obsignaret, for, *sigillum.*

3 Vvhich is also the cause vvhy not only he, but the English Bibles (for commonly they ioyne handes and agree together) to make no difference betvvene Iohns Baptisme and Christs, translate thus concerning

certaine

certaine that had not yet receiued the holy Ghoſt: *Vnto vvhat then vvere ye baptized? And they ſaid, vnto Iohns Baptiſme.* Vvhich Beza in a long diſcourſe proueth to be ſpoken of Iohns doctrine, and not of his baptiſme in vvater. As though it vvere ſaid, *vvhat doctrine then do ye profeſſe? and they ſaid, Iohns.* Vvhereas in deede the queſtion is this, and ought thus to be tranſlated, *In vvhat then or vvherein vvere you baptized? And they ſaid, In Iohns Baptiſme.* As vvho ſhould ſay, vve haue receiued Iohns Baptiſme, but not the holy Ghoſt as yet. and therfore it folovveth immediatly, *then they vvere baptized in the name of Ieſus*, & after impoſition of handes *the Holy Ghoſt came vpon them.* Vvhereby is plainely gathered, that being baptized vvith Iohns baptiſme before, and yet of neceſſitie baptized aftervvard vvith Chriſts baptiſme alſo, there muſt needes be a great differēce betvvene the one baptiſme and the other, Iohns being inſufficient. And that this is the deduction vvhich troubleth theſe Bezites, and maketh them tranſlate accordingly, Beza (as commonly ſtill he vttereth his greefe) telleth vs in plaine vvordes thus. *It is not neceſſarie, that vvhereſoeuer there is mention of Iohns Baptiſme, vve ſhould thinke it to be the very ceremonie of Baptiſme. therfore they that gather Iohns Baptiſme to haue been diuers from Chriſts, becauſe theſe a litle after are ſaid to be baptized in the name of Ieſus Chriſt, haue no ſure foundation.* Loe, hovv of

Act. 19, 3.

Annot. in Act. 19.

purpose he translateth and expoundeth it Iohns doctrine, not Iohns Baptisme, to take avvay the foundation of this Catholike conclusion, that his baptisme differeth and is far inferior to Christs.

4 But doth the Greeke leade him or force
εἰς τί him to this translation, *In quid? vnto vvhat?* First him self confesseth in the very same place the contrarie, that the Greeke phrase is often vsed in the other sense, *vvherein*, or *vvherevvith*, as it is in the vulgar Latin and Erasmus: but that in his iudgement it doth not so signifie here, and therfore he refuseth it. Yet in the very next verse almost, vvhere
εἰς τὸ ὄνομα it is said by the same Greeke phrase, *that they vvere baptized in the name of Iesus Christ*, there both he and his, so translate it as vve doe, & not, *vnto the name of Christ.* Is it not plaine, that al is voluntarie, and at their pleasure? For (I beseeche them) if it be a right translation, *baptized in the name of Iesus*: vvhy is it not right, *baptized in the baptisme of Iohn?* Is there any difference in the Greeke? none. Vvhere then? in their commentaries and imaginations only, against vvhich vve oppose and set both the text and the commentaries of al the fathers.

5 But no maruel if they disgrace the baptisme of Christ, vvhen they are bold also to take it avvay altogether: interpreting this Scrip-

Scripture, *Vnles a man be borne againe of vvater and the Spirit, he can not enter into the kingdom of God,* vvhich a man vvould thinke vvere plaine ynough to proue that Baptisme in vvater is necessarie: interpreting (I say) this Scripture, *Of vvater and the Spirit,* thus: of vvater, that is, the Spirit: making vvater to be nothing els in this place but the Spirit allegorically, and not material vvater. As though our Sauiour had said to Nicodemus, *Vnles a man be borne of vvater, I meane, of the spirit, he can not enter, &c.* According to this most impudent exposition of plaine Scriptures, Caluin translateth also as impudently for the same purpose in the epistle to Titus, making the Apostle to say, that God povvred the vvater of regeneration vpon vs aboundantly, that is, the holy Ghost. And lest vve should not vnderstand his meaning herein, he telleth vs in his commentarie vpon this place, that vvhen the Apostle saith, *Vvater povvred out aboundantly,* he speaketh not of material vvater, but of the holy Ghost. Novv in deede the Apostle saith not, that vvater vvas povvred vpon vs, but the holy Ghost. neither doth the Apostle make vvater and the holy Ghost al one, but most plainely distinguisheth them, saying, that God *of his mercie hath saued vs by the lauer of regeneration and renouation of the Holy Ghost, vvhom he hath povvred vpon vs aboundantly.* See hovv plainely the Apostle

Io. 3. v. 5.

Beza in. 4. Io. v. 10. & in Tit. 3. v. 5.

c. 3. v. 5. *Per lauacrũ regenerationis Sp. sancti* QVOD *effudit in nos abunde.*

Quem effudit as Beza him self translateth.

ſtle ſpeaketh both of the material vvater or vvaſhing of Baptiſme, and of the effect thereof vvhich is the holy Ghoſt povvred vpon vs. Caluin taketh avvay vvater cleane and vvil haue him ſpeake only of the holy Ghoſt, vvhich Flaccus Illyricus the Lutheran him ſelf vvondereth at, that any man ſhould be ſo bold, and calleth it plaine ſacrilege againſt the efficacie of the Sacraments.

Comment. in hunc locum.

6 And if vve ſhould here accuſe the Engliſh tranſlatours alſo, that tranſlate it thus, *by the fountaine of the regeneration of the holy Ghoſt,* VVHICH *he ſhedde on vs, &c.* making it indifferent, either *vvhich fountaine*, or, *vvhich holy Ghoſt he ſhedde, &c:* they vvould anſvver by & by that the Greeke alſo is indifferent: but if a man ſhould aſke them further, vvhether the holy Ghoſt may be ſaid to be ſhedde, or rather a fountaine of vvater, they muſt needes confeſſe, not the holy Ghoſt, but vvater: and conſequently that they tranſlating, *vvhich he ſhedde*, vvould haue it meant of the fountaine of vvater, & ſo they agree iuſt vvith Caluins tranſlation, and leaue Beza, vvho in his tranſlation referreth it only to the holy Ghoſt, as vve doe: but in his commentarie plaieth the Heretike as Caluin doth.

Sp. ſancti, quē effudit.

7 Of

7 Of the Sacrament of penance I haue ſpoken before, concerning that part ſpecially vvhich is ſatisfaction : here I vvill only adde of Confeſſion, that to auoid this terme (namely in ſuch a place vvhere the reader might eaſily gather Sacramental cōfeſſion) they tranſlate thus, *Acknovvledge your faultes one to an other*. Iac. 5. It is ſaid a litle before, If any be diſeaſed, *let him bring in Prieſts, &c.* And then it folovveth, *Confeſſe your faultes. &c.* But they to make al ſure, for, *Confeſſe*, ſay, *Acknovvledge*: & for *Prieſts*, *Elders*. Vvhat meane they by this? If this acknovvledging of faultes one to an other before death be indifferently to be made to al men, vvhy do they appoint in their Communion-booke (as it ſeemeth out of this place) that the ſicke perſon ſhal make a ſpecial confeſſion to the Miniſter, and he ſhal abſolue him in the very ſame forme of abſolution that Catholike Prieſts vſe in the Sacrament of Cōfeſſion. againe, if this acknovvledging of faultes be ſpecially to be made to the Miniſter or Prieſt, vvhy tranſlate they it not by the vvord Confeſſing and confeſſion, as vvel as by, *Acknovvledging*, & vvhy is not this confeſsion a Sacrament, vvhere them ſelues acknovvledge forgiuenes of ſinnes by the Miniſter? Theſe contradictions and repugnance of their practiſe and tranſlation, if

ἐξομολογεῖσθε, Whereof Confeſſion is called in S. Cyprian and other fathers, *Exomologêſis.*

In the order of viſitation of the ſicke.

if they can vvittely and vvisely reconcile, they may perhaps in this point satisfie the reader. But vvhether the Apostle speake here of Sacramental confession or no, sincere translators should not haue fled from the proper and most vsual vvord of confession or confessing, consonant bothe to the Greeke and Latin, and indifferent to vvhatsoeuer the holy Ghost might meane, as this vvord, *acknovvledge*, is not.

CHAP. XV.

Heretical translation against the Sacrament of HOLY ORDERS, *and for the* MARIAGE OF PRIESTS *and* VOTARIES.

I AGAINST the Sacramēt of Orders what can they doe more in trāslation, then in al their Bibles to take avvay the name of *Priest* and *Priesthod* of the Nevv Testament altogether, and for it to say, *Elder* and *Eldership*? Whereof I treated more at large * in an other place of this booke. Here I adde these fevv obseruations, that both for Priests and Deacons, vvhich are tvvo holy orders in the Catholike Church, they translate, *Ministers*, to commend that nevv degree deuised by

* Chap. 6.

by them ſelues. As when they ſay in al their bibles, *Feare the Lord vvith al thy ſoule, and honour his miniſters.* in the Greeke it is plaine thus, *& honour his Prieſts.* as the vvord alvvaies ſignifieth, and in the very next ſentence them ſelues ſo tranſlate, *Feare the Lord and honour the Prieſts.* but they vvould needes borovv one of theſe places for the honour of Miniſters. As alſo in the epiſtle to Timothee, vvhere S. Paul talketh of Deacons, and nameth them tvviſe: they in the firſt place tranſlate thus, *Likevviſe muſt the Miniſters be honeſt &c.* And a litle after, *Let the Deacons be the huſbāds of one vviſe.* Loe, the Greeke word being one, and the Apoſtle ſpeaking of one Eccleſiaſtical order of Deacons, and Beza ſo interpreting it in both places, yet our Engliſh tranſlatours haue allovved the firſt place to their Miniſters, and the ſecond to Deacōs. and ſo (becauſe Biſhops alſo vvent before) they haue found vs out their three orders, Biſhops, Miniſters, & Deacons. Alas poore ſoules, that can haue no place in Scripture for their Miniſters, but by making the Apoſtle ſpeake three things for tvvo.

Eccli. c. 7. v. 31.
ἱερεῖς.
ἱερέα.
1. Tim. 3.
Bib. 1562. and 1577.
Διάκονοι.

2 There are in the Scripture that are called miniſters in infinite places, and that by three Greeke vvordes commonly: but that is a large ſignification of miniſter, attributed to al that miniſter, vvaite, ſerue, or attend

ὑπηρέται.
λειτουργοί.
διάκονοι.

tend to doe any seruice Ecclesiastical or tẽporal, sacred or prophane. If the vvord be restrained to any one peculiar seruice or function, as one of the Greeke vvordes is, then doth it signifie Deacōs only. Vvhich if they knovv not, or vvil not beleeue me, let them see Beza him self in his Annotations

Annot. c. 5. v. 25.

vpon S. Matthevv, vvho protesteth that in his translation he vseth alvvaies the vvord, *Minister*, in the general signification: and, *Diaconus*, in the special and peculiar Ecclesiastical function of Deacons. So that yet vve can not vnderstād, neither can they tell vs, vvhence their peculiar calling & function of Minister commeth, vvhich is their secōd degree vnder a Bishop, & is placed in steede of Priests.

3 Againe, vvhat can be more against the dignitie of sacred orders and Ecclesiastical

* ἰδιῶται, Act. 4. Bib. 1562.

ἀπόστολος. For messen-ger & legate the Scriptu-re vseth the-se vvordes, ἄγγελος, πρέσβευτὴς, πρεσβεύειν.

degrees, then to make them profane & secular by their termes and translations? For this purpose, as they translate, *Elders* & *Eldership*, for, *Priests* and *Priesthod*, so do they most impudently terme S. Peter and S. Iohn, * *lay men*: they say for Apostle, *Embassadour*, & *Messenger*: Io. 13. v. 16. and for Apostles of the Churches, *Messengers* of the same: 2 Cor. 8. for Bishops, *ouerseers*. Act. 20. Why my maisters, doth *idiota* signifie a lay man? Suppose a lay man be as vvise and learned as any other, is he he *idiota?* or that one of your Miniſters be as vnlearned and ignorant as any ſhepheard, is he not *idiota?* ſo then *idiota* is neither clerke nor lay man, but euery ſimple and ignorant man. They that ſpake vvith miraculous tõgues in the primitiue Church, vvere they not lay men many of them? yet the Apoſtle plainely diſtinguiſheth them from *idiota.* So that this is more ignorantly or vvilfully tranſlated, then Neophytus, *a yong ſcholer,* in al your Bibles.

1 Cor. 14. 23. 24.

1 Tim. 3.

4 Novv for changing the name Apoſtle into Meſſenger, though Beza do ſo alſo in the foreſaid places, yet in deede he controuleth both him ſelf and you in other places, ſaying of the ſame vvord, *Apoſtles: A man may ſay in Latin, legates, but vve haue gladly kept the Greeke vvord* (Apoſtle) *as many other vvordes familiar to the Church of Chriſt.* And not only of the principal Apoſtles, but alſo of the other Diſciples he both tranſlateth and interpreteth in his commentarie, that they are *notable Apoſtles.* and he proueth that al *Miniſters of the vvord* (as he termeth them) are and may be ſo called. And for your *Ouerſeers,* he ſaith, *Epiſcopos,* and not, *Superintendentes.* Vvhich he might as wel haue ſaid, as you, *Ouerſeers.* But to ſay the truth, though he be to to profane, yet he doth much more keepe & vſe the Eccleſiaſtical receiued termes, then you doe, often prote-ſting

Annot in c. 10. Mat. v. 2.

Annot. in Ro. 16. v. 7. & in 2 Cor. 8. v. 23.

In tit. Euãg. Math. & in c.3.v.11.& c. 10.v.2.&c. 5.v.25. sting it and as it vvere glorying therein, against Castaleon especially. As, vvhen he saith *Presbyterum*, vvhere you say *Elder*: *Diaconũ*, vvhere you say, *Minister*, & so forth. Vvhere if you tel me that hovvsoeuer he translate, he meaneth as prophanely as you, I beleeue you, and therfore you shal goe together, like Maister, like Scholers, al false and profane translatours. for, this Beza (vvho sometime so gladly keepeth the name of Apostle) yet calleth Epaphroditus *legatum Philippensium*, Philip.2. v.15. Vvherevpon the English Bezites translate, *your messenger*, for, *your Apostle*. As if S. Augustine vvho vvas our Apostle, should be called, *our messenger*.

5 As also, vvhen you translate of S. Matthias the Apostle, that *he vvas by a common consent counted vvith the eleuen Apostles*: Act. 1. v. 26. (No. Test. 1580.) vvhat is it els but to make onely a popular election of Ecclesiastical degrees, as Beza in his Annotations vvould haue vs to vnderstand, (Annot. ibid. & Act. 14. v.23.) saying, *that nothing vvas done here peculiarly by Peter as one of more excellent dignitie then the rest, but in common by the voices of the vvhole Church.* though in an other place vpon this election he noteth Peter to be the cheefe or Corypheus. And as for the Greeke vvord in this place, (συγκατεψηφίσθη.) if partialitie of the cause vvould suffer him to consider of it, he should finde, that the proper signification thereof in this phrase of

of ſpeache, is, as the vulgar Latin interpreter, Eraſmus, and Valla (al vvhich he reiecteth) tranſlate it, to vvit, *He vvas numbred*, or, *counted vvith the eleuen Apoſtles*, vvithout al reſpect of common conſent or not conſent. as you alſo in your other bibles do tranſlate.

Annumeratus eſt. cooptatus eſt.

6 Vvhich diuerſitie may procede of the diuerſitie of opinions among you. For vve vnderſtād by Maiſter vvhitegiftes bookes againſt the Puritanes, that he and his fellovves deny this popular election, & giue preeminence, ſuperioritie, and difference in this caſe to Peter, and to Eccleſiaſtical Prelates. and therfore he proueth at large the vſe and Eccleſiaſtical ſignification of the Greeke vvord χειροτονία, not to be the giuing of voices in popular elections, but to be the Eccleſiaſtical impoſing of handes vpon perſons taken to the Churches miniſterie. Vvhich he ſaith very truely, and needeth the leſſe here to be ſpoken of, ſpecially being touched * els vvhere in this booke.

His defenſe, or 2 booke pag. 157.

* chap. 6. nu. 7.

7 One thing onely vve vvould knovv, vvhy they that pleade ſo earneſtly againſt their brethren the Puritanes, about the ſignification of this vvord, pretending herein only the primitiue cuſtome of impoſition of handes in making their Miniſters, vvhy

 (I ſay)

Bib.1577. (I say) them selues translate not this word accordingly, but altogether as the Puritanes, thus: *VVhen they had ordained them elders by* χειροτονήσαντες. *election in euery Church.* Act.14. v. 23. For if the Greeke vvord signifie here the peoples giuing of voices (as Beza forceth it only that vvay out of Tullie & the popular custome of old Athens) then the other signification of imposing handes is gone, vvhich Maister Whitgift defendeth, and the popular election is brought in, vvhich he refelleth: and so by their translation they haue in my opinion ouershot them selues, and giuen aduantage to their brotherly Aduersaries. Vnles in deede they trāslate as they thinke, because in deede they thinke as heretically as the other, but yet because their state of Ecclesiastical regiment is othervvise, they must mainteine that also in their vvritings, hovv so euer they translate. For an exāple, They al agree to translate Elder for Priest:

Beza ibid.

Pag.200. ad rat. Camp. and M. Whitakers telleth vs a fresh in the name of them all, that there are no Priests novv in the Church of Christ, that is (as he interpreteth him self) *This name Priest is neuer in the Nevv Testamēt peculiarly applied to the Ministers of the Gospel,* this is their doctrine. But vvhat is their practise in the regiment of their Church? cleane contrarie. For in the order of the communion booke, vvhere it is appointed

pag. 210.

pointed vvhat the Minister shal doe, it is indifferetly said, *Then shal the Priest doe or say this & that* : &, *Then shal the Minister, &c.* Vvhereby it is euident that they make Priest a proper and peculiar calling applied to their Ministers, & so their practise is contrarie to their teaching and doctrine.

8 Novv concerning imposition or laying on of handes in making their Ministers (vvhich the Puritanes also are forced to allovv by other vvordes of Scripture, hovvsoeuer they dispute and iangle against χειροτονία) none of them all make more of it, then of the like Iudaical ceremonie in the old Lavv, not acknovvledging that there is any grace giuen withal, though the Apostle say there is, in expresse termes. but they vvill ansvver this text (as they are vvont) vvith a fauorable translation, turning *grace*, into *gift*. As, vvhen the Apostle saith thus, *Neglect not* THE GRACE *that is in thee, vvhich is giuen thee by prophecie, vvith imposition of the handes of Priesthod*, they translate, *Neglect not the* GIFT. and Beza most impudently for, *by prophecie*, translateth, *to prophecie* : making that only to be this gift, & vvithal adding this goodly exposition, that he had the gift of prophecie or preaching before, and now by imposition of handes vvas chosen only to execute that function. But because it might be

Beza Annot. Act. 6, v. 6.

1 Timoth. 4. v. 14.

τοῦ χαρίσματος.

διὰ προφητείας.

obiected that the Apostle saith, *Vvhich vvas giuen thee vvith the imposition of handes,* or (as he
2 Tim. 1. speaketh in an other place) *by impositiō of hādes,* making this imposition of handes an instrumental cause of giuing this grace, he saith that it did only confirme the grace or gift before giuen.

9 Thus it is euident that, though the Apostle speake neuer so plaine for the dignitie of holy Orders, that it giueth grace, & consequently is a Sacrament, they peruert all to the contrarie, making it a bare ceremonie, suppressing the vvord *grace*, vvhich is much more significant to expresse the
χάρισμα. Greeke vvord, then *gift* is, because it is not euery gift, but a gratious gift, or a gift proceding of maruelous and mere grace. as
Phil. cap. 1. v. 29. when it is said, *To you it is giuen not only to beleeue, but also to suffer for him.* the Greeke vvord signifieth this much, *To you this grace is giuen, &c.* So
ἐχαρίσθη. Act. 27. vvhen God gaue vnto S. Paul al that sailed vvith him, this Greeke vvord is vsed, because it vvas a great grace or gratious gift giuen vnto him. Vvhen S. Paul pardoned
2 Cor. 2. the incestuous person before due time, it is
κεχάρισμαι expressed by this vvord, because it vvas a
χάρισμα. grace (as * Theodorete calleth it) giuen vnto him. & therfore also the almes of the
τὴν χάριν ὑμῶν. Corinthians, *1 Cor. 16. v. 3.* are called, *their grace,* vvhich the Protestants translate, *liberalitie,*

neg-

neglecting altogether the true force and ſignification of the Greeke vvordes.

10 But concerning the Sacrament of orders, as in the firſt to Timothee, ſo in the 2. Tim. 1.
ſecond alſo, they ſuppreſſe the vvord *grace*, v. 6.
and call it barely and coldly, *gift*, ſaying: *I put thee in remembrance, that thou ſtirre vp the gift of God vvhich is in thee, by the putting on of my handes.* Vvhere if they had ſaid, *the grace* of God vvhich is in thee by the putting on of my handes: then vvere it plaine that S. Paul by the ceremonie of impoſing handes vpon Timothee in making him Prieſt or Biſhop, gaue him grace: and ſo it ſhould be a very Sacrament of holy Orders. for auoiding vvhereof they tranſlate othervviſe, or els let them giue vs an other reaſon thereof, ſpecially the Greeke vvord much more ſignifying grace, then a bare gift, as is declared.

11 The more to profane this ſacred order, vvherevnto continencie & ſingle life hath been alvvaies annexed in the nevv Teſtament for the honour and reuerence of the functions therevnto belonging, to profane the ſame (I ſay) and to make it mere laical & popular, they vvil haue all to be maried men, yea thoſe that haue vovved the contrarie: and it is a great credite among them, for our Prieſts Apoſtataes to take vviues.

 This

This they would deduce from the Apostles custom, but by most false and impudent translation: making S. Paul say thus as of his ovvne vvife and the other Apostles vviues,

1 Cor. 9. v. 5. No. Test. 1580.

Haue not vve povver to lead about a vvife being a sister, as vvel as the rest of the Apostles? Vvhereas the Apostle saith nothing els but, *a vvoman a sister,* that is, a Christian vvoman, meaning such holy vvomen as folovved Christ, and the Apostles, to finde and mainteine them of their substance. So doth S. Hierom interpret it, and S. Augustine, both directly prouing that it can not be translated, *vvife,* but, *vvoman:* & the Greeke fathers most expresly. And as for the Greeke vvord, if they say it is ambiguous, S. Augustine telleth them that as the Apostle hath put it dovvne with al the circumstances, there is no ambiguitie at al that might deceiue any man. yea let vs set a part the circumstances, & consider the Greeke vvord alone in it self, and Beza vvil tell vs in other places, that it signifieth a vvoman rather then a vvife: reprehending Erasmus for translating it, *vvife, because there is no * circumstance annexed vvhy it should so signifie:* thereby declaring that of it self it signifieth, *vvoman,* and therfore much more vvhen the circumstance also (as S. Augustine saith) maketh it certaine, that so it doth signifie.

ἀδελφὴν γυναῖκα. Mat. 27.

Li. 1. aduers. Iouin. De op. mon. cap. 4.

In Collectá. Oecu. super húc locum.

Annot. Mat. 5. v. 28. & 1. Cor. 7. v. 1.

* Quia non additur τινὸς, aut ἀδελφοῦ.

12 Vvherfore great must the impudencie

of

of Beza be (and of the Engliſh Bezites) that knovving this and proteſting it els vvhere in his Annotations, yet here tranſlateth, *ſororem vxorem, a ſiſter a vvife*, and ſaying after his lordly manner, I doubted not ſo to trāſlate it, diſputing and reaſoning againſt al other interpreters both auncient and later, for the contrarie, yea and affirming that S. Paul him ſelf, *did fooliſhly*, if he ſpake there of other riche vvomē. Such a fanſie he hath to make the Apoſtles not only maried men, but that they caried about their vviues vvith them, and that they vvere the Apoſtles vviues, (for ſo he tranſlateth it *Act.1.v.14.*) that returned vvith them after our Lords aſcēſion to Hieruſalem, and continued together in praier til the Holy Ghoſt came vpon them. Whereas S. Luke there ſpeaketh ſo euidētly of the other holy & faithful women which are famous in the Goſpel (as the Maries & other) that the Engliſh Bezites them ſelues dare not here folovv his tranſlation. For I beſeeche you Maiſter Beza (to turne my talke vnto you a litle) is there any circumſtāce or particle here added vvhy it ſhould be tranſlated *vviues?* none. then by your ovvne reaſon before alleaged it ſhould rather be tranſlated, *vvomen.* Againe, did Eraſmus tranſlate vvel, ſaying, *It is good for a man not to touch a vvife?* 1 Cor. 7. v. 1. No, ſay

ineptè faceret.

Cum vxoribus.

σὺν γυναιξὶ.

Vxorē non tangere.

γυναικὸς μὴ ἅπτεσθαι.

 you

you, reprehending this translation, because it dehorteth from mariage. if not, shevv your commission vvhy you may translate it in the foresaid places, *vvife*, and, *vviues*, at your pleasure: the Greeke being all one, both vvhere you vvill not in any wise haue it translated, *vvife*, and also vvhere you vvill haue it so translated in any vvise.

σύζυγε γνήσιε.

13 Againe, to this purpose they make S. Paul say as to his vvife, *I beseeche thee also faithful yokefellovv* Phil. 4. v. 3: for in English what doth it els sound but man and vvife? but that S. Paul should here meane his vvife, most of the Greeke fathers count it ridiculous and folish, S. Chrysostom, Theodorete, Oecumenius, Theophylactus. Beza & Caluin both mislike it, translating also in the masculine gender, S. Paul him self saith the contrarie that he had no vvife, 1 Cor. 7. And as for Clemens Alexandrinus vvho alleageth it for Paules wife, Eusebius plainely insinuateth, and Nicephorus expresly saith, that he did it ἀνταγωνιστικῶς, by the vvay of contention and disputation, vvhiles he earnestly vvrote against them that oppugned matrimonie.

Socie germane. Theophylacte saith, if he spake to a vvomã, it should be γνήσια in the Greeke.

Li. 2. c. 24.

14 Againe, for the mariage of Priests & of al sortes of men indifferētly, they translate the Apostle thus: *vvedlocke is honorable among al men.* Vvhere one falsification is, that they

Hebr. 13.

they ſay, *among al men*, and Beza, *inter quoſuis*, and in the margent, * *in omni hominũ ordine, in euery order or condition of men*, and in his Annotation he raileth, to make this tranſlation good: vvhereas the Greeke is as indifferent to ſignifie, that mariage is honorable by al meanes, in al reſpectes, vvholy, throughly, altogether. So doth not only Eraſmus, but alſo the Greeke fathers expound it, namely Theophylacte, vvhoſe vvordes in the Greeke be very ſignificãt, but to long here to trouble the reader vvith them. *Not in part* ſaith he, *honorable, & in part not: but vvholy, throughout, by al meanes honorable and vndefiled, in al ages, in al times.* Therfore to reſtraine it in tranſlation to perſons only (though it may alſo very vvel be vnderſtood of al perſons that haue no impediment to the contrarie) that is to tranſlate falſely.

No. Teſt. an. 1565.

ἐν πᾶσι.

See Oecum. in catena.

15 An other and the like falſification in this ſame ſhort ſentence, is, that they make it an affirmatiue ſpeache, by adding, *is*: vvhereas the Apoſtles vvordes be theſe, *Mariage honorable in al, and the bed vndefiled.* Vvhich is rather an exhortation, as if he ſhould ſay, *Let mariage be honorable in al, and the bed vndefiled.* How honorable? that (as S. Peter ſpeaketh, 1 *Pet. c. 3.*) men conuerſe vvith their vviues according to knovvledge, imparting *honour*, vnto them as to the vveaker veſſels: that is

τίμιος ὁ γάμος.

τιμὴν.

(as

(as S.Paul also explicateth it, *1 Thess. c. 4.*) possessing euery man his vessel in sanctification and *honour*, not in the passion or lust of concupiscence, as the Gentiles, &c. Loe vvhat honorable mariage is, to vvit, vvhen the husband vseth his vvife honorably and honestly in al respectes, not beastly and filthily according to al kinde of lust & concupiscence. And that the Apostle here exhorteth to this honorable vsage of vvedlocke, rather then affirmeth any thing, it is most probable both by that which goeth before & that which immediatly foloweth, al vvhich are exhortations. & let the Protestants giue vs a reason out of the Greeke text, if they can, vvhy they translate the vvordes folovving by vvay of exhortatiō, *Let your cōuersation be vvithout coueteousnes*: and not these vvordes also in like maner, *let mariage be honorable in al.* Certaine it is that the Greeke in both is al one phrase and speache, and Beza, is much troubled to finde a good reason against Erasmus vvho thinketh it is an exhortation. The sentence then being ambiguous and doubtful at the least, vvhat ioly fellovves are these, that wil so restraine it in translation, that it can not be taken in the other sense, and not rather leaue it indifferently, as in the Greeke and vulgar Latin it is, lest the sense of the holy Ghost be

ἐν τιμῇ.

ἀφιλάργυρος ὁ τρόπος.

τίμιος ὁ γάμος.

be not that, or not only that, vvhich they tranſlate.

16 Moreouer it is againſt the profeſſion of cōtinencie in Prieſts & others, that they tranſlate our Sauiours vvordes of ſingle life and the vnmaried ſtate, thus: *Al men can not receiue this ſaying*: as though it were impoſſible to liue continent. Vvhere Chriſt ſaid not ſo, that al men can not, but, *Al men do not receiue this ſaying*. But of this I haue ſpoken more in the chapter of free vvill. Here I adde only cōcerning the vvordes folovving, that they tranſlate them not exactly, nor perhaps vvith a ſincere meaning. for if there be chaſtitie in mariage as vvel as in the ſingle life, as Paphnutius the Confeſſor moſt truely ſaid, and they are vvont much to alleage it, then their trāſlation doth nothing expreſſe our Sauiours meaning, vvhen they ſay, *There are ſome chaſt, vvhich haue made them ſelues chaſt for the kingdom of heauens ſake*. for a man might ſay, al do ſo that liue chaſtly in matrimonie. but our Sauiour ſpeaketh of them that are impotent and vnable to generation, called *eunuches or gelded men, and that in three diuers kindes: ſome that haue that infirmitie or maime frō their birth, otherſome that are gelded aftervvard by men, & other that geld them ſelues for the kingdom of heauen, not by cutting of thoſe partes vvhich

Mat. 19. v. 11.

Bibl. 1562. 1577.

* εὐνοῦχοι.

vvhich vvere an horrible mortal sinne, but
εὐνούχισαν ἑαυτούς. hauing those partes as other men haue, yet
geld them selues (for so is the Greeke) and
make them selues vnable to generation.
Vvhich hovv it can be but by voluntarie
profession, promis, and vovv of perpetual
continencie which they may neuer breake,
let the Protestants tell vs. Christ then as it
is most euident speaketh of gelded men,
either corporally, or spiritually (vvhich are
al such as professe perpetual continencie:)
and they tel vs of some that vvere borne
chast, and some that vvere made chast by
men, and some that make them selues chast:
a most folish and false translation of the
Gréeke vvordes, εὐνοῦχος and εὐνουχίζειν.

17 The Bezites here, are blamelesse, vvho
trãslate it vvord for vvord, *eunuches*: but they
are more to blame in an other place, vvhere
Mal. 2. v. 7. in derogation of the priuilege and dignitie
of Priests, they translate thus: *The Priests lippes*
φυλάξεται ἐκζητήσουσιν. *should preserue knovvledge, and they should seeke the*
Lavv at his mouth. vvhere in the Hebrue and
Greeke it is as plaine as possibly can be
ישמרו יבקשו spoken, *The Priests lippes shal keepe knovvledge, and*
they shal seeke the Lavv at his mouth. Vvhich is a
maruelous priuilege giuen to the Priests of
The infallible iudgemẽt of the Priests, in questions of religion. of the old Lavv, for true determination of
matters in controuersie, and right expoun-
ding of the Lavv, as vve reade more fully

Deutero.

Deutero. 17. Vvhere they are commaunded vnder paine of death to stand to the Priests iudgement, vvhich in this place God by the Prophet Malachie calleth his couenant v.4.
vvith Leui, and that he vvil haue it to stand, to vvit, in the nevv Testamẽt, vvhere Peter hath such priuilege for him and his succes-sors, that his faith shal not faile, vvhere the holy Ghost is president in the Councels of Bishops and Priests. Al vvhich these Here-tikes vvould deface and defeate, by transla-ting the vvordes othervvise then the holy Ghost hath spoken them.

18 And vvhen the Prophet addeth imme-diatly the cause of this singular prerogatiue of the Priest, *quia angelus Domini exercituum est, because he is the Angel of the Lorde of hostes*, vvhich is also a wonderful dignitie, so to be called: they after their cold maner of profane trãs-lation say, *because he is the messenger of the Lord of hostes.* So doe they in the next chapter call Malach. 3.
S. Iohn the Baptist, *messenger*: vvhere the v.1.
Scripture no doubt speaketh more hono-rably of him as being Christs precursor, then of a messenger, vvhich is a terme for postes also and lackies. The Scripture I say speaketh thus of S. Iohn, *Behold I send mine an-gel before thee*: and our Sauiour in the Gospel, *Mat.* 11. *Luc.* 7: telling the people the vvonder-ful dignities of S. Iohn, and that he vvas more

τὸν ἄγγε-λόν μου. angelum meum.

more then a prophet, citeth this place and giueth this reason, *For this is he of vvhom it is vvritten, Behold I send mine Angel before thee.* Vvhich S. Hierom calleth *meritorum αὔξησιν, the encrease and augmenting of Iohns merites or priuileges, that in Malachie he is called an Angel:* & S. Gregorie saith, he vvhich came to bring tidings of Christ him self, *vvas vvorthely called an Angel, that in his very name there might be a dignitie.* and al the fathers, and al vvit and reason conceiue a great excellencie in this name: only our profane Protestants that thinke of al diuine things and persons most basely, translate accordingly, euen in the foresaid Gospel also, making our Sauiour to say, that Iohn vvas more then a prophet, because he vvas *a messenger.* Yea vvhere our Sauiour him self is called, *Angelus Testamenti, the Angel of the Testament,* there they translate, *the messenger of the couenant.*

Comment. in hunc locum.

Hom. 6. in Euang.

Malach. 3. v. 1.

19 If S. Hierom in al these places had translated, *nũtium*, then the English vvere, *messenger*: but translating it, *angelum*, and the Church and al antiquitie so reading and expounding it as a terme of more dignitie & excellencie, [c] vvhat meane these base companions to disgrace the very eloquence of the Scripture, vvhich by such termes of amplification vvould speake more significantly and emphatically? vvhat meane they

c See Apoc. c. 2. and 3. In the English Bibl. 1562. *To the messenger of the congregation, &c. Angelo Ecclesiæ.*

they (I say) that so inueigh against Castaleo for his profanenesse, them selues to say, for Angel, *Messenger,* for Apostle, *Legate* or *Embassadour*, and the like? Are they afraid, lest by calling men Angels, it vvould be mistaken, as though they vvere Angels in deede by nature? then S. Paul spake dangerously, vvhen he said to the Galatians, *As Gods Angel you receiued me, as Christ Iesus.* But to procede. Gal. 4. v. 14.

20 It is much for the authoritie and dignitie of Gods Priests, that they do binde and loose, and execute al Ecclesiastical function as in the person & povver of Christ, vvhose ministers they are. So S. Paul saith, *2 Cor. 2. v. 10.* that vvhen he pardoned or released the penance of the incestuous Corinthian, he did it *in the person of Christ.* that is (as S. Ambrose expoundeth it) in the name of Christ, in his steede, as his Vicar and deputie. but they translate it, *In the sight of Christ.* Vvhere it is euident they can not pretend the Greeke, & if there be ambiguitie in the Greeke, the Apostle him self taketh it avvay interpreting him self in the very same case, whē he excōmunicateth the said incestuous person, saying, that he doth it, *in the name and vvith the vertue of our Lord Iesus Christ*: so expounding vvhat he meaneth also in this place. ἐν προσώπῳ Χριστοῦ. 1 Cor. 5. v. 4.

21 And it may be, that for some such purpose they change the auncient and accustomed

stomed reading in these vvordes of S. Mat-
Mat. 2. thevv, *Ex te enim exiet dux qui regat populum meum*
No. Test. *Israel*: translating thus, *Out of thee shal come the Go-*
1580. *uernour that shal feede my people Israel.* for, *that shal*
rule my people Israel. This is certaine that it is
τοῦ εἶναι εἰς a false translation, because the Prophets
ἄρχοντα vvordes *Mich.* 5. (cited by S. Matthevv) both
τοῦ Ἰσραήλ in Hebrue & Greeke, signifie only a ruler or
לִהְיוֹת Gouernour, & not a Pastor or feeder. Therfore it is either a great ouersight, vvhich is
מוֹשֵׁל. a small matter in cōparison of the least corruption: or rather because they doe the like
Act. 20. v. 28, it is done to suppresse the
significatiō of Ecclesiastical povver and gouernement, that concurreth vvith feeding,
first in Christ, and from him in his Apostles
and Pastors of the Church, both vvhich are
here signified in this one Greeke vvord, to
ποιμαίνω. vvit, that Christ our Sauiour shal rule and
feede, (*Psal. 2. Apoc. 2. v. 27*) yea he shal rule
in a rod of yron: and from him, Peter and
the rest, by his cōmission giuen in the same
ποίμαινε. vvord *feede and rule my sheepe*: Io. 21: yea and
that in a rod of yron, as vvhen he strooke
Ananias and Sapphîra to corporal death, as
Act. 5. 1 Cor. 4. v. his successors doe the like offenders to spiri-
21. & c. 5. v. tual destruction (vnles they repent) by the
5. & 2 Cor. 10. v. 4. & 8. terrible rod of excōmunication. This is im-
ported in the double signification of the
Greeke vvord, vvhich they to diminish
Eccle-

Ecclesiastical authoritie, they translate, *feede*, then, *rule*, or *gouerne*.

22 To the diminishing of this Ecclesiastical authoritie, in the later end of the reigne of king Henrie the eight, & during the reigne of king Edvvard the sixt, the only translation of their English Bibles, vvas, *Submit your selues vnto al maner ordināce of man: vvhether it be* VNTO THE KING, AS TO THE CHEEFE HEAD. 1 Pet. 2. Vvhere in this Queenes time, the later translatours can not finde those wordes novv in the Greeke, but do trāslate thus, *To the king as hauing preeminence*: or, *to the king as the Superior*. Vvhy so? because then the King had first taken vpon him this name of *supreme head* of the Church, and therfore they flattered both him and his sonne, til their heresie vvas planted, making the holy Scripture to say that the king vvas, *the Cheefe head*, vvhich is al one vvith, *supreme head*: but novv being better aduised in that point (by Caluin I suppose and the Lutherans of Magdeburge, vvho doe ioyntly inueigh against such title, and Caluin against that by name, vvhich vvas first giuen to king Henrie the eight) and because they may be bolder vvith a Queene then vvith a king, and because novv they thinke their kingdom is vvel established, therfore they suppresse this title in their later

βασιλεῖ ὡς ὑπερέχοντι.

Bibl. 1577. 1579.

Calu. in c. 7. Amos. Magdeb. in præf. Cent. 7. fo. 9. 10. 11.

ter translations, & vvould take it from her altogether if they could, to aduance their ovvne Ecclesiastical iurisdiction, vvithout any dependence of the Queenes supreme gouernement of their church, vvhich in their conscience (if they be true Caluinists, or Lutherans, or mixt of both) they do and must mislike.

23 But hovvsoeuer that be, let them iustifie their translation, or confesse their fault. and as for the kings supremacie ouer the Church, if they make any doubt, let them read S. Ignatius vvordes, who vvas in the Apostles time, euen vvhen S. Peter gaue the foresaid admonition of subiection to the king, and knevv very vvel hovv far his preeminence extended, and therfore saith plainely in notorious vvordes, that, vve must first honour God, then the Bishop, & thē the king. because in al thinges nothing is comparable to God, & *in the Church, nothing greater then the Bishop, vvho is consecrated to God for the saluation of the vvhole vvorld*, and [c] among magistrates & temporal rulers, none is like the king. See his [b] other vvordes immediatly folovving, vvhere he preferreth the Bishops office before the kings and al other thinges of price among men.

Epist. 7. ad Smyrnenses.

c ἐν ἄρχουσιν.

b ἱερωσύνη ἐστὶν, τὸ πάντων ἀγαθῶν ἐν ἀνθρώποις ἀναβεβηκός.

24 But in the former sentence of S. Peter, though they haue altered their transla-

tion

tion about the kings headſhip, yet there is one corruption remaining ſtill in theſe vvordes, *Submit your ſelues* VNTO AL MANER ORDINANCE OF MAN. Vvhereas in the Greeke it is vvord for vvord as in the old vulgar Latin tranſlation, *omni humanæ creaturæ*, and as vve haue tranſlated, *to euery humane creature*: meaning temporal Princes and Magiſtrates, as is plaine by the exemplification immediatly folovving, of *king, and dukes* and other *ſent* or appointed *by him.* But they in fauour of their temporal ſtatutes, actes of Parliament, Proclamations & Iniunctions made againſt the Catholike religion, do tranſlate all vvith one conſent, *Submit your ſelues to al maner ordinance of man.* Doth κτίσις ſignifie *ordinance?* or is it al one to be obedient to euery one of our Princes, and to al maner ordinance of the ſaid Princes?

πάσῃ ἀνθρωπίνῃ κτίσει.

1 Pet. 2. v. 13. 14.

25 A ſtrange caſe and much to be conſidered, hovv they vvring and vvreſt the holy Scriptures this vvay and that vvay and euery vvay to ſerue their heretical proceedings. For vvhen the queſtion is of due obedience to Eccleſiaſtical canons, and decrees of the Church and general Councels, vvhere the holy Ghoſt by Chriſts promis is aſſiſtant, and vvhereof it is ſaid, *If he heare not the Church, let him be vnto thee as an hethen & Publicane.* and, *He that heareth you, heareth me: he that* Mat. 18. Luc. 10.

 deſpi-

despiseth you, despiseth me: there they crie out aloud, and odiously terme al such ordinances, *Mens traditions*, and, *commaundements of men*, & most despitefully contemne and condemne them. but here, for obedience vnto tẽporal edictes & Parliament-statutes daily enacted in fauour of their schisme and heresies, they once malitiously forged, and still vvickedly reteine vvithout alteration, a text of their ovvne, making the Apostle to commaund submission vnto al maner ordinãce of man, vvhereof hath ensued the false crime of treason and cruel death for the same, vpon those innocent men and glorious martyrs, that chose to obey God and his Churches holy ordinances, rather then mans statutes and lavves directly against the same.

CHAP. XVI.

Heretical translation against the Sacrament of MATRIMONIE.

1 BVT as they are iniurious translatours to the sacred Order of Priesthod, so a mã vvould thinke they should be very frendly to the Sacrament of Matrimonie. for they would seeme to make more of Matrimonie then vve doe, making it equal at the least vvith virginitie. Yet the truth is, vve make it, or rather the Church of God esteemeth it

it as a holy Sacrament, they doe not: as giuing grace to the maried perſons to liue together in loue, concord, and fidelitie: they acknovvledge no ſuch thing. So that Matrimonie vvith them is highly eſteemed in reſpect of the fleſh, or (to ſay the beſt) only for a ciuil cōtract, as it is among Iewes & Pagans: but as it is peculiar to Chriſtians, and (as S. Auguſtine ſaith) *in the ſanctification alſo and holines of a Sacrament*, they make no account of it, but flatly deny it.

2 And to this purpoſe they tranſlate in the epiſtle to the Epheſians, 5. vvhere the Apoſtle ſpeaketh of Matrimonie, *This is a great ſecrete.* Vvhereas the Latin Church and al the Doctors thereof haue euer read, *This is a great Sacrament*: the Greeke Church and al the fathers thereof, *This is a great myſterie.* becauſe that vvhich is in Greeke, myſterie: is in Latin, Sacrament: & contrarievviſe, the vvordes in both tongues being equiualent. ſo that if one be taken in the large ſignification, the other alſo: as, Apoc. 17. *I vvil ſhevv thee the ſacramēt of the vvoman.* & *I vvil ſhevv thee the myſterie of the vvoman.* and ſo in ſundrie places. againe if one be reſtrained from the larger ſignification, and peculiarly applied, ſignifie the Sacraments of the Church, the other alſo. As, *the Sacrament* of the body and bloud of Chriſt: or, *the Myſterie* of the body

Sacramentū hoc magnū eſt.

μυστήριον.

Sacramentū

μυστήριον.

Duo Sacramenta. δύο μυστήρια.

and bloud of Christ: and the Caluinists in their Latin and Greeke Catechisme say, *tvvo Sacraments*. or, *tvvo Mysteries.*

3 This being so, vvhat is the fault of their translation in the place aforesaid? this, that they translate neither, *Sacrament*, nor, *Mysterie*. As for the vvord *Sacrament*, they are excused, because they translate not the Latin: but translating the Greeke, vvhy said they not, *Mysterie*, vvhich is the Greeke vvord here in the Apostle? I meane, vvhy said they not of Matrimonie, *This is a great Mysterie?* No doubt there can be no other cause, but to auoid both those vvordes, vvhich are vsed in the Latin and Greeke Church, to signifie the Sacraments. For in the Greeke Church the Sacrament of the body and bloud it self is called but a mysterie or mysteries, vvhich yet the Protestants them selues call a true Sacrament. Therfore if they should haue called Matrimonie also by that name, it might easily haue sounded to be a Sacrament also. But in saying it is a great secrete, they put it out of doubt, that it shal not be so taken.

Vvere it honest or lavvfull to translate, *Baptiso*, I vvash: or *Baptismus*, vvashing: or *Euāgeliū*, good nevves? yet the vvords prophanely taken, signifie no more.

4 They vvil say vnto me, Is not euery sacrament and mysterie, in english a secrete? yes, as Angel, is a messenger: and Apostle, one that is sent. but vvhen the holy Scripture vseth these vvordes to signifie more excellent

cellent

cellent and diuine thinges then those of the common sort, doth it become translators to vse baser termes in steede therof, and so to disgrace the vvriting & meaning of the holy Ghost? I appeale to them selues, when they translate this vvord in other places, vvhether they say not thus, *And vvithout doubt great was that* MYSTERIE *of godlines: God was shewed manifestly in the flesh &c.* againe, *The* MYSTERIE *vvhich hath beene hid since the vvorld began, but novv is opened to his saincttes.* againe, *I shevv you a* MYSTERIE, *vve shal not al sleepe, but vve shal al be changed.* and the like. Vvhere if they should trãslate, secrete, in steede of, mysterie, as the Bezites doe in one of these places, saying, *I vvil shevv you a secrete thing:* vvhat a disgracing and debasing vvere it to those high mysteries there signified? And if it vvere so in these, is it not so in Matrimonie, vvhich the Apostle maketh such a mysterie, that it representeth no lesse matter then Christ and his Church and vvhatsoeuer is most excellent in that coniunction? Novv then, if in al other places of high mysterie they translate it also mysterie, as it is in the Greeke, and only in Matrimonie do not so, but say rather, *This is a great secrete*, vsing so base a terme in so high & excellent a mysterie, must vve not needes thinke (as no doubt it is) that they doe it because of their Heretical opinion against

1 Tim. 3.

Col. 1. v. 26.
Eph. 3. v. 9.
1 Cor. 15. v. 51.

the Sacrament of Matrimonie, and for their base estimation thereof?

5 But they vvil yet replie againe, & aske vs, vvhat vve gaine by translating it either Sacrament, or mysterie? Doth that make it one of the Sacraments properly so called, to vvit, such a Sacrament as Baptisme is? no surely. but hovvsoeuer vve gaine othervvise, at least vve gaine the commendation of trew translators, vvhether it make vvith vs or against vs. for othervvise it is not the name that maketh it such a peculiar Sacrament. for (as is said before) Sacrament is a general name in Scripture to other things. neither do vve therfore so translate it, as though it vvere forthvvith one of the 7 Sacraments, because of the name: but as in other places vvheresoeuer vve finde this vvord in the Latin, vve translate it, Sacra-

Apoc. 17. ment (as in the Apocalypse, *the Sacrament of the vvoman*) so finding it here, vve do here also so translate it. and as for the diuers taking of it here, and els vvhere, that vve examine othervvise, by circumstance of the text, and by the Churches and Doctors interpretation: and vve finde that here it is taken for a Sacrament in that sense as vve say, *seuen Sacraments:* not so in the other places.

6 As vvhen vve read this name *Iesus* in Scripture common to our Sauiour and to other

other men, vve tranſlate it alvvaies alike, *Ieſus*: but vvhen it is [b] IESVS Chriſt, and vvhen ſome other Ieſus, [c] vve knovv by other circumſtances. likevviſe preſuppoſe Baptiſme in the Scripture vvere called a ſacrament: yet the Proteſtants them ſelues would not, nor could thereby conclude, that it vvere one of their tvvo Sacraments. yet I trovv they vvould not auoid to tranſlate it by the vvord ſacrament, if they foũd it ſo called: euen ſo vve finding Matrimonie ſo called, do ſo tranſlate it, neither concluding thereby that it is one of the Seuen, nor yet ſuppreſſing the name, vvhich no doubt gaue ſome occaſion to the Church and the holy doctors to eſteeme it as one of the Seuen. They cõtrarievviſe, as though it vvere neuer ſo called, ſuppreſſe the name altogether, calling it *a ſecrete*, to put it out of al queſtion, that it is no Sacrament: vvhich they vvould not haue done, if the Scripture had ſaid of Baptiſme or the Euchariſt, *This is a great Sacrament.* So partial they are to their ovvne opinions.

b Iude. v. 5.
c Act. 7. v. 45. Coloſ. 4. v. 11.

CHAP. XVII.

Heretical tranſlation againſt the B. SACRAMENT, *and* SACRIFICE, *and* ALTARS.

NOVV

1 NOvv let vs see concerning the Eucharist, vvhich they allovv for a Sacrament, hovv they handle the matter to the disgracing and defacing of the same also. They take avvay the operation and efficacie of Christes blessing pronounced vpon the bread & vvine, making it only a thankes-giuing to God: and to this purpose they translate more gladly, *thankes-giuing*, then, *blessing*. as Matth. 26. the Greeke vvordes being tvvo, the one signifying properly, to blesse: the other, to giue thankes: they translate both thus, *vvhen he had giuen thankes.* likevvise Marc. 14. in the Bible printed 1562. And vvhen they translate it, *blessing*, they meane nothing els but giuing thankes, as Beza telleth vs in his Annotations Mat. 26. v. 26. We reply and by most manifest Scripture proue vnto them, that the former Greeke vvord doth not signifie thankes-giuing properly, but blessing, and a blessing of creatures to the operation of some great effect in them: as vvhē Christ tooke the fiue loaues & tvvo fishes, to multiplie them, *he blessed them* Luc. 9. Vvhat say they to this thinke you? Doth not the Greeke vvord here plainely signifie, blessing of creatures? No, (saith Beza) *no doubt but here also it signifieth giuing-thankes.* Hovv Beza? he

εὐλογήσας. εὐχαριστήσας. Bib. 1562. 1577.

Great difference in the scriptures, betvvene blessing, and geuing of thankes.

Benedixit eis. εὐλόγησεν αὐτούς. Annot. in 9. Luc. v. 16.

he addeth, *Not as though Christ had giuen thankes to the bread, for that vvere to absurd: but vve must mollifie this interpretation thus, that he gaue thankes to God the father for the loaues and the fishes.* Is not this a notable exposition of these vvordes, *benedixit eis?*

2 Vve aske him in the like cases, vvhen God blessed Adam and Eue, Gen. 1. & 9. Noe and his children, saying, *Increase and multiplie:* vvhen *he blessed the children of Israël, and they multiplied excedingly,* vvhen *he blessed the later things of Iob more then the first.* Iob 42. Vvas this also a giuing of thankes, and not an effectual blessing vpon these creatures? Vvhat vvil they say, or vvhat difference vvil they make? As God blessed here, so he vvas God and man that blessed the loaues and fishes there. If they vvil say he did it as man, and therfore it was a giuing of thankes to God his father: to omit that he blessed them as he multiplied them, that is, rather according to his diuine nature then humane: vve aske them, vvhen he blessed as man, vvas it alvvaies giuing of thankes? he blessed the litle children, he blessed his disciples, vvhen he ascended: vvas this giuing thākes for them, as Beza expoundeth his blessing of the loaues & fishes? Vvhen * vve blesse the table or the meate vpon the table, vvhen S. Paul saith, 1 Timoth. 4. al meate is lavvful

εὐλόγησεν αὐτούς. Psal. 106. εὐλόγησεν τὰ ἔσχατα.

Luc. 24.

* Beza loco citato.

ἁγιάζειν, Which word cã neuer signifie, giuing thankes.

lavvful that * is sanctified by the vvord & by praier: is al this nothing but giuing thankes? So saith Beza in expresse vvordes.

3 Vve goe forvvard, and proue the contrarie yet more manifestly, in the very matter of the B. Sacrament, for the vvhich they multiplie al the foresaid absurdities. Vve tell them that S. Paul saith thus, *The chalice of blessing, vvhich vve blesse*, is it not &c. hovv could he speake more plainely, that the chalice or cuppe (meaning that in the cuppe) is blessed? Vvhich S. Cyprian *de Cœn. Do.* explicateth thus, *Calix solenni benedictione sacratus, The Chalice consecrated by solemne blessing.* Oecumenius thus, *The Chalice vvhich blessing, vve prepare.* that is, which vve blesse & so prepare. for so it must signifie, & not as Beza vvould haue it, *vvhich vvith thankes giuing vve prepare.* and that I proue by his ovvne vvordes immediatly before, vvhere he saith that the Greeke vvord being vsed of the Apostle transitiuely, that is, vvith a case folovving, can not signifie giuing thankes. Hovv then can it so signifie in Oecumenius vvordes, vvho doth interprete the Apostles meaning by the Apostles ovvne vvordes and phrase? yea (that you may note a notorious contradiction) hovv doth Beza then in the place of Luke before alleaged (vvhere the same Greeke vvord is a plaine transitiue as in this place

τὸ ποτήριον τῆς εὐλογίας ὃ εὐλογοῦμεν.

ὃ εὐλογοῦντες κατασκευάζομεν.

Annot. in 1 Cor. 10. v. 16.

εὐλόγησεν αὐτούς.

place) expound it of giuing thankes for the bread and fishes? A lyer (they say) must be mindeful, to make his tale agree in euery point. He that before forced the vvord in euery sentēce to be nothing els but thankes giuing, euen vvhen it vvas a plaine transitiue, novv confesseth that he neuer read it in that signification, vvhen it is a transitiue. and so vve haue that the blessing of the cuppe or of the bread, is not giuing thankes as they either translate, or interprete it.

4 And surely in the vvord εὐλογεῖν this is most euident, that it signifieth in this case the blessing & consecration of the creature or element: in so much that S. Basil and S. Chrysostom in their Liturgies or Masses, say thus by the same Greeke vvord: *Blesse ô Lord the sacred bread.* and, *Blesse ô Lord the sacred cuppe.* and vvhy or to vvhat effect? It folovveth, *changing it by the holy Spirit.* Vvhere is signified the transmutation and cōsecration thereof into the body and bloud. But in the other vvord εὐχαριστεῖν there may be some questiō, because it signifieth properly to giue thankes, and therfore may seeme to be referred to God only, and not to the element and creature. But this also vve finde contrarie in the Greeke fathers, vvho vse this vvord also transitiuely, saying, *panem & calicem eucharistisatos*, or, *panem in quo gratiæ actæ sunt.* that is the bread

εὐλόγησον τὸν ἄρτον. τὸ ποτήριον. μεταβαλών.

τὸν ἄρτον εὐχαριστηθέντα.

bread and the cuppe made the Eucharist: the bread ouer vvhich thankes are giuen: that is, *vvhich by the vvord of praier and thankes-giuing is made a consecrated meate, the flesh and bloud of Christ*, as S. Iustine *in fine 2 Apolgo.* and S. Irenæus *li. 4. 34.* in the same places expound it. Vvhereas it may also signifie that, for vvhich thankes are giuen in that most solemne sacrifice of the ἀξίων εὐχαριστειῶν τῶν δωρεῶν. Eucharist, as S. Denys in one place seemeth to take it. *Eccl. Hier. c.3 in fine.* Vvho in the self same chapter speaketh of the consecration thereof most euidently.

5 Vvhereby vve haue to note that the Heretikes in vrging the vvord, *Eucharist*, as mere thankes-giuing, thereby to take avvay blessing and consecration of the elements of bread and vvine, do vnlearnedly and deceitfully. because al the fathers make mention of both: S. Paul also calleth it, blessing of the chalice, which the Euãgelists call, giuing of thankes. Vvhose vvordes Theophylacte explicateth thus, THE CHALICE OF BLESSING, *that is, of the Eucharist.* For holding it in our handes, vve blesse it, & giue thankes to him that shed his bloud for vs. See here both blessing, & Eucharist, blessing the chalice, and thankes-giuing to Liturg. S. Iac. Basil. Chrys. Christ. S. Iames and the Greeke fathers in their Liturgies, put both vvordes in the consecration of eche element, saying thus, *giuing thankes, sanctifying, breaking*: and, *giuing thankes, blessing.*

bleßing, ſanctifying : and, *taking the cuppe, giuing* εὐχαριστήσας,
thankes, ſanctifying, bleßing, filling it vvith the holy εὐλογήσας,
Ghoſt, he gaue it to vs his Diſciples. S. Chryſoſtom ἁγιάσας.
vvho in many places of his vvorkes ſpea- Hom. 2. in
keth much of thankes-giuing in theſe holy Tim. 2.
myſteries, doth he not as often ſpeake of Hom. 83. in
Mat.
the bleſſing, conſecration, yea and the tranſ- Ho. de Iuda
proditore.
mutation thereof, & that vvith vvhat vvordes, and by vvhat povver it is done? Doth
not S. Auguſtine ſay of the ſame, *benedicitur* Aug. ep. [illegible].
& ſanctificatur, it is bleſſed and ſanctified, vvho often
ſpeaketh of the ſolemne giuing of thankes *De bono viduit. c. 16.*
in the ſacrifice of the Church? Doth not the Church at this day vſe the very ſame termes, as in S. Auguſtines time, *Gratias agamus Domino Deo noſtro, Let vs giue thankes to the Lord our God.* and, *Verè dignum & iuſtum eſt, ſemper & vbique tibi gratias agere &c. It is very meete and right, alvvaies and in al places to giue thee thankes*: Vvhich the Greeke Church alſo in their Liturgies expreſſe moſt aboundantly? yet doth there folovv bleſſing & conſecration, and vvhatſoeuer S. Ambroſe deſcribeth to be done in this holy ſacrifice, touching this point, vvriting thereof moſt excellently in his booke *de ijs qui initiantur myſterijs. c. 9.*

6 Of al vvhich, this is the concluſion, that the Euchariſt is a ſolemne name, taken of the vvord εὐχαριστεῖν, ſo called, becauſe this Sacrament and ſacrifice is bleſſed and conſecrated vvith praier & thankes-giuing,

as

as S. Iustine speaketh, and because in this sacrifice so blessed and consecrated into the body and bloud of Christ, him vve offer vp a most acceptable oblation of thankes-giuing, and a memorie of al Gods maruelous benefites tovvard vs. In this sense the fathers and the holy Church speake of the Eucharist, including al the rest, to vvit Sacrament, sacrifice, blessing, & consecration, vvithout vvhich this vvere no more to be called Eucharist, then any other common giuing of thãkes, as S. Irenæus doth plaine-
Li.4.c.34. ly signifie, vvhen he declareth, *hat being before bread, and receiuing the inuocation of God ouer it, novv is no more common bread, but the Eucharist, consisting of tvvo things, the earthly, and the heauenly.* So that it is made the Eucharist by circumstance of solemne vvordes and ceremonies, & therfore is not a mere giuing of thankes: and further vve learne, that S. Iustines and S. Irenæus
εὐχαριστηθείς. vvordes before alleaged, *Panis & calix Eucharistisatus,* signifie, *the bread and chalice made the Eucha-*
εὐχαριστεῖν. *rist*: and consequently vve learne that the actiue thereof, is, by thankes-giuing to make the Eucharist. and because the other vvord of blessing & this of thankes-giuing are vsed indifferently one for an other in Christs action about this Sacrament, vve learne vndoubtedly, that vvhen it is said, εὐλογήσας, or, εὐχαριστήσας, the meaning is, blessing, & giuing thankes, he made the Eucharist

rist of his body and bloud, that is the Sacrament and Sacrifice of a singular thankes-giuing, vvhich (as S. Augustine often is vvont to say) the faithful only do knovv & vnderstand in the sacrifice of the Church: and because the faithful only vnderstand, therfore the Protestants and Caluinistes are so ignorant in this mysterie, that to take away al the dignitie thereof they bend both their expositions and translations.

7 After they haue turned blessing or consecration into bare thankes-giuing, vvhich is one steppe tovvard the denying of the real presence, they come neerer, and so include Christ in heauen, that he can not be vvithal vpon the altar, translating thus, *Vvhom heauen must conteine, vntil the times that al things be restored.* Act. 3. v. 21. and yet Beza vvorse, and he that alleageth him, M. Vvhitakers: *vvho must be conteined in heauen.* Vvhich is so far from the Greeke, that not only Illyricus the Lutheran, but Caluin him self doth not like it. Beza protesteth that he so trāslateth of purpose to keepe Christs presence from the altar: and vve maruel the lesse, because vve are wel acquainted vvith many the like his impudēt Protestatiōs. M. Vvhitak. only vve do maruel at, that he should be either so deceiued by an other mans translation, or him self be so ouerseen in the Greeke

ὃν δεῖ οὐρανὸν δέξασθαι

ad rat. camp. pag. 43.

R vvord

ἀξαδαι. vvord, that he knovveth not a mere deponent and onely deponent, from a passiue.

Ibid. pa. 84

8 This doth not become him that * obiecteth ignorance of the Greeke to an other man, and that after he had vvel tried by publike conference, that he vvas not ignorant: & so obiecteth it as though he knevv not three vvordes in that tongue, vvhereas he had heard him reade & interpret S. Basil, not the easiest of the Greeke Doctors. This is palpable impudencie and a face that can not blush, and ful of malice against the sainctes of God, vvho if they knevv not a vvord in the Greeke tongue, vvere neuer the vvorse, nor the lesse learned, but among fooles and children, that esteeme learning by such trifles, vvhich Grammarians knovv far better then great Diuines. For vvere not he a vvise man that vvould prefer one Maister Humfrey, Maister Fulke, Maister Whitakers, or some of vs poore mē, because vve haue a litle smack in the three tonges, before S. Chrysostom, S. Basil, S. Augustin, S. Gregorie, or S. Thomas, that vnderstoode vvel, none but one? Hovvbeit if they esteeme learning by knovvledge of the tongues, they vvil not (I trovv) compare vvith Catholikes, either of former time, or of these later age, specially since their nevv Gospel began: & if they vvil cō-

If he had not yet tried him, he presumed to belye him, before he knevv him.

pare

pare with vs herein for their ſimple credite, vve may perhaps giue them occaſion ere it be long, to muſter their men al at once, if they dare ſhevv their face before our campe of excellent Hebricians, Grecians, Latiniſtes, of abſolute linguiſtes in the Chaldee, Syriake, Arabike &c. vvhom they muſt needes confeſſe to haue been, and to be euen at this day, their Maiſters and teachers.

9 But to returne to you M. Vvhitakers, greater is your fault in diuinitie, then in the tonges, vvhen you make your argument againſt the real preſence out of this place, as out of the Scripture & S. Peter, vvhereas they are Bezas vvordes, and not S. Peters. Againe, vvhether you take Bezas vvordes, or S. Peters, your argument faileth very much, when you conclude that Chriſts natural body is not in the Sacrament, becauſe it is placed and conteined in heauen. For S. Chryſoſtom telleth you, that *Chriſt aſcending into heauen, both left vs his fleſh, and yet aſcending hath the ſame.* and againe, *O miracle,* ſaith he: *He that ſitteth aboue vvith the Father, in the ſame moment of time is handled vvith the handes of al.* This is the faith of the auncient fathers, M. Whitakers, and this is the Catholike faith, and this is (I trovv) an other maner of faith and far greater, thus to beleeue the preſence of

Ho. 2 ad po. Antioch.

Li. 3 de Sacerdotio.

Christ in both places at once, because he is omnipotent and hath said the vvord: then your faith (vvhereof you boast so much) vvhich beleeueth no further then that he is ascended, and that therfore he cannot be present vpon the altar, nor dispose of his body as he list.

10 Againe it is a very famous place for the real presence of the bloud (vvhich vve
* Chap. 1. numb. 38. haue handled at large * els vvhere, but here also must be breifely touched) vvhen our
τὸ ποτήριον τὸ ἐκχυνόμενον. Sauiour saith, Luc. 22. *This is the Chalice the nevv Testamẽt in my bloud, vvhich* (Chalice) *is shed for you.* For so (vvhich) must needes be referred according to the Greeke. In which speache, Chalice must needes be taken for that in the chalice, and that in the chalice must needes be the bloud of Christ, & not wine, because his bloud only vvas shed for vs. & so vve do plainely proue the real presence.
in 1 Cor. ca. 10. ho. 24. according as S. Chrysostom also said, *Hoc quod est in calice, illud est quod fluxit de latere. That vvhich is in the Chalice, is the same that gushed out of his side.* Al vvhich most necessarie deduction Beza vvould defeate, by saying the Greeke is corrupted in al the copies that are extant in the vvorld, and by trãslating thus cleane
ἐν τῷ ἐμῷ αἵματι τὸ ἐκχυνόμενον. othervvise then the Greeke vvil beare, *This cuppe is the nevv Testamẽt in my bloud, vvhich* (bloud) *is shed for you,*

11 But

11 But what pertaineth this to the English Heretikes, Who translate, *Vvhich is shed*, so indifferētly that it may signifie, *Vvhich cuppe* or, *vvhich bloud* is shed? Thus far it pertaineth, because they do not only defend this translatiō by al meanes, but they tel vs plainely namely Fulke, that they referre (vvhich) to the vvord *bloud*, and not to the vvord *cuppe*, euen as Beza doth, asking vs vvhat Grammarian vvould referre it othervvise. in vvhich questiō he sheweth him self a very simple Grāmariā in the Greeke, or a madde heretike, that either knovveth not, or vvil not knovv, that in the Greeke it can not be so referred, and consequently neither in latin nor English, vvhich in true translation must folovv the Greeke. but of these and other their foule and manifold shiftes to auoid this place, * I haue spokē in an other place of this booke. Ad rat. Cāp. pag. 34. Against D. Sand. Rocke pag. 309. Chap. 1. nu. 37. 38. &c.

12 Only M. Whitakers (to say truely) hath brought somevvhat to the purpose, to vvit, that S. Basil readeth the Greeke as they translate. But he doth vvel to make light of it, because it is euident that S. Basil cited not the text of the Euangelist, but the sense, vvhich Beza noteth to be the custom of the auncient fathers, telling vs vvithal that therfore the reading of the fathers, is no certaine rule to reforme or alter the wordes Pag. 35. Præf. in no. Test. an. 1556.

of Scripture according to the same: and it is very like that if Beza or Fulke his aduocate had thought S. Basils reading of any importance, they vvould haue vsed it long since, rather then so many other shiftes and so absurd, as they doe: vnles vve may thinke they knevv it not, and therfore could not vse it. But for S Basil, according to the sense he citeth it very truely: for, vvhether vve say, *the Cuppe that is shed*, or, *the bloud that is shed*, both signifieth the bloud of Christ shed for vs, as S. Basil citeth it. the differēce is, that referring it to the cuppe, as S. Luke hath it, it signifieth the bloud both present in the cuppe, and also then shed in a Sacrament at the last supper: but referring it to the vvord *bloud*, as S. Basil doth, & as they translate, it may signifie the bloud shed on the crosse also, yea (as these translatours meane and vvould haue it) only that on the Crosse, not considering that the Greeke vvord is the present tense, and therfore rather signifieth the present sheding of his bloud then in mystical sacrifice, then the other visible sheding thereof, vvhich vvas to come in the future tense. Lastly, they translate S. Lukes Gospel, and not S. Basil: and therfore not folovving S. Luke, they are false translators, hovvsoeuer S. Basil readeth.

13 As

13 As this falſhod is both againſt Sacrament and Sacrifice, ſo againſt the Sacrifice alſo of the altar it is, that they controule S. Hieroms tranſlation in the old Teſtament concerning the ſacrifice of Melchiſedec, *Vvho brought forth bread and vvine*: Gen. 14. v. 18. that is, offered or ſacrificed bread & vvine: vvhich vve proue to be the true ſenſe and interpretation (& that this bringing forth of bread & vvine, vvas ſacrificing thereof) not only by al the fathers expoſitions that vvrite of Melchiſedeks prieſthod, (*Cypr. epiſt. 63. Epiph. har. 55. & 79. Hiero. in Mat. 26. & in epiſt. ad Euagrium.*) & by the Hebrue vvord vvhich is a vvord of ſacrifice, Iud. 6. v. 18: and * by the greateſt Rabbines and Hebricians that vvrite thereof, but vve proue it alſo by theſe vvordes of the very text it ſelf, *He brought forth bread and vvine, for he vvas the Prieſt of God moſt high.* Vvhich reaſon immediatly folovving, *Becauſe he vvas Gods Prieſt*, proueth euidētly that he brought it not forth in cōmon maner as any other man might haue done, but as Gods Prieſt, vvhoſe office is to offer ſacrifice. This cōſequence is ſo plaine, that for auoiding thereof, the Aduerſaries vvil not haue it tranſlated in any vviſe, *For he vvas the Prieſt*, as though the Scripture gaue a reaſon vvhy he brought forth bread and vvine: but, *and he vvas a Prieſt, &c.* Vvrangling

The ſacrifice of Melchiſedec.

הוציא

* See Pet. Galat. libro c. 4. et 5. et Chro. Genebrardi pag. 13.

ἦν δὲ ἱερεύς.

והוא כהן

about the signification of the Hebrue coniunction.

14 Vvherein the reader may see their exceding partiality & wilfulnes. For, besides infinite like places of Scripture, whereby vve do easily shevv that this Hebrue particle is vsed to giue a reason or cause of a thing, them selues also in an other place proue it for vs, and that by the authoritie of Theophylacte, & allegation of examples out of the Scripture, and translate accordingly thus: *Blessed art thou among vvomen, because the fruite of thy vvombe is blessed.* Let them giue vs a reason, vvhy the said Coniunction is here by their translation, *quia*, or, *enim*, vvhere it vvas neuer so translated before, and it must not be in any case in the other place of Genesis, vvhere it hath been so translated and generally receiued euē in the primitiue Church. In other places of Scripture also vvhich Theophylacte alleageth, and many moe may be alleaged, they cōfesse and like very vvell it should so signifie: only in the place of Genesis, they can not abide any such sense or translation thereof: but, *He brought forth bread and vvine, and he vvas the Priest, &c.* not, *because he vvas the Priest*: Vvhat is the cause of this their dealing? None other vndoubtedly (and in al these cases I knocke at their consciences) but that here they vvould auoid

Beza annot. in 1 Luc. v. 42.

No. Test. an. 1580. Benedicta tu &c. & benedictus. &c. καὶ εὐλογημένος.

Gen. 14. v. 18.

auoid the neceſſarie ſequele of Melchiſedecks ſacrifice, vpon ſuch tranſlation, vvhich typical ſacrifice of bread and vvine if it ſhould be graũted, then vvould folow alſo a ſacrifice of the nevv Teſtamẽt, made of bread and vvine anſvvering to the ſame, and ſo vve ſhould haue the ſacrifice of the altar, and their bare communion ſhould be excluded.

15 For vvhich purpoſe alſo their partial tranſlation about, *altar*, and, *table*, is notorious. For, the name of altar (as they knovv very vvel) both in the Hebrue and Greeke, and by the cuſtome of al peoples both Ievves and Pagans, implying and importing ſacrifice, therfore vve in reſpect of the ſacrifice of Chriſts body & bloud, ſay, *altar*, rather then, *table*, as al the auncient fathers (*Chryſ. ho. 53 ad po. Antioch.* and *ho. 20 in 2 Cor.* and *in Demoſt. q Chriſtus ſit Deus, to. 5. Nazianz. de Gorgonia ſorore. Baſil. in Liturg. Socrat. li. 1. Hiſt. c. 20 & 25. Theodoret. hiſt. li. 4. c. 20. Theophyl. in 23 Mat. Cypr. epiſt. 63. Optat. cont. Parm. Aug. ep. 86. & li. 9. Confeſſ. c. 11 & 13. & alibi ſæpe*) are wont to ſpeake & vvrite, (namely vvhen S. Hierom calleth the bodies or bones of SS. Peter & Paul the altars of Chriſt, becauſe of this ſacrifice offered ouer and vpon the ſame) though in reſpect of eating & drinking the body and bloud, it is alſo called a table: ſo that vvith vs it is both an altar and a table, vvhether

θυσιαστήριον.

מִזְבֵּחַ

it,

it be of vvood or of ſtone. but the Proteſtants, becauſe they make it only a communion of bread and vvine, or a ſupper, and no ſacrifice, therfore they call it *table* only, and abhorre from the vvord, *altar*, as Papiſtical. For the vvhich purpoſe, in their firſt tranſlation, (*Bible an.* 1562.) vvhen altars vvere then in digging dovvne through out England, they tranſlated vvith no leſſe malice, then they threvve them dovvne, putting the vvord, *temple*, in ſteede of *altar*: vvhich is ſo groſſe a corruption, that a man vvould haue thought it had been done by ouerſight, and not of purpoſe, if they had not done it thriſe immediatly vvithin tvvo chapters, 1 *Cor.* 9. & 10. ſaying: *Knovv you not that they vvhich vvaite of the* TEMPLE, *are partakers of the* TEMPLE? and, *Are not they vvhich eate of the ſacrifice, partakers of the* TEMPLE? in al vvhich
θυσιαστή- places the Apoſtles vvord in Greeke is, *altar*,
ριον. and not, *temple*. and ſee here their notorious
c. 9. v. 13. peeuiſhnes. vvhere the Apoſtle ſaith, *temple*,
ἱερὸν. there the ſame tranſlation ſaith, *ſacrifice*: vvhere the Apoſtle ſaith, *altar*, there it ſaith, *temple*.

16 Thus vve ſee hovv they ſuppreſſe the name of altar, vvhere it ſhould be: novv let vs ſee how they put it in their tranſlatiõ, vvhere it ſhould not be. this alſo they do thriſe in one chapter, & that for to ſaue the honour of their communion table. namely in

in the storie of Bel, vvhere we haue it thrise called the *table* of that idol, vnder vvhich Bels priests *had made a priuie entrance* and, *that the king looked vpon the table*, and, *that they did eate vp such things as vvere vpon the table*: these vvicked trāslators fearing lest the name of Bels table might redound to the dishonour of their Communion table, translate it, *altar*, in al these places. Vvherein I cannot but pitie their follie, and vvonder excedingly hovv they could imagin it any disgrace either for table or altar, if the Idols also had their tables and altars, vvhereas S. Paul so plainely nameth both together, *The table of our Lord, and the table of Diuels.* If the table of Diuels, vvhy not the table of Bel? if that be no disgrace to the table of our Lord, vvhy are you afraid of Bels table, lest it should disgrace yours? Or if you had no such feare, then you must tell vs some other good reason of your vnreasonable trāslation in this place, vvhy you translate, *altar*, for, *table*, that is, chaulke for cheese.

Dan. 14. v. 12.17.20.

τράπεζα.

See the Bib. 1562. and 1577.

1 Cor. 10. v. 21.

17 And here by the vvay the Reader may note an other exceding folly in them, that thinke the name of table, maketh against altar & sacrifice, their ovvne translation here condemning them, vvhere they call Bels table, an altar. and S. Paul, hauing said to the Corinthians, *the table of our Lord*, saith

* Haimo. Oecumen.

saith to the Hebrues * of the self same, *vve haue an altar.* & againe he saith, *the table of Diuels*, vvhich I am sure they wil not deny to haue been a true altar of Idololatrical sacrifice. & Malach. 1. v. 7. in one sentence it is called both altar & table, vvherevpon the Ievves offered their external and true sacrifices. & al the fathers both Greeke and Latin speaking of the sacrifice of the nevv Testamēt, call that wherevpon it is offered, both altar & table: but the Greekes more often *table*, the Latin fathers more often *altar*: and vvhy or in vvhat respectes it is called both this and that, vve haue before declared, & here might adde the very same out of S. Germanus Arch. B. of Constantinople, in his Greeke commentaries (called *mystica theoria*) vpon the Liturgies or Masses of the Greeke fathers. but to procede.

18 There are also some places lesse euidēt, yet such as smatche of the like heretical humor against the B. Sacrament. In the prophet Hieremie c. 11. v. 19. vve reade thus according to the Latin and the Greeke, *Let vs cast * vvood vpon his bread*, that is, saith S. Hierom in comment. huius loci, *the crosse vpon the body of our Sauiour. For it is he that said, I am the bread that descended from heauen.* Vvhere the Prophet so long before saying, *bread*, and meaning his body, alludeth prophetically to his body in the B. Sacra-

* Lignum in panem eius. ξύλον εἰς τὸν ἄρτον αὐτοῦ.

B.Sacrament made of bread and vnder the forme of bread, and therfore alſo called bread of the Apoſtle. So that both in the Prophet and the Apoſtle, his bread and his body is al one. (1 Cor.10.) and leſt vve ſhould thinke that the bread only ſignifieth his body, he ſaith, *let vs put the Croſſe vpon his bread*, that is, vpō his very natural body vvhich hung on the croſſe. Novv for theſe vvordes of the Prophet ſo vſual and vvel knovven in the Church and al antiquitie, hovv thinke you do theſe nevv Maiſters tranſlate? in one bible thus, *Let vs deſtroy the tree vvith the fruite therof.* An other, *vve vvil deſtroy his meate vvith vvood.* or as they ſhould haue ſaid rather, *the vvood vvith his meate* Do you ſee how properly they agree, vvhiles they ſeeke nouelties, and forſake the auncient vſual tranſlation?

19 They vvil ſay, the firſt Hebrue vvord can not be as S.Hierom tranſlateth, and as it is in the Greeke, and as al antiquitie readeth: but it muſt ſignifie, *Let vs deſtroy.* They ſay truely, according to the Hebrue vvord vvhich novv is. But is it not euidēt thereby, that the Hebrue vvord novv is not the ſame vvhich the Septuaginta trāſlated into Greeke, and S.Hierom into Latin? and conſequently the Hebrue is altered and corrupted from the original copie vvhich they had: perhaps by the Ievves (as * ſome other places

ἐμβάλωμεν. mittamus. נַשְׁחִי־תָה

Pſ.21.

places) to obſcure this prophecie alſo of Chriſts Paſſion, and their crucifying of him vpon the Croſſe. Such Ievviſh Rabbines and nevv Hebrue vvordes do our nevv maiſters gladly folovv in the tranſlation of the old Teſtament, vvhereas they might eaſily conceiue the old Hebrue vvord in this place, if they vvould employ their ſkill that vvay, and not only to nouelties. For who ſeeth not that the Greeke Interpreters in number 70, and al Hebrues of beſt ſkill in their ovvne tongue, S. Hierom alſo a great Hebrician did not reade as novv vve haue in the Hebrue, *Naſhchitha*, but, *Naſhitha*, or, *Naſhlicha*? Againe the Hebrue vvord that novv is, doth ſo litle agree vvith the vvordes folovving, that they cannot tel hovv to tranſlate it, as appeareth by the diuerſitie and difference of their tranſlations thereof before mentioned, and tranſpoſing the vvordes in Engliſh othervviſe then in the Hebrue, neither of both their tranſlations hauing any commodious ſenſe or vnderſtanding.

Deſtruamus. ponamus. mittamus.

20 But yet they vvil pretend that for the firſt vvord at the leaſt, they are not to be blamed, becauſe they folovv the Hebrue that novv is. not conſidering that if this vvere a good excuſe, then might they as vvel folovv the Hebrue that novv is. Pſal.

21.

21.v.18 : and so vtterly suppresse and take out of the Scripture this notable prophecie, *They pearced my handes and my feete*: Vvhich yet they doe not, neither can they doe it for shame, if they vvil be counted Christians. So that in deede, to folovv the Hebrue sometime vvhere it is corrupt, is no sufficient excuse for them, though it may haue a pretence of true translation, and vve promised in the preface, in such cases not to call it heretical translation.

21 But concerning the B. Sacrament, let vs see once more hovv truely they folovv the Hebrue. *The holy Ghost* (saith S. Cyprian ep.63 nu.2.) *by Salomon foreshevveth a type of our Lordes sacrifice, of the immolated host of bread and vvine, saying, Vvisedome hath killed her hostes,* SHE HATH MINGLED HER VVINE INTO *the cuppe. Come ye, eate of my bread, and drinke the vvine that* I HAVE MINGLED *for you. Speaking of* VVINE MINGLED (saith this holy doctor) *he foreshevveth prophetically the cuppe of our Lord,* MINGLED VVITH VVATER AND VVINE. So doth S. Hierom interprete this mixture or mingling of the vvine in the chalice, so doth the author of the commentaries vpon this place among S. Hieroms vvorkes, so doe the other fathers. So that there is great importance in these prophetical vvordes of Salomon. *She hath mingled her vvine into the cuppe*, and, *the vvine vvhich I haue mingled*, as being a manifest prophecie of Christs mingling vvater

That vvater and vvine ought to be mingled in the chalice. Pro. 9.

See S. Augustine de Ciuit. Dei li.17 c.20.

vvater and vvine in the Chalice at his last supper, vvhich the Catholike Church obserueth at this day, and vvhereof S. Cyprian vvriteth the foresaid long epistle.

22 But the Protestants counting it an idle superstitious ceremonie, here also frame their translation accordingly, suppressing altogether this mixture or mingling, and in steede thereof saying, *she hath drawen her vvine*, and, *drinke the vvine that I haue drawen*: or (as in other of their bibles) *she hath povvred out her vvine*, and *the vvine vvhich I haue povvred out*: neither trāslation agreing either vvith Greeke or Hebrue. not vvith the Greeke, vvhich doth euidently signifie, mingling and mixture, as it is in the Latin, & as al the Greeke Church from the Apostles time hath vsed this vvord in this very case vvhereof vve novv speake, of mingling vvater & vvine in the chalice. S. Iames and S. Basil in their Liturgies expresly testifying that Christ did so, as also S. Cyprian in the place alleaged. S. Iustine in the end of his second apologie, calling it of the same Greeke vvord, κρᾶμα, that is (according to Plutarche) vvine mingled vvith vvater: likevvise S. Ireneus in his fifth booke neere the beginning. See the 6 general Councel most fully treating hereof and deducing it from the Apostles & auncient

Bibl. 1579.

an. 1577.

ἐκέρασεν, miscuit.

κεκέρακα, miscui.

λαβὼν τὸ ποτήριον, κεράσας.

mixtus calix.

Conc. Constantinop. 6. can. 32.

cient fathers, and interpreting this Greeke μεῖγνυμι
vvord by an other equiualent, and more
plaine to signifie this mixture
23 Thus thē the Greeke is neither drawing
of vvine, nor povvring out thereof, as they
trāslate, but mingling. but the Hebrue perhaps signifieth both, or at the least one of
the tvvo, either to dravv, or to povver out.
Gentle reader, if thou haue skill, looke the
Hebrue Lexicon of Pagnine esteemed the מָסַךְ
best: if thou haue not skil, aske, and thou
shalt vnderstand that there is no such signification of this vvord in al the bible, but
that it signifieth only mixture & mingling.
A strange case, that to auoide this mingling
of the cuppe, being a most certaine tradition of the Apostles, they haue inuented
tvvo other significations of this Hebrue
vvord, vvhich it neuer had before.

CHAP. XVIII.

Heretical translation against the honour of SAINCTS, *namely of our* B. LADIE.

1 LET vs passe from Gods holy Sacraments to his honorable Saincts in heauen, and vve shal finde that these transla- tions plucke from them also as much honour as they may. In the Psalme

Psal. 138. 138 vvhere the Catholike Church & al antiquitie readeth thus, *Nimis honorati sunt amici tui Deus* &c. *Thy frendes ô God are become exceding honorable, their princedom is excedingly strengthened:* vvhich verse is sung and said in the honour of the holy Apostles, agreably to that in an

Ps. 44. other Psalme, *Constitues eos principes super omnem terram*, Thou shalt appoint them Princes ouer al the earth: vvhat meane they in al their English Bibles to alter it thus: *Hovv deere are thy counsels (or thoughtes) to me ô God: ô hovv great is the summe of them?* Doth not the Hebrue

רֵעֶיךָ make more for the old receiued Latin translation, then for theirs, because the Hebrue vvord is vsed more cõmonly for to signifie frendes then cogitations? doth not S. Hierom so translate in his translation of the Psalmes according to the Hebrue? doth not the great Rabbine R. Salomon? Doth not

οἱ φίλοι σου the Greeke put it out of doubt, vvhich is altogether according to the said auncient Latin translation?

2 And you my Maisters that translate

עָצְמוּ otherwise, I beseeche you, is it in Hebrue,

רָאשֵׁי- *Hovv great is the summe of them* & not rather word for vvord most plainely, *hovv are the heads of*

הֶם *them strengthened*, or *their princedoms*, as in the

αἱ ἀρχαὶ Greeke also it is most manifest? Vvhy do

αὐτῶν. you then hunt after nouelties, and forsake the troden pathe of the auncient, and passe the

the boundes vvhich our holy forefathers haue ſet and appointed, preferring your ovvne ſingularities and nevv deuiſes euen there vvhere you can not iuſtly pretend either the Hebrue or Greeke? Vvhen the Hebrue Lexicon hath giuen the common interpretation of this place, and then ſaith, *Quidam exponunt*, Some expound it otherwiſe: vvhy had you rather be of that leſſer, *ſome that expound othervviſe*, then of the great ſocietie of al auncient interpreters?

Epito. Theſau. Pagn. an. 1570. in radice. רצח

3 But this nevv fangled ſingularitie of teaching and tranſlating othervviſe then al antiquitie hath done, ſhal better appeare in their dealing about our B. Lady, vvhoſe honour they haue ſought ſo many vvaies to diminiſh & deface, that the defenſe and maintenance thereof againſt the Heretikes of our time is grovven to a great booke learnedly vvritten by the great Clerke and Ieſuite, father Caniſius, entitled, *Mariana.*

4 Concerning our purpoſe, vvhat vvas euer more common, and is novv more general and vſual in al Chriſtian Countries, then in the *Aue Marie* to ſay, *Gratia plena, ful of grace*, in ſo much that in the firſt Engliſh Bible it hath continued ſo ſtill, and euery childe in our Countrie vvas taught ſo to ſay, till the *Aue Marie* vvas baniſhed altogether and not ſuffered to be ſaid neither in

Latin nor Engliſh? Vvhat auncient father of the Latin Church hath not alvvaies ſo read and expounded? Vvhat Church in al the vveſt hath not euer ſo ſung and ſaid? Onely our nevv Tranſlators haue found a nevv kinde of ſpeache, tranſlating thus:
Bib. 1579. and 1577. *Haile thou that art freely beloued.* and, *Haile thou that art in high fauour.* Vvhy this, and that, or any other thing, rather then, *Haile ful of grace?*
Luc. 1. v. 15. S. Iohn Baptiſt vvas ful of the holy Ghoſt
Act. 7. v. 8. euen from his birth, S. Steuen vvas ful of grace, as the Scripture recordeth of them both: vvhy may not then our Lady much
Ambr. li. 2 in 1 Luc. more be called ful of grace, vvho (as S. Ambroſe ſaith) *onely obteined the grace, vvhich no other vvomen deſerued, to be repleniſhed vvith the author of grace?*

5 They vvil ſay, the Greeke vvord doth not ſo ſignifie. doth it not? I make them ſelues vvitneſſes of the contrarie, and their owne tranſlation in other places ſhal confute them, vvhere they tranſlate an other vvord of the ſelf ſame nature and forme
Luc. 16. v. 20 and in al reſpectes like to this, *ful of ſores.* If ἡλκωμένος be ful of ſores, vvhy is not κεχαριτωμένη ful of grace? Let any Grecian of them al make me a difference in the nature and ſignificancie of theſe tvvo vvordes. Againe if *vlceroſus* (as Beza tranſlateth) be ful of ſores, vvhy is not *gratioſa* (as Eraſmus tranſlateth) ful

ful of grace? or vvhy doth Beza maruel that
Eraſmus tranſlated, *gratioſa*, vvhen him ſelf
trãſlateth the like vvord, *vlceroſus*. Al vvhich
adiectiues in *oſus* (you knovv) ſignifie fulnes,
as, *periculoſus*, *ærumnoſus*. Yet vvhat a ſturre doth
Beza keepe here in his Annotatiõs to make
the Greeke vvord ſignifie, *freely beloued*?

6 But hath it in deede any ſuch ſignification? tell vs you that profeſſe this great
ſkill of the tongues, vvhat ſyllable is there χαριτῶσαι
in this vvord that ſoundeth to that ſignification? S. Chryſoſtom and the Greeke Do- Comment. in Eph. 1.
ctors that ſhould beſt knovv the nature
of this Greeke word, ſay that it ſignifieth, to
make gratious, & acceptable, and beloued,
and beautiful, and amiable, and ſo to be deſired as vvhen the Pſalme ſaith, *The king ſhal* Pſal. 44.
deſire thy beautie. Beza him ſelf ſaith, that it is
vvord for vvord, *gratificata*, *made grateful*,
and yet he expoundeth it, *accepted before God*,
and tranſlateth it, *freely beloued*, becauſe he
vvill haue no ſingular grace or goodnes or
vertue reſident in our B. Lady, but al by
imputation & acceptation, vvhereof I haue
ſpoken before. S. Athanaſius a Greeke Do- S. Athan. de S. Deip.
ctor ſaith that ſhe had this title κεχαριτω-
μένη, becauſe the HOLY Ghoſt deſcended into
the Virgin, filling her vvith al graces and
vertues. and I beſeeche the reader to ſee his
vvordes, vvhich are many moe concerning

this fulnes of grace and al spiritual-giftes.

Ep. 140 in expos. Psal. 44.

S. Hierom that knevv the Greeke vvord as vvel as the Protestants, readeth, *Gratia plena,* and findeth no fault vvith this interpretation. but saith plainely she vvas so saluted, *ful of grace,* because she conceiued him in vvhom al fulnes of the deitie dvvelt corporally.

John Keltridge *preacher of the vvord* in London. in his sermons vvithin the toure, printed. fo. 14.

Grosse ignorance & singular pride in many of the nevv cleargie.

So he called the Priests of the Seminarie, as if one vvold cal a monke a Monasterie or a nonne a Nonry.

7 Novv let the English Bezites come vvith their nevv terme, *freely beloued,* and controule these and al other auncient fathers both Greeke and Latin, and teache them a nevv signification of the Greeke vvord, vvhich they knevv not before. Let Iohn Keltridge one of their great preachers in London, come and tel vs, *that the Septuaginta and the best translations in Greeke haue no such vvordes as vve vse in the Aue Marie,* but that the vvord vvhich the Septuaginta vse, is κεχαριτωμένη &c. Vvho euer heard such a ieast, that the preacher of the vvord of God in London (so he is called in the title of his booke) and preacher before the Iesuites and Seminaries in the tovver, vvhich is next degree to the disputers there, vvhose sermons be solemnely printed, and dedicated to one of the Queenes Councel, vvho seemeth to be such a Grecian that he confuteth the vulgar Latin translation by the signification of the Greeke vvorde, and in other places of his booke

booke alleageth the Greeke text: that this man for al this, referreth vs to the Septuaginta either as authors of S. Lukes Gospel vvhich is to ridiculous: or as translators thereof, as though S. Luke had vvritten in Hebrue, yea as though the vvhole nevv Testament had been vvritten in Hebrue (for so no doubt he presupposed) and that the Septuaginta had translated it into Greeke as they did the old, vvho vvere dead three hundred yeres before S. Lukes Gospel and the nevv Testament vvas vvritten. Pag. 37. of the 2 part.

8 Al this is such a pitiful ieast, as vvere incredible, if his printed booke did not giue testimonie. Pitiful I say, because the simple people count such their preachers ioly fellowes & great Clerkes, because they can talke of the Greeke & of the Hebrue text, as this man doth also concerning the Hebrue letter *Tau*, vvhether it had in old time the forme of a crosse or no, euen as vvisely and as skilfully, as he did before of the Septuaginta and the Greeke vvord in S. Lukes Gospel. Vvhose incredible follie and ignorance in the tongues perhaps I vvould neuer haue mentioned (because I thinke the rest are sorie and ashamed of him) but that he boasteth of that vvhereof he hath no skil, and that the people may take him for a very paterne and example of many Fol. 11. parte. 2.

other like boasters and braggers among them, and that vvhen they heare one talke lustely of the Hebrue and Greeke, and cite the text in the said tongues, they may alvvaies remember Iohn keltridge their preacher, and say to them selues, vvhat if this fellovv also be like Iohn keltridge?

9 But to procede: these great Grecians and Hebricians that controule al antiquitie and the approued aunciẽt Latin translation by scãning the Greeke & Hebrue vvordes, that thinke it a great corruption Gen. 3. to reade, *Ipsa conteret caput tuum, she shal bruise thy head*, because it pertaineth to our Ladies honour, calling it* a corruption of the Popish Church, whereas S. Ambrose, S. Augustine, S. Gregorie, S. Bernard, & the rest reade so, as being the cõmon receiued text in their time (though there hath been also alvvaies the other reading euen in the vulgar Latin trãslatiõ, & therfore it is not any late reformation of these new correctors, as though the Hebrue and Greeke text before had been vnknovven) these controulers I say of the Latin text by the Hebrue, against our Ladies honour, are in an other place content to dissemble the Hebrue vvord, and that also for smal deuotion to the B. Virgin: namely Hierem 7 and 44. Vvhere the Prophet inueigheth against them that offer sacrifice

*Sand. Rocke discou. pag. 145.

crifice

crifice to the *Queene of heauen.* this they thinke is very vvel, becauſe it may ſound in the peoples eares againſt the vſe of the Catholike Church, vvhich calleth our Lady, *Queene of heauen.* but they knovv very vvel that the Hebrue vvorde doth not ſignifie, *Queene* in any other place of the Scripture, and that the Rabbines and later Hebricians (vvhom they gladly folovv) deduce it othervviſe, to ſignifie rather the vvhole corps and frame of heauen, conſiſting of al the beautiful ſtarres and planets, and the Septuaginta call it not onely βασίλισσαν, See Pagn. in radice.
Queene, but τὴν στρατιὰν, *the hoſt of heauen,* c. 7. מְלַךְ
Hierem: and S. Hierom not only, *reginam,* and
but rather, *militiam cœli*: & vvhen he nameth לְאַךְ
it *reginam, Queene,* he ſaith vve muſt vnderſtand it of the moone, to vvhich and to the other ſtarres they did ſacrifice and commit idolatrie. but the Proteſtants (againſt their cuſtom of ſcanning the Hebrue and the Greeke) tranſlate here, *Queene of heauen,* for no other cauſe in the vvorld, but to make it ſound againſt her, vvhom Catholikes truely call and vvorthily honour as Queene of heauen, becauſe her ſõne is king, and ſhe exalted aboue Angels and al other creatures. See the Nevv Teſt. Annot. Act. 1. v. 14.

10 Againe, vvhy doth the Geneua nevv An. 1580.
Teſtament make S. Mathevv to ſay, that *He* Cap. 1. v. 25.

(to

(to vvit, Ioseph) *called his name Iesus?* Vvhy
Cap.1. v.31. not she, as vvel as he? For in S. Luke the
Angel saith to our Lady also, *Thou shalt call his name Iesus.* S. Matthevv then speaking indifferently, and not limiting it to him or her, vvhy doe they giue this preeminence to Ioseph rather then to the B. Virgin? did
Luc. 1. v. 60 and 63. not both Zacharie and also Elisabeth his vvife by reuelation giue the name of Iohn to Iohn the Baptist? yea did not Elisabeth the mother first so name him, before Zacharie her husbād? much more may vve thinke that the B. Virgin the natural mother of our Sauiour, gaue him the name of Iesus, then Ioseph his putatiue father. specially if vve consider that the Angel reuealed the name first vnto her, saying, that she should so call him: and the Hebrue vvord Esa.7. vvherevnto the Angel alludeth, is the fœminine gender, and referred by the great Rabbines, Rabbi Abraham and Rabbi Dauid, vnto her, saying expresly in their commentaries, *Et vocabit ipsa puella: and the maide her self shal call.* and surely the vsual pointing of the Greeke text (for Beza maketh other points of his ovvne) is much more for that purpose. Novv if they vvil say that Theophylacte vnderstandeth it of Ioseph, true it is, and so it may be vnderstood very wel: but if it may be vnderstood of our Lady also

alſo, and rather of her then of him, vvhy doth your tranſlation exclude this other interpretation?

11 Vvhere, by the vvay I muſt tel you (and els vvhere perhaps more at large) that it is your common fault to make ſome one doctors interpretation, the text of your tranſlation, and ſo to exclude al the reſt that expound it othervviſe, vvhich you knovv is ſuch a fault in a tranſlator as can by no meanes be excuſed. Secōdly the reader may here obſerue and learne, that if they ſhal hereafter defend their tranſlation of any place, by ſome doctors expoſitiō agreable therevnto, that vvil not ſerue nor ſuffice them, becauſe euery Doctor may ſay his opinion in his cōmentaries, * but that muſt not be made the text of Scripture, becauſe other doctors expound it othervviſe: and being in it ſelf and in the original tōge ambiguous and indifferent to diuers ſenſes, it may not be reſtrained or limited by tranſlation, vnles there be a mere neceſſitie, vvhen the tranſlation can not poſſibly or hardly expreſſe the ambiguitie and indifferencie of the original text.

See chap. 1. nu. 3. 43. Cha 10. nu. 1.2. chap. 19. nu. 1.

12 As (for example) in this controuerſie cōcerning Saincts, S. Peter ſpeaketh ſo ambiguouſly, either that he wil remember thē after his death, or they ſhal remember him, that

2 Pet. 1. v. 15.

μέμνηνται τῶν τῆδε, καὶ πρεσβεύουσιν ὑπὲρ τῶν ζώντων.

that some of the Greeke fathers gathered and concluded therevpon (*Oecum. in Caten. Gagneius in hunc locũ*) that the Saincts in heauen remember vs on earth, and make intercession for vs. Vvhich ambiguitie both in the Greeke and the Latin, should be also kept and expressed in the English translation, and vve haue endeuoured as neere as vve could possibly so to make it, because of the diuers interpretations of the auncient fathers. But it may seeme perhaps to the reader that the said ambiguitie can not be kept in our English tongue, and that our ovvne translation also can haue but one sense. If it be so, and if there be a necessitie of one sense, then (as I said) the translator in that respect is excused. But let the good reader consider also, that the Caluinists in restraining the sense of this place, folovv not necessitie, but their heresie, That Saincts pray not for vs. Vvhich is euident by this, that they restraine it in their Latin translations also, vvhere there is no necessitie at al, but it might be as ambiguous & indifferẽt, as in Greeke, if it pleased them: yea when they print the Greeke Testament only vvithout any translation, yet here they put the Latin in the margent, according as they vvil haue it read, and as though it might be read no othervvise then they prescribe.

Beza.

No. Test. Gr. Henr. Steph. an. 1576.

CHAP.

CHAP. XIX.

Heretical tranſlation againſt the diſtinction of LATRIA *and* DVLIA.

IN this reſtraining of the I
Scripture to the ſenſe of
ſome one Doctor, there is a
famous example in the epi-
ſtle to the Hebrues, vvhere Heb.11.v.21
the Apoſtle ſaith either Iacob adored the
toppe of Ioſephs ſcepter, as many read and
expound: or els, that he adored tovvard the
toppe of his ſcepter, as other read and interpret: and beſide theſe there is no other interpretation of this place in al antiquitie,
but in S. Auguſtine only, as Beza cōfeſſeth: Quæſt. in Gen.
yet are they ſo bold to make his expoſition
only, and his commentarie peculiar to him Bib.1579.
alone, the text of the Scripture in their trāſlation, ſaying, *Iacob leaning on the end of his ſtaffe,
vvorſhipped God*, and ſo excluding al other
ſenſes & expoſitions of al the other fathers,
excluding and condemning their ovvne
former tranſlations, adding tvvo vvordes Bib. 1562.
more then are in the Greeke text, *leaning, God*: 1577.
forcing αὐτοῦ to ſignifie αὑτοῦ, vvhich may
be, but is as rare, as *virga eius*, for *virga ſuæ*:
turning the other vvordes cleane out of
their order and place and forme of conſtruction vvhich they muſt needes haue correſ-
pondent

Gen. 47. v. 31 pondent and ansvverable to the Hebrue
וישתחו text from vvhence they vvere translated:
על vvhich Hebrue vvordes them selues translate in this order, *He vvorshipped tovvard the*
ראש *beddes head.* If *he vvorshipped tovvard the beddes head,*
המטה according to the Hebrue: then *did he vvorship*
προσεκύνησεν ἐπὶ τὸ ἄκρον τῆς ῥάβδου αὐτοῦ. *tovvard the toppe of his scepter*, according to the
Greeke: the difference of both being only
in these vvordes, *scepter*, and, *bedde* (because
the Hebrue is ambiguous to both) and not
in the order or construction of the sentence.

2 To make it more plaine, vvhen the Pro-
πρὸς ναόν. phet Dauid saith, *Adorabo ad templum sanctum*
tuum Psal. 5. & 137. is not the true translation,
and grāmatical sequele of the vvordes thus:
I vvil adore tovvard thy holy temple? Is it not a
common phrase in the Scripture, that the
εἰς ὄρος. people of God adored tovvard Hierusalem,
Dan. 6. 3 Reg. 8. tovvard his holy mount, before the arke,
Psal. 98. tovvard the place vvhere his feete stood?
Iosu. 7. May any man be so bold, by adding and
εἰς τὸν τόπον. transposing to alter and obscure al such
Ps. 131. places of holy Scripture, that there may
appeare no maner of adoration tovvard or
before a creature? and for vvorshipping or
adoring tovvard the things aforesaid and
the like, may vve say, leaning vpon those
things to vvorship or adore God? Vvere
they afraid lest those speaches of holy Scripture

ture might vvarrant and confirme the Catholike & Christian maner of adoring our Sauiour Christ toward the holy Roode, at, or before his image and the Crucifixe before the altar, and so forth? For had they not feared this, vvhy should they translate ἐπὶ, *leaning vpon*, rather then, *tovvards*, yea, vvhy in Genesis, *tovvards his beddes head*, & here not, *tovvards*?

3 And (vvhich is more) vvhen the auncient Greeke fathers, *Chrys. Oecum. in Collectan. Damasc. li. 1. pro imaginibus, Leont. apud Damasc.* put so litle force either in this preposition ἐπὶ (or the other alleaged) that they expound al those speaches as if the prepositions vvere of phrase only and not of signification, saying, *Iacob adored Iosephs scepter, the people of Israel adored the temple, the Arke, the holy mount, the place vvhere his feete stoode*, and the like, vvhereby S. Damascene proueth the adoration of creatures named *Dulia*, namely of the crosse and of sacred images: if I say they make so litle force of the prepositions, that they inferre not only adoration towards the thing, but adoratiō of the thing: hovv do these goodly translatours, of al other vvordes so straine and racke the litle particle ἐπὶ to signifie, *leaning vpon*, that it shal in no vvise signifie any thing tending tovvards adoration?

προς, εἰς.

τῇ ῥάβδῳ προσκυνῆσαι. τοῖς τόποις θεοῦ, τῷ ναῷ προσκυνεῖν.

4 And

4 And if the Greeke Doctors suffise not to satisfie these great Grecians herein, tel me you that haue skil in the Hebrue, vvhether in the foresaid speaches cited out of the Psalmes, there be any force in the
לְהַר Hebrue prepositions? surely no more then
Psal. 98. 131. if vve should say in English vvithout prepositions, *Adore ye his holy hil: vve vvil adore the*
לַהֲדוֹם *place vvhere his feete stoode: Adore ye his footestoole:*
רַגְלָיו For you knovv that there is the same pre-
Psal. 95. or 96. position also vvhen it is said, *Adore ye our Lord:* or as your selues translate, *vvorship the Lord:*
לַיהוָה vvhere there can be no force nor signification of the prepositiō. And therfore in these places also your translation is corrupt and vvilful, vvhen you say thus: *Vve vvil fall dovvne before his footestoole. fall ye dovvne before his footestoole, before his holy mount, or vvorship him vpon his holy hil:* Vvhere you shunne and auoid first the terme of adoration, vvhich the Hebrue and Greeke duely expresse by termes
προσκυνεῖν correspondent in both languages, through
לְשְׁתַּחֲוֺת out the Bible, and are applied for the most part to signifie adoring of creatures. Secondly you auoid the Greeke phrase, vvhich is at the least, to adore tovvards these holy things and places: & much more the Hebrue phrase, vvhich is, to adore the very things rehearsed: *to adore Gods footestoole*
Psal. 98. (as the Psalme saith) *because it is holy*, or, *because he*

he is holy, vvhose footestoole it is, as the Greeke readeth.

5 This being most manifest to al that haue skil in these tongues, it is euident that you regard neither Hebrue nor Greeke, but only your heresie: & that in S. Paules place aforesaid of adoring Iosephs scepter, you alter it by your ovvne fansie, and not by S. Augustines authoritie, vvhom I am sure you vvil not admit reading in the Psalme, *Adore ye his footestoole:* and so precisely and religiously reading thus, that he examineth the case, and findeth thereby that the B. Sacrament must be adored, and that no good Christian doth take it, before he adore it. Neither vvil you admit him vvhen he readeth thus of Dauid, *He vvas caried i his ovvne handes*, & interpreteth it mystically of Christ, that he vvas caried in his ovvne handes, vvhen he gaue his body and bloud to his disciples. Yet are S. Augustines interpretations (hovvsoeuer you like or mislike them) very good, as also that aboue named of Iacobs leaning vpon his staffe, and adoring, may be one good sense or commentarie of that place, but yet a commentarie, and one Doctors opinion, not the sacred text of Scripture, as you would make it by so translating.

Præf. in Ps. 33.

T 6 And

6 And if S. Hierom like not the Greeke Doctors interpretation in this place of adoring Ioseph and his scepter, yet he also saith that Iacob adored tovvard Iosephs rodde, or tovvard the beds head, and not *leaning vpon his staffe he adored*, vvhich you make the text of Scripture. And though he thinke that in this place is not meant any adoratiō of Ioseph, yet I am sure, for adoration of holy things, namely Relikes, the holy land, and al the holy places and monuments of Christs being & doing vpon the earth, you vvil not be tried by S. Hierom. And againe, why S. Paul should say, that by faith he adored, & in respect of things to come, it is not othervvise easie to vnderstand, but that he partly foresaw the kingdom of Ephraim, in the posteritie of Ioseph: partly the kingdom of Christ prefigured in Ioseph then Prince of Ægypt, & so by faith adored his scepter or tovvard his scepter (vvhich is al one) as the greeke fathers for the most part expoūd it. But let vs hasten tovvard an end.

CHAP. XX.

Heretical translation by ADDING TO THE TEXT.

BECAVSE

1

BECAVSE in the last corruption I spake of adding to the text, though it be their common and vniuersal fault in euery controuersie, as is to be seen in euery chapter of this booke: yet here I vvil adde certaine places not yet mentioned. As, *The rest of the actes of Iehoakim, and his abominations vvhich he did, and* CARVED IMAGES THAT VVERE LAID TO HIS CHARGE, BEHOLD THEY ARE WRITTEN *&c.* these vvordes, *carued images laid to his charge*, are more then is either in the Greeke or the Hebrue.

2 Paral. 36. v. 8. in Bib. 1562.

Against images.

2 Againe, *Saul confounded the Ievves prouing (by conferring one Scripture vvith an other) that this is very Christ.* These vvordes, *by conferring one scripture vvith an other*, are added more then is in the Greeke text: in fauour of their presumptuous opinion, that conference of Scriptures is ynough for any man to vnderstand them, and so to reiect both the commentaries of the Doctors, & exposition of holy Councels and Catholike Church. it is so much more I say then is in the Greeke text, and a notorious corruption in their Bible read daily in their churches as most authentical. See the rest of their Bibles, and thou shalt finde no more for al those vvordes, but, *affirming*, or, *confirming*. and the self same Bible in the first epistle to the Corinthians translateth the same Greeke vvord thus,

Act. 9. v. 22. Bib. 1577.

For Conference of Scriptures, against fathers, Councels &c.

συμβιβάζων

c. 2. v. 16.

τίς συμβιβάσει. συμβιβάσεις. הורע

Vvho shal instruct? And in deede that is the true and vsual signification of the vvord, both in the old Testament, and in the nevv. as Deut. 4. *Thou shalt teach them thy children.* And Esa. 40. *Vvho shal instruct our Lord?* the Hebrue vvord also in both places signifying no more but instructing and teaching. And so doth the Apostle cite it to the Corinthians out of Esay, & he vseth it to the Colos. (c. 2. v. 2) in the same signification, as the Church readeth and expoundeth it, and so consequently S. Luke in the place vvhereof vve novv treate, saith nothing els, but that S. Paul earnestly taught or instructed them that Iesus is Christ. And yet our nevv Translators vvithout respect of Hebrue or greeke, haue coined a nevv signification, of conferring one Scripture vvith an other. So ignorant they are in the signification of Greeke vvordes, or rather so vvilfully malitious.

1 Pet. 1. v. 25. Bib. 1562. 1577. Against traditions.

3 Againe, in the first epistle of S. Peter they translate thus: *The vvord of the Lord endureth euer: and this is the vvord vvhich by the Gospel vvas preached vnto you.* vvhere these vvordes, *by the Gospel,* are added deceitfully and of il intent, to make the reader thinke that there is no other vvord of God but the vvritten vvord, for the common reader hearing this vvord, *Gospel,* conceiueth nothing els. But in

in deede al is the Goſpel vvhatſoeuer the Apoſtles taught either by vvriting, or by tradition and vvord of mouth, as S. Paul ſpeaketh 2. Theſſ. 2. and S. Peter ſaith nothing els in the place alleaged, but, *This is the vvord vvhich is preached among you,* as the Geneua bibles tranſlate, or more ſignificantly, *vvhich is euangelized* among you, as vve tranſlate. for though there be greater ſignificancie in the Greeke vvord, then is expreſſed by bare preaching or telling a thing, as hauing a goodly relation and alluſion to the vvord, *Euangelium, Goſpel*: yet neither do they in any other place, neither can they tranſlate it, *to preach by the Goſpel*: but ſimply, to preache, to tel, to ſhevv. as, *preaching peace by Ieſus Chriſt,* Act. 10. v. 36. ſo them ſelues tranſlate it. and Pſ. 95 (or 96. v. 2) *Be telling of his ſaluation from day to day.* Vvhich in other places is ſpoken by other Greeke vvordes, that haue no ſignification at al of Goſpel. as immediatly in the ſaid Pſ. 95 (or 96. v. 3) & Pſ. 104. (or 105. v. 1.) & Act. 13. v. 5. and c. 17. v. 23. and Io. 1. verſ. 3.

τὸ ῥῆμα τὸ εὐαγγελισθὲν.

Euangelizo.

εὐαγγελιζόμενος.

εὐαγγελίζεσθε.

ἀναγγείλατε.

ἀπαγγείλατε, κατήγγελον, καταγγέλλω ἀπαγγέλλομεν.

4 Al vvhich vvordes ſignifie only to tel, to ſhevv, to declare, and are vſed indifferently for & with the other word vvhich they here only tranſlate, *to preache by the Goſpel.* Vvhereas in al others places vvhen they

Luc. 2. v. 10. Act. 13. v. 32. Gal. 3, 8. Dominus dabit verbũ *euangelizantibus*. Qui *Euangelizas* Hierusalem. Ps. 67. Isa. 40.

vvil translate it most significantly, they expresse it by *bringing glad tidings*: and in some places vvhere it should be expressed most significantly in respect of euangelizing or preaching the Gospel, there they trãslate it barely, *preachers*, & *preaching*. Only S. Peters place aforesaid, must be stretched to signifie, *The word preached by the Gospel*, to insinuate & vphold their heresie of the vvritten Gospel only, or only vvritten vvord, against Apostolical traditions not vvritten. If this be not their meaning, let them giue vs a good reason vvhy they translate it so in this one place only.

Lind. Dubit. pag. 88.

5 It is vvritten of Luther that he for the self same heresie, in his first translation into the Germane tonge, left out these vvordes of S. Peter altogether, *This is the vvord vvhich is euangelized or preached to you.* Vvhy so? because S. Peter doth here define vvhat is the vvord of God: saying, *that vvhich is preached to you*, & not that only vvhich is vvritten. Vvhich false dealing of Luther is no smal presumption against the like heretical meaning of our English Protestants, vvho (I am sure) in this point of controuersie of the vvord vvritten & vnvvritten, vvil not deny that they agree vvith the Lutherans.

Ia. 4. v. 6.

6 Againe in the epistle of S. Iames, they adde the vvord, *Scripture*, into the text, saying,

ing, *But the Scripture offereth more grace*. Vvhere the Apostle may say as vvel, and indifferently, *The Spirit or holy Ghost giueth more grace,* and it is much more probable, and is so expounded of many. Let the good reader see the circũstance of the place, and abhorre their saucines in the text of holy scripture.

7 One addition of theirs I vvould not speake of, but only to knovv the reason vvhy they doe it, because it is very strange, and I knovv not vvhat they should meane by it. this I am sure, if they do it for no purpose, they doe it very folishly and forgetfully and contrarie to them selues. In the Gospel of S. Marke, in the reckening of the Apostles, they adde these vvordes, *And the first vvas Simon,* more then is in their Greeke text. Vvhich addition they learned of Beza, vvhose contradictions in this point are worthie noting. In S. Matthew where these vvordes are, he suspecteth that, *first,* vvas added by some Papist, for Peters primacie: here, vvhere the vvord is not, he auoucheth it to be the true text of the Gospel, & that because Matthevv readeth so. there he alleaged this reason, vvhy it could not be said *the first, Simon,* because there is no consequẽce nor coherence of second, third, fourth, &c: here he saith, that is no impediment, be-

Marc. 3. v. 16
Bibl. 1579.
Mat. 10. v. 2.

cause there be many exāples of such speach, & namely in the said place of S. Matthevv. there he saith it is not so, though al Greeke copies haue it so: here it must needes be so, though it be only found in certaine odde Greeke copies of Erasmus, vvhich Erasmus him self (as Beza confesseth) allovved not, but thought that these vvordes vvere added in them out of S. Matthevv. Vvhat these contradictions meane I knovv not, and I vvould learne the reason thereof, of his scholers our English translators, vvho by their Maisters authoritie haue made the self same addition in their English translation also.

8 There is also an other addition of theirs, either proceding of ignorance, or of the accustomed humor, vvhen they trans-
Col. 1. v. 23. late thus: *If ye continue stablished in the faith, and be not moued avvay from the hope of the Gospel, vvhich ye haue heard hovv it vvas preached to euery creature:* or, *vvhereof ye haue heard hovv that it is preached:* or, *vvhereof ye haue heard, and vvhich hath been preached to euery creature, &c.* For, al these varieties they haue, and none according to the Greeke text, vvhich is vvord for vvord, as the vulgar Latin interpreter hath most sincerely translated it, *Vnmoueable from the hope of the Gospel*
οὗ ἠκούσατε, *vvhich you haue heard, vvhich is or hath been preached*
τοῦ κηρυχ- *among al creatures, &c.* So that the Apostles ex-
θέντος. hortation is vnto the Colossians, that they

con-

continue grounded and ſtable in the faith and Goſpel vvhich they had heard and receiued of their firſt Apoſtles: as in the epiſtle to the Romanes, and to the Galatians, and to the Theſſalonians, and to the Hebrues, and to Timothee, and S. Iohn in his firſt epiſtle c. 2. v. 24: and S. Iude v. 3. & 20: al vſe the like exhortations.

Ro. 16. Ga. c. 1. & 2. 2 Theſſ. 2. Heb. 13. 1 Tim. 6. 2 Tim. 1. & 2.

9 But this doth not ſo vvel like the Proteſtants vvhich * vvith Hymenæus & Alexander and other old Heretikes haue fallen from their firſt faith, and therfore they alter the Apoſtles plaine ſpeache vvith certaine vvordes of their ovvne, and they vvil not haue him ſay, Be vnmoueable in the faith and Goſpel vvhich you haue heard and receiued: but, *vvhereof you haue heard hovv that it is preached*: as though he ſpake not of the Goſpel preached to them, but of a Goſpel vvhich they had only heard of, that vvas preached in the vvorld. Certaine it is, theſe vvordes, *vvhereof you haue heard hovv it vvas preached*, are not ſo in the Greeke: but, *vvhich you haue heard, vvhich hath been preached.* Vvhich is as much to ſay, as that they ſhould continue conſtant in the faith and Goſpel vvhich them ſelues had receiued, and vvhich vvas then preached and receiued in the vvhole vvorld. So ſay vve to our deere countriemen, Stād faſt in the faith & be vnmoueable

* 1 Tim. 1. & 6.

from

from the hope of the Gospel vvhich you heard of your first Apostles, vvhich vvas & is preached in al the vvorld. If the Protestants like not this exhortation, they do according to their translation.

CHAP. XXI.

Certaine other heretical TREACHERIES *and* CORRVPTIONS, *vvorthie of obseruation.*

1 THEY hold this position, that the Scriptures are not hard to be vnderstood, that so euery one of them may presume to interprete and expound them. And because S. Peter

2 Pet. 3. Corruption concerning the easines of the scriptures. Beza in Annot.

saith plainely, that S. Paules Epistles are hard, and other Scriptures also, vvhich the vnlearned (saith he) peruert to their ovvne destruction, therfore they labour tooth and naile to make this subtil difference, that S. Peter saith not, Paules epistles are hard but some thinges in S. Paules epist. are hard (as though that vvere not al one) and therfore they translate so, that it must needes be vnderstood of the things, and not of the Epistles, pretending the Greeke, vvhich yet

ἐν οἷς. ἐν αἷς. Test. Gr. Crisp.

they knovv in some copies can not be referred to the things, but must needes be vnderstood of the Epistles. VVherfore, the Greeke copies being indifferent to both,

and

and the thing alſo in very deede being al one, vvhether the hardnes be in the Epiſtles or in the matter (for vvhen vve ſay the Scripture is hard, vve meane ſpecially the matter) it is not only an Heretical but a fooliſh & peeuiſh ſpirit that maketh them ſo curious and preciſe in their tranſlations, as here to limite and abridge the ſenſe to the things only, Beza tranſlating, *inter quæ ſunt multa difficilia*, and not, *in quibus*, as it is in the old vulgar tranſlation, moſt ſincere, and indifferent both to epiſtles and things.

ἐν οἷς.
ἐν αἷς.

2 An other faſhion they haue, vvhich can not procede of good meaning, that is, vvhen the Greeke text is indifferent to tvvo ſenſes, and one is receiued, read, and expounded of the greater part of the auncient fathers, and of al the Latin Church, there to folovv the other ſenſe not ſo generally receiued & approued. as in S. Iames epiſtle vvhere the common reading is, *Deus intentator malorum eſt, God is no tempter to euil,* they tranſlate, *God can not be tempted vvith euil,* vvhich is ſo impertinent to the Apoſtles ſpeache there, as nothing more. But vvhy vvil they not ſay, God is no tempter to euil, as vvel as the other? is it becauſe of the Greeke vvord vvhich is a paſſiue? Let them ſee their Lexicon, and it vvil tel them that it is both an actiue and paſſiue. ſo ſay other learned

Corruption to make God the author of ſinne.

ἀπείραστος κακῶν.

Gre-

Gagneius.

Grecians, interpreters of this place. so saith the very circumstance of the vvordes next going before, *Let no man say that he is tempted of God.* Vvhy so? *Because God is not tempted vvith euil,* say they. is this a good reasõ? nothing lesse. how then? *Because God is no tempter to euil,* therfore let no man say that he is tempted of God.

3 This reason is so coherent and so necessarie in this place, that if the Greeke vvord vvere only a passiue (as it is not) yet it might beseeme Beza to translate it actiuely, vvho hath turned the actiue into a passiue vvithout scrupulositie, as him self confesseth, and is before noted, against the real presence. Much more in this place might he be bold to translate that actiuely, vvhich is both an actiue and a passiue, specially hauing such an example and so great authoritie as is al the auncient Latin Church vntil this day. But vvhy vvould he not? surely because he vvould fauour his and their heresie, vvhich saith cleane contrarie to these vvordes of the Apostle, to vvit, *that God is a tempter to euil.* Is that possible to be proued? yea it is possible and plaine. Bezas vvordes be these, *Inducit Dominus in tentationem eos quos Satanæ arbitrio permittit, aut in quos potius Satanam ipsum inducit, vt cor eorum impleat, vt loquitur Petrus Act. 5. v. 3.* that is, *The Lord leadeth into tentation those vvhom he permitteth to Satans arbitrement, or into vvhom rather he leadeth or bringeth in Satan him self to fill their hart, as Peter speaketh.* Marke that he saith God brin-

Annot. No. Test. an. 1556. Mat. 6. v. 13.

geth Satan into a man, to fill his hart, as Peter said to Ananias, *Vvhy hath Satan filled thy hart, to lie vnto the Holy Ghost?* So then by this mans opinion God brought Satan into Ananias hart, to make him lie vnto the holy ghost, & so ledde him into tentation, being author & causer of that heinous sinne.

4 Is not this to say, God is a tempter to euil: cleane contrarie to S. Iames the Apostle? or could he that is of this opinion, translate the contrarie, *that God is no tempter to euil?* Is not this as much to say as that God also brought Satan into Iudas to fil his hart, and so vvas author of Iudas treason, euen as he vvas of Paules conuersion? Let Beza novv and Maister Whitakers or any other Heretike of them al, vvrest & vvring them selues from the absurditie of this opinion, as they endeuour and labour to doe excedingly, because it is most blasphemous: yet shal they neuer be able to cleere & discharge them selues from it, if they vvil allovv & mainteine their foresaid exposition of Gods leading into tentation. Doth not Beza for the same purpose trāslate, *Gods prouidēce,* for, *Gods prescience?* Vvhich is so false, that the English Bezites in their translation are ashamed to folovv him.

See Beza Annot. in Ro. c. 1. v. 24 Act. 2. v. 23. Vvhit. ad rat. Camp. pag. 139. 145.

προγνώσει Act. 2. v. 23.

5 An other exceding treacherie to deceiue the reader, is this: that they vse Catholike termes and speaches in such places vvhere

Corruption in abusing Catholike vvordes. they may make them odious, and vvhere they must needes sound odiously in the peoples eares. As for example, this terme, 2 Mach. 6. v. 7. *procession*, they put very maliciously & falsely thus: *Vvhen the feast of Bacchus vvas kept, they vvere constrained to goe in the procession of Bacchus.* Bib. 1570. πεμπεύειν τῷ Διονύσῳ Let the good reader see the Greeke Lexicō, if there be any thing in this vvord like to the Catholike Churches processions: or procession. Bib. 1562. 1577. vvhether it signifie so much as, *to goe about*, as their other bibles are translated, vvhich meant also heretically, but yet durst not name, *procession*.

Founded. נִתְּנוּ כְּמָרִים 6 Againe, *He put dovvne the Priests (of Baal) vvhom the kings of Iuda had founded to burne incense.* 4 Reg. 23. v. 5. So they translate (the Hebrue being simply to giue, make, appoint) because in the Catholike Church there are foundations of chauntrie Priests, Chapples, diriges, &c. Neither is it sincerely and vvithout il meaning that they say here the *Priests* of Baal vvhom, &c. Because the Hebrue word signifieth al those that ministred in the temples of false gods.

Shrines, ναούς. 7 Againe, *Siluer shrines for Diana*, Act. 19. v. 24. Because of the shrines & tabernacles made to the image of our B. Ladie: the Greeke vvord signifying, *temples*, and Beza saith, he can not see hovv it may signifie shrines.

Deuotions σεβάσματα 8 Againe, *As I passed by, & beheld your deuotiōs,*

I found

I found an altar, Act. 17. v. 23. So they call the superstition of the Athenians toward their false gods, because of Catholike peoples deuotiōs toward the true God, his Church, altars, Saincts, &c, the Greeke vvord signifying the things that are vvorshipped (as σέβασμα. 2 Thess. 2. v. 4. and Sap. 15. v. 17.) not the maner of vvorshipping.

9 Againe, *The Ievves had agreed, that if any mā did confesse that he vvas Christ, he should be excommunicate,* Ioh. 9. v. 22. And *Iesus heard that they had excōmunicated him,* v. 35. to make the Ievves doing against them that confessed Christ, found like to the Catholike Churches doing against Heretikes in excōmunicating them, and so to disgrace the Priests povver of excommunication: vvhereas the Ievves had no such spiritual excommunication, but (as the Greeke must needes only signifie) they did, *put them out of the Synagogue,* and so they should haue translated, the Greeke vvord including the very name of Synagogue. But they, as though the Church of Christ and the Synagogue of the Ievves vvere al one, so translate, *excommunicating,* and *putting out of the Synagogue,* as al one.

ἵνα ἀποσυνάγωγος γένηται.

Excommunication.

Aposynagogum facere.

10 I omit here as spoken before, that they call an Idol, *the Queene of heauen,* because vve call our Lady by that title: so to make both seeme like. Also, that they say Bels altar thrise,

Altars.

Images. thrise, for Bels table, to disgrace altars: and that for idols, they say images, in despite of the Churches images: that they say traditiõ
Traditions. duely in the il part, yea sometime when it is not in the Greeke, to make traditions odious, and such like. Thus by similitude & like sound of vvordes they beguile the poore people, not only in their false expositions concerning Iudaical fastes, meates, obseruatiõ of daies (as is els where shevved) but also in their translations. So doth Cal-
Mat. 23. uins nevv Testament in frenche, for, *Nolite vocari Rabbi*, translate, Be not called, *nostre maistre* or, *Magister noster*: in derision and disgrace of this title and calling, vvhich is peculiar to Doctors of Diuinitie in the Catholike Vniuersities beyond the seas: euen as Wicleffe their grand-father did vpon the same vvordes condemne such degrees in Vniuersities. But their Rabbines can tel them that *Rabbi* signifieth, *Magister*, and not, *Magister noster.* and S. Iohn telleth them so chap.1. v.38. and chap.3. v.2. and chap.20. v.16. and yet it pleaseth them to translate othervvise and to abuse Christs ovvne sacred vvordes against Catholike Doctors & schooles: not considering that as Christ forbadde them to be called *Rabbi*, so he forbadde them the name of father & fathers, and yet I trovv they vvil not scoffe at this name

name either in their ovvne fathers, or in them selues so called of their children: though in Religious men, according to their heretical humor, they scoffe also at this name, as they do at the other in Doctors.

A heape of corruptiōs.

11 Contrarievvise as they are diligent to put some vvordes odiously vvhere they should not, so they are as circumspect not to put other vvordes and termes, vvhere they should. In their first bible (printed againe an. 1562.) not once the name of Church: in the same, for charitie, loue: for altar, temple: for heretike, an author of sectes: & for heresie, sect: because in those beginnings, al these vvordes sounded excedingly against them. The Church they had then forsaken, Christian charitie they had broken by schisme, altars they digged dovvne, heresie & heretike they knevv in their conscience vvere like in the peoples eares to agree vnto them, rather then to the old Catholike faith and professors of the same. Againe in al their bibles indifferently, both former & later, they had rather say, *righteous*, then, *iust*: *righteousnes*, then, *iustice*: *gift*, then, *grace*, specially in the sacrament of holy orders: *secrete*, rather then *mysterie*, specially in matrimonie: *dissension*, then, *schisme*: & these vvordes not at al, *Priest*, (to vvit, of the new

Testament) *Sacrament, Catholike, hymnes, confession, penance, iustifications*, and *traditions* in the good part: but in steede thereof, *Elders, secrete, general, praises, acknovvledging, amendement of life, ordinances, instructions.* and vvhich is, somevvhat vvorse, *carcas*, for *soule*, and *graue* for *hel*. vve may say vnto you as Demosthenes said to Æschines. τί ταῦτα; ῥήματα ἢ θαύματα; vvhat are these? vvordes or vvonders? certainly they are vvonders, and verie vvonderful in Catholike mens eares. and vvhether it be sincere and not heretical dealing, I appeale to the vvise and indifferent reader of any sort.

Demosth. περὶ στεφάνου.

CHAP. XXII.

Other faultes Iudaical, prophane, *mere* vanities, follies *&* noueltics.

1 NOVV leauing matters of cōtrouersie, let vs talke a litle vvith you familiarly, and learne of you the reason of other points in your translation, vvhich to vs seeme faultes, and sauour not of that spirit vvhich should be in Christian Catholike translators.

2 First, you are so profane, that you say, *The ballet of ballets of Salomon*, so terming that diuine booke *Canticum Canticorum*, conteining the high mysterie of Christ & his Church, as if it vvere a ballet of loue betvvene Salomon

lomon and his cõcubine, as Caſtaleo vvantonly tranſlateth it. But you ſay more profanely thus, *vve haue conceiued, vve haue borne in paine, as though vve ſhould haue brought forth vvinde.* I am aſhamed to tel the literal commentarie of this your tranſlation. Vvhy might you not haue ſaid, *Vve haue conceiued and as it vvere trauailed to bring forth, and haue brought forth the ſpirit?* is there any thing in the Hebrue to hinder you thus far? Vvhy vvould you ſay, *vvinde,* rather then, *ſpirit:* knovving that the Septuaginta in Greeke, & the auncient fathers, and S. Hierom him ſelf vvho tráſlateth according to the Hebrue, yet for ſenſe of the place, al expound it both according to Hebrue & Greeke, of the ſpirit of God, vvhich is firſt cõceiued in vs & beginneth by feare, vvhich the Scripture calleth the beginning of vviſedom. in ſo much that in the Greeke there are theſe goodly vvordes, famous in al antiquitie: *Through the feare of thee ô Lord vve cõceiued, and haue trauailed vvith paine, and haue brought forth the ſpirit of thy ſaluation, vvhich thou haſt made vpon the earth.* Which doth excellently ſet before our eies the degrees of a faithful mans increaſe and proceding in the ſpirit of God, vvhich beginneth by the feare of his iudgements, & is a good feare, though ſeruile, and not ſufficient. & it may be that you condemning vvith Luther this

Eſa. 26. v. 18.

Ambr. li. 2. de Interpel. c. 4. Chryſ. in Pſ. 7. prope finem. See S. Hier. vpon this place.

seruile feare as euil and hurtful, meane also some such thing by your translation. But in deede the place may be vnderstood of the other feare also, which hath his degrees more or lesse.

3 But to say, *vve haue brought forth vvinde*, can admit no such interpretation. but euen as if a mere Ievv should translate or vnderstand it, vvho hath no sense of Gods spirit, so haue you excluded the true sense vvhich cōcerneth the Holy Ghost, & not the cold terme of vvinde, and vvhatsoeuer naked interpretation thereof. And it is your fashion in al such cases, where the richer sense is of Gods holy spirit, there to translate *vvinde*, as Ps. 147. v. 18. as you number the psalmes.

4 And it is not vnlike to this, that you vvil not translate for the Angels honour that caried Abacuc, *He sette him into Babylon, ouer the lake by the force of his spirit*: but thus, *through a mightie vvinde*: so attributing it to the vvinde, not to the Angels povver, and omitting cleane the Greeke pronovvne αὐτοῦ, *his*, vvhich shevveth euidently that it vvas the Angels spirit, force, and povver.

ἐν ῥοιζῳ τοῦ πνεύματος αὐτοῦ.

5 Againe, vvhere the Prophets speake most manifestly of Christ, there you translate cleane an other thing: as Esa. 30 v. 20.
Bib. 1579. Vvhen S. Hierom translateth thus, and the Church

Church hath alvvaies read accordingly, *Non faciet auolare a te vltra Doctorem tuum: & erunt oculi tui videntes praeceptorem tuum.* that is, *And* (our Lord) *shal not cause thy Doctor to flie from thee any more: and thine eies shal see thy Maister.* Vvhich is al one in effect vvith that vvhich Christ saith, *I vvil be vvith you vnto the end of the vvorld*: there you translate thus, *Thy raine shal be no more kept backe: but thine eies shal see thy raine.* So likevvise Ioel 2.v.23. where the holy church readeth, *Reioyce ye children of Sion in the Lord your God: because he hath giuen you the Doctor of iustice*: there you translate, *the raine of righteousnes.* Doth the Hebrue vvord force you to this? you knovv that it signifieth a teacher or Maister. and therfore the Ievves them selues, partly vnderstand it of Esdras, partly of Christs Diuinitie. Vvhy are you more profane (I vvil not say more Iudaical) then the Iewes them selues? vvhy might not S. Hierom a Christian Doctor and lacking no skil in the Hebrue (as you vvel knovv) satisfie you, vvho maketh no doubt but the Hebrue in these places is, *Doctor, Maister, teacher?* Vvho also (in Psal. 84,7:) translateth thus, *Vvith blessings shal the Doctor be araied*: meaning Christ. Vvhere you vvith the later Rabbines the enemies of Christ translate, *The raine couereth the pooles.* Vvhat cold stuff is this in respect of that other translation so cleerely pointing to Christ our Maister and Doctor?

מוֹרֶיךָ

See יֹרֶה

Lyra in 30 Esa.

6 And

6 And againe, vvhere S. Hierom transf-
Es. 33. lateth, and the Church readeth, and al the fathers interpret and expound accordingly, *There shal be faith in thy times*: to expresse the maruelous faith that shal be then, in the first Christians specially, euen vnto death, and in al the rest concerning the hidden mysteries of the nevv Testament: there you translate, *There shal be stabilitie of thy times.* The Prophet ioyneth together there, iudgemēt, iustice, faith, vvisedom, knovvledge, the feare of our Lord: you for a litle ambiguitie of the Hebrue vvord, turne faith into stabilitie.

7 If I should burden you vvith transf-
Esa. 2. lating thus also concerning Christ, *Cease from the man vvhose breath in his nostrels: for vvherein is he to be esteemed?* You vvould say I did you wrong, because it is so pointed novv in the Hebrue.
במח Vvhereas you knovv very vvell by S. Hieroms commentarie vpon that place, that this is the Iewes pointing or reading of the vvord, against the honour of Christ: the true reading and translation being as he interpreteth it, *for he is reputed high*: and therfore bevvare of him. Othervvise (as S. Hierom saith) vvhat a consequence vvere this, or vvho vvould commend any man thus, *Take heede ye offend not him, vvho is nothing esteemed?* yet that is your translation. Neither doth the

the Greeke helpe you vvhich (if the accent ἐν τινὶ ἐλο-
be truely put) is thus, *becauſe he is reputed for ſome* γίσθη.
body or ſome thing: as S. Paul ſpeaketh of the Gal.2.v.6.
cheefe Apoſtles, and it is our phraſe in the commendation of a man.

8 The like excuſe you vvould haue by alleaging the Hebrue vovvels, if you vvere told that you much obſcure a notable ſaying of the prophet concerning Chriſt, or rather the ſpeache of Chriſt him ſelf by
his prophet, ſaying: *I haue ſpoken by the Prophets,* Oſee 12, 10.
and I haue multiplied viſion, & in the hand of the Prophets (that is, by the Prophets) *haue I been reſembled.* Vvhich later vvordes doe excedingly expreſſe, that al the Prophets ſpake of Chriſt:
as our Sauiour him ſelf declareth, *beginning* Luc.24.v.
from Moyſes and al the Prophets to interpret vnto the tvvo 27.
diſciples, the things that concerned him. and as S. Peter Act.3.
ſaith in theſe vvordes, *Al the Prophets from Samuel and that ſpake after him, did tel of theſe daies.* This prophecie then being ſo conſonant to theſe ſpeaches of the nevv Teſtament, the
Greeke alſo being vvord for vvord ſo, the ἐν χερσὶ
Hebrue by chāging one litle pricke (vvhich προφητῶν
the later Ievves haue added at their ovvne ὡμοιώθην
pleaſure) being fully ſo as vve read vvith אֲדַמֶּה
the Catholike Church: vvhy pretend you אֲדָמֶה
the Ievves authoritie to mainteine an other leſſe Chriſtian tranſlation, vvhich is thus: *I vſe ſimilitudes by the miniſterie of the Prophets.* as

though there vvere nothing there concerning Christ or the second person peculiarly?

9 You vvil also perhaps alleage not only the later Ievves, but also some later Catho-
The Hebrue text, is no certaine rule to interprete by.
like men that so translate the Hebrue. But the difference betvvene them and you, is, that they, vvith reuerence and preferment alvvaies of S. Hieroms and the Churches auncient translation, tel vs hovv it is novv in the Hebrue: you, vvith derogation and disanulling the same altogether, set dovvne your ovvne as the only true interpretation according to the Hebrue: auouching the Hebrue that novv is, and as novv it is printed, to be the only authentical truth of the old Testament. Vvhere you can neuer ansvver vs, hovv that in the Psalme 22, *As a lion my hand and my feete* (as novv it is in the
כָּאֲרִי
Hebrue) can be the true and old authentical Hebrue, vvhich none of the fathers knevv, the auncient Rabbines condemne as a corruption, your selues translate it not, but after the old accustomed reading, *They haue pearced my handes and my feete* Vvhich is a notable prophecie of our Sauiours kinde and maner of Passion, being crucified on the Crosse. Only the later Ievves, and such Heretikes as thinke he died vpon a gallous or gibbet, and not vpon the Crosse, they like this

this Hebrue text vvel, and ſtand vpon it, as you do vpon al vvithout exception, & yet vvhen it commeth to certaine particulars, you are cōpelled to forſake it. as in certaine other places, for example.

10 Vvhere the Hebrue ſaith, *Achaz king of Iſrael,* 2 Paralip. 28. v. 19. which is not true, you are compelled to tranſlate, *Achaz king of Iuda,* as the truth is, and as it is in the Greeke and the vulgar Latin. yet * ſome of your Bibles folovv the falſhod of the Hebrue.

Faultes in the Hebrue text.

Bib. 1579.

11 Likevviſe, vvhere the Hebrue ſaith, *Zedecias his brother,* meaning the brother of Ioachin, you trāſlate, *Zedecias his fathers brother,* as in deede the truth is, according to the Greeke, and to the Scripture 4 Reg. 24. v. 19. and therfore your Bible vvhich folovveth the Hebrue here alſo, tranſlating, *his brother,* yet in the margent putteth dovvne as more true, *vncle.*

Bib. 1579.

12 Likevviſe in an other place, the Hebrue is ſo out of frame, that ſome of your Bibles ſay, *he begat Azuba of his vvife Azuba.* and otherſome tranſlate, *he begat Ierioth of his vvife Azuba:* the Hebrue being thus, *he begat Azuba his vvife and Ierioth,* vvhich neither you nor any man els can eaſily tel vvhat to make of. Thus you ſee hovv eaſie it vvere (if a man vvould multiplie ſuch examples) to ſhevv by your ovvne teſtimonies the corruption

of

In the preface of the nevv Test.

of the Hebrue, and that your selues do not, nor dare not exactly folovv it, as of the Greeke text of the nevv Testament also is declared els vvhere.

13 But it is greater maruel, vvhy you folovv not the Hebrue in other places also, vvhere is no corruption. You protest to translate it according to the pointes or vovvels that novv it hath, and that you call the Hebrue veritie. Tel me then I beseeche you, vvhy do you in al your Bibles translate

Esa. 37. v. 22

thus, *O Virgin daughter of Sion, he hath despised thee, and laughed thee to scorne: ô daughter of Hierusalem he hath shaken his head at thee.* In the Hebrue,

παρθένος, θυγάτηρ. τὴν κεφαλὴν αὐτῆς.

Greeke, S. Hieroms translation and commentarie, it is cleane contrarie, *The Virgin daughter of Sion hath despised thee* (ô Assur:) *the daughter of Hierusalem hath shaken her head at thee.* Al are the fœminine gender, and spoken of Sion literally, and of the Church spiritually trium-

בָּזָה לָעֲגָה לָךְ

phing ouer Assur and al her enemies: you trãslate al as of the masculine gẽder, & apply it to Assur insulting against Hierusalem. &c. I can not conceiue vvhat this translation meaneth, & I vvould gladly know the reason, & I vvould haue thought it some grosse ouersight, but that I finde it so in al your English Bibles, & not only in this place of Esay, but also in the bookes of the kinges,

4 Reg. 19.

vvhere the same wordes are repeated. And it is no lesse maruel vnto vs that knovv not the reason of your doings, vvhy you haue [c] left out *Alleluia* nine times in the sixe last Psalmes, being in the Hebrue nine times more then in your translation: specially vvhen you knovv that it is the auncient and ioyful song of the primitiue Church. See the nevv English Testament, Annot. Apoc. 19.

Alleluia.
c Bib. 1577.
הַלְלוּיָה

14 Againe, you translate thus: *Many vvhich had seen the first house, vvhen the foundation of this house vvas laid before their eies, vvept &c.* Looke vvel to your Hebrue, and you shal finde it according both to the Greeke & the Latin, thus: *Many vvhich had seen the first house in the foundation thereof* (that is, yet standing vpon the foũdation, not destroied) *and this temple before their eies, vvept.* You imagined that it should be meant, they savv Salomons temple, vvhen it vvas first founded, vvhich because it vvas vnpossible, therfore you translated othervvise then is in the Hebrue, Greeke, and Latin. But yet in some of your Bibles you should haue considered the matter better, and translated accordingly.

15 And surely vvhy you should translate (4 Reg. 23. v. 13.) *On the right hand of mount Oliuete*, rather then as it is in the vulgar Latin: and why, *Ye abiect of the Gentiles*, Esa. 45. v. 20. rather then, *ye that are saued of the Gentiles*: you belike knovv some reason, vve do not, neither

לְהַר הַמַּשְׁחִית
οἱ σωζόμενοι ἀπὸ τῶν ἐθνῶν.
פְּלִיטֵי גוֹיִם

ther by the Hebrue nor the Greeke.

16 Hovvbeit in theſe leſſer things (though nothing in the Scripture is to be counted litle) you might perhaps more freely haue taken your pleaſure, in folovving neither Hebrue nor Greeke: but vvhen it cōcerneth a matter no leſſe then vſurie, there by your falſe tranſlation to giue occaſion vnto the reader, to be an vſurer, is no ſmal fault either against true religion or againſt good

Bib. 1562. 1577. Deut. 23. v. 19.

maners. This you doe moſt euidently in your moſt authentical tranſlations, ſaying thus: *Thou ſhalt not hurt thy brother by vſurie of money, nor by vſurie of corne, nor by vſurie of any thing that he may be hurt vvithal.* What is this to ſay, but that vſurie is not here forbidden, vnles it hurt the partie that borovveth, vvhich is ſo

לא תשיך לאחיך נשך

rooted in moſt mēs hartes, that they thinke ſuch vſurie very lavvful, and daily offend mortally that vvay. Vvhere almightie God in this place of holy Scripture hath not a vvord of hurting or not hurting (as may be ſeen by the Geneua bibles) but ſaith ſimply thus: *Thou ſhalt not lend to thy brother to vſurie, vſurie of money, vſurie of meate, vſurie of any thing that is put to vſurie.*

ὀυκ ἐκτοκιεῖς τῷ ἀδελφῷ σου τόκον ἀργυρίου, &c.

17 Marke the Hebrue and the Greeke, and ſee, and be aſhamed, that you ſtraine and peruert it, to ſay for, *Non fœnerabis fratri tuo,* vvhich is vvord for vvord in the Greeke and Hebrue, *Thou ſhalt not hurt thy brother by*

vsurie. If the Hebrue vvord in the vse of holy
Scripture do signifie, to hurt by vsurie, vvhy
do you in the very next vvordes folowing,
in the self same Bibles translate it thus, *vnto* ibid.v.20.
a stranger thou maist lend vpon vsurie, but not vnto thy
brother? Vvhy said you not, *A stranger thou ma-*
ist hurt vvith vsurie, but not thy brother? Is it not al
one vvord and phrase here and before? And
if you had so translated it here also, the
Ievves vvould haue thanked you, vvho by
forcing the Hebrue vvord as you doe,
thinke it very good to hurt any stranger,
that is, any Christian by any vsurie be it
neuer so great.

18 Vvhat shal I tel you of other faultes,
vvhich I vvould gladly accoũt ouersightes
or ignorances, such as vve also desire pardon of, but al are not such, though some
be. As, *Tvvo thousand,* (vvritten at length) *to* Cant. Cãtic.
them that keepe the fruite thereof. In the Hebrue & c.8.v.12,
Greeke, *tvvo hundred.* Againe in the same Bib.1579.
booke c.1. v.4. *As the fruites of Cedar.* in the
Hebr. and Greeke. *tabernacles.* And, *Aske a signe* Isa. 7. v. 11.
either in the depth or in the height aboue, for, *in the*
depth of Hel. And, *Great vvorkes are vvrought by him.* Mat.14.v.2.
for, *do vvorke in him,* as S. Paul vseth the same
vvord 2 Cor. 4. v.12. And, *To make ready an* ἐνεργοῦσιν
horse. Act.23.v.24. in the Greeke, *beastes,* And, ἐν αὐτῷ.
If a man on the Sabboth day receiue circumcision vvithout Bib. 1577.
breaking of the lavv of Moyses. Io. 7.v. 23. For, *to the* ἵνα μὴ λυ-
end that the lavv of Moyses be not broken. And, *The* θῇ ὁ νόμος.
sonne

ἀποδοκιμα- *sonne of man must suffer many things, and be reproued of*
σθῆναι. *the elders.* Mar. 8. v. 31. For, *be reiected.* as in the
psalme, *The stone vvhich the builders reiected,* vve
say not, *reprouing* of the said stone, vvhich
1 Tim. 3. is Christ. And, νεόφυτος, a yong scholer, in al
your trãslatiõs, falsely. And, *Simõ of Chanaan* or
Mar. 3. *Simon the Cananite,* vvho is called otherwise, Ze-
lótes, that is Zelous, as an interpretation of
the Hebrue vvord, *Cananæus:* vvhich I maruel
you cõsidered not, specially cõsidering that
ק. כ. the Hebrue vvord for Zelous, & the other
for a Cananite, beginne with diuers letters.
Heb. 2. v. 1. and, *lest at any time vve should let them slippe.* for,
lest vve slippe or runne by, and so be lost.
An. 1562. 19 And as for the first bible, vvhich vvas
done in hast, and not yet corrected, but is
Mat. 22. printed still a fresh: that saith, *Vvith Herods seruants,* as though that vvere the only sense:
a Mat 24. that calleth *idiotas* lay men: [a] κιβωτὸν, a ship:
b Mar. 5. [b] θόρυβον, vvondering: [c] σβέννυνται, are gone
c Mat. 25. out: ἐξουσίαν, his substance: and, *To knovv the*
Eph. 3. *excellent loue of the knovvledge of Christ.* For, *the loue
of Christ that excelleth knovvledge.* And, *of men that*
Tit. 1. *turne avvay the truth.* For, *that shunne the truth and
turne avvay from it.* And, *Mount Sina is Agar in Ara-
bia.* For, *Agar is Mount Sina.* &c.

20 Let these and the like be smal negli-
gences or ignorances, such as you vvil pardon vs also, if you finde the like. Neither
do vve greatly mislike, that you leaue these
vvordes

vvordes, a *Vrim* and *Thummim* and b *Chemarim* and c *Ziims*, & *Iims*, vntranslated, because it is not easy to expresse them in English: and vve vvould haue liked it as vvel in certaine other vvordes, vvhich you haue translated, *images, images,* and stil, *images*, being as hard to expresse the true signification of them, as the former. And vve hope you vvil the rather beare vvith the late Catholike translatiō of the English Testamēt, that leaueth also certaine vvordes vntrāslated, not only because they can not be expressed, but also for reuerence and religion (as S. Augustine saith) and greater maiestie of the same.

21 Of one thing vve can by no meanes excuse you, but it must sauour vanitie, or noueltie, or both. As vvhen you affectate nevv strange vvordes vvhich the people are not acquainted vvithal, but it is rather Hebrue to them then English: μάλα σεμνῶς ὀνομάζοντες, as Demosthenes speaketh, vttering vvith great countenāce and maiestie, *Against him came vp Nabucadnezzar king of Babel*, 2 Par. 36. v.6. for, *Nabuchodonosor king of Babylon*: *Saneherib*, for *Sennacherib*: *Michaiahs* prophecie, for *Michæas*: *Iehoshaphats* praier, for *Iosaphats*: *Vzza* slaine, for *Oza*. *Vvhen Zerubbabel vvent about to build the Temple*, for *Zorobabel*: Remēber vvhat the Lord did to *Miriā*, for *Marie*, Deut. 34. And in your first trāslatiō, *Elisa* for *Elisæus*, *Pekahia* & *Pekah* for *Phaceia* & *Phacee*, *Vziahu* for *Ozias*, *Thiglath-peleser* for *Teglath-*

Phalasar,

a Deut. 33.
b 4 Reg. 23.
Ierem. 50.

Hamanim. *Esa.* 17.
Gillulim. *Ier.* 50.
Miphletseth. 3 *Re.* 15.

Bib. 1579.
Demosth.
2 Par. 36. v.6.
c. 32.
Fo. 172. 173.
Fo. 160.
Epistle to the Queene.
Bib. 1562.
4 Reg. c. 15. 16.

phalasar, Ahaziahu for Ochozias: *Peka the sonne of Remaliahu*, for, *Phacee the sonne of Romelia.* And vvhy say you not as vvel *Shelomoh* for *Salomon*, and *Coresh* for *Cyrus*, and so alter euery vvord from the knovven sound and pronunciation thereof? Is this to teach the people, vvhen you speake Hebrue rather then English? Vvere it a goodly hearing (thinke you) to say for IESVS, *Ieshuah*, and for MARIE his mother, *Miriam*: and for *Messias Meshiach*, and for *Iohn*, *Iachannan*, and such like monstruous nouelties? vvhich you might as vvel doe, and the people vvould vnderstand you as vvel, as when your preachers say, *Nabucadnezer king of Bábel.*

Calfil.

Præfat. in Esa.

22 Vvhen Zuinglius your great Patriarke did reade in Munsters translation of the old Testamét, Iehizkiahu, Iehezchel, Choresh, Darianesch, Beltzezzer, and the like. for, Ezechias, Ezechiel, Cyrus, Darius, Baltasar: he called them barbarous voices, & vnciuil speaches, & said the vvord of God vvas soiled and depraued by them. Knovv you not that proper names alter & chaúge, and are vvritten and sounded in euery language diuersely? Might not al antiquitie & the general custom both of reading and hearing the knovven names of Nabuchodonosor, and Michæas, and Ozias, suffice you, but you must needes inuent other vvhich

vvhich the people neuer heard, rather for vaine oſtentation to amaſe and aſtoniſh them, then to edification and inſtruction. Vvhich is an old Heretical faſhion, noted by Euſebius lib. 4. c. 10: and by the author of the vnperfect cōmentaries vpon S. Matthevv, ho. 44: and by S. Auguſtine lib. 3. c.26. contra Creſconium.

23 Vvhat ſhal I ſpeake of your affectation of the vvord *Iehôua* (for ſo it pleaſeth you to accent it) in ſteede of *Dominus*, *The Lord*: vvhereas the auncient fathers in the very Hebrue text did read and ſound it rather, *Adonai*, as appeareth both by S. Hieroms tranſlation and alſo his cōmētaries, and I vvould knovv of them the reaſon, vvhy in the Hebrue Bible, vvhen ſo euer this vvord is ioyned vvith *Adonai*, it is to be read *Elohim*, but only for auoiding *Adonai*, tvviſe together. This I ſay vve might iuſtly demaund of theſe that take a pride in vſing this vvord *Iehôua* ſo oft both in Engliſh & Latin: though otherwiſe we are not ſuperſtitious, but as occaſion ſerueth, only in the Hebrue text vve pronounce it and reade it. Againe vve might aſke them, vvhy they vſe not as vvel *Elobim* in ſteede of *Deus*, *God*: and ſo of the reſt, changing al into Hebrue, that they may ſeeme gay fellovves, and the people may vvonder at their vvonderful

Iehouah. יְהוָֹה

and myſtical diuinitie.

24 To conclude, are not your ſcholers (thinke you) much bound vnto you, for giuing them in ſteede of Gods bleſſed worde and his holy Scriptures, ſuch tranſlations, heretical, Iudaical, profane, falſe, negligent, phantaſtical, nevv, naught, monſtruous? God open their eies to ſee, and mollifie your hartes to repent of al your falſhod & treacherie, both that vvhich is manifeſtly conuinced againſt you and can not be denied, as alſo that vvhich may by ſome ſhevv of anſvver be ſhifted of in the ſight of the ignorant, but in your conſciences is as manifeſt as the other.

FINIS.

The faultes correcte thus.

	For	Read
Page	46. fecit honem	fecit hominem.
	53 Abac, 2.v.13.	Abac 2.v.18.
	80 πρεσβυίτέρους,	πρεσβυτέρους.
	117 Prou.3,15.marg.	Prou.30,15.
	ibid.Prou.27,30. marg.	Prou.27,20.
	124 mur- in marg.	murder.
	186	178.
For	187	179.
	178 Io. 5,3.	1 Io.5,3.
	194	186.
	195	187.
	241 (line 2) then,	rather then.
	256 hat being,	that being.
	255 εὐχαρήσας in marg.	εὐχαριστήσας.

210 and 316 in the Hebrue, of necessitie, because the printer could not supplie them, there vvanteth the vovvel *Holem.* and for like reason pa.211. and 134. there vvanteth *Kibuts.* Vvhich also caused vs to leaue some wordes vvithout vovvels, as once in the Preface. & alibi.

49 in some fevve copies ther vvanteth *Segol.*

A BRIEF TABLE TO DIRECT THE READER TO SVCH PLACES

as this booke proueth to be corrupted in diuers translations of the English Bibles: by order of the bookes, chapters, & verses of the same. With some other corrupted by Beza & others, in their Latin translations.

and

chap.5

S. *Iames*

BEZAS CORRVPTIONS.